DATE DUE			

*The Latin Poetry
of English Poets*

The Latin Poetry
of English Poets

Edited by
J. W. Binns

Routledge & Kegan Paul
London and Boston

First published in 1974
by Routledge & Kegan Paul Ltd
Broadway House, 68–74 Carter Lane,
London EC4V 5EL and
9 Park Street,
Boston, Mass. 02108, USA
Set in Monotype Baskerville 11 pt 1 pt leaded
and printed in Great Britain by
The Camelot Press Ltd, Southampton
© Routledge & Kegan Paul Ltd 1974

ISBN 0 7100 7845 5
Library of Congress Catalog Card No. 13–93635

Contents

Introduction

A surprisingly large number of English poets wrote Latin poetry, down to the time of Walter Savage Landor in the nineteenth century, the last major poet to compose a substantial number of Latin verses. By Landor's time, and even a century earlier, the fitness for poetry of the English language was indisputable, and there is to some extent an air of preciosity, of literary trifling, in much of the Latin verse then produced. Nonetheless a substantial amount of Latin poetry even from that period has survived; it was appreciated by the polite taste of the times; and it can still today enrich our understanding of the authors who wrote it.

In the sixteenth and seventeenth centuries, however, the prestige of the Latin language was still enormous. Only hindsight enables us to laugh at poets who were in doubt whether to entrust their works to the English language. Milton's own consideration of the merits of English, as against Latin, as the language appropriate for his major poetry is well known. Latin, in the sixteenth and seventeenth centuries, was after all still the international language of diplomacy, science and learning. As late as the 1670s it was in a Latin version that Anthony à Wood's *History and Antiquities of the University of Oxford* was accepted for publication, whilst as the language even of science Latin held sway for well over a century beyond that date. Latin was too the language of the vast and immeasurable body of neo-Latin literature, to which the authors discussed in this volume made their conscious contribution. No one has ever counted the number of books written in Latin in the two centuries from 1500, but it runs into tens of thousands. Moreover, any book written in Latin by its very nature had as its author a man of some education, and was addressed to a like audience.

There was then a simple but compelling reason for a sixteenth- or seventeenth-century English poet to wish to write in Latin: the desire for an international audience and international recognition. The population of England was small, and the language, in those pre-imperial days, little disseminated in the lands beyond the seas. Knowledge in Europe of English was rare; of Latin, commonplace. The great work of Milton, *Paradise Lost,* was at an early date appreciated in seventeenth-century Europe in Latin versions. A poet thus seemed justified in writing in a language whose future seemed assured by a millennium and a half of pre-eminence, a language in which, across the frontiers, he could speak to a cultivated European audience. A poet from the new Commonwealth finds himself in a similar position today *vis-à-vis* English. If he wishes to be talked about in the literary circles of London and New York, it were well that he write in English, not in Urdu nor Malay, nor in the dialect of an African tribe. And Latin, being then quite without rival as an international language, enjoyed a position surpassing even that of English today.

There was too another reason for writing in Latin. It made possible a much closer imitation of the Latin models so much admired. Languages have different structures and, as every translator knows, it is not possible to carry over from one language into another the totality of a passage's effect. 'English Seneca' is as much English as Seneca. A closer imitation of a hexameter of Vergil, or of an ode of Horace, can be attained in Latin than in English, and this is important if praise for poetry is to be measured out for close adherence to a classical model. Such imitations of Latin authors may seem today to be mere pastiches. There is a tendency for Renaissance Latin poetry to be dismissed as 'faded flowers': and perhaps it does not stand up well to the techniques of literary criticism now in vogue. A poet is likely to be less able to mould the Latin language into a new style, less able to stamp the impress of his personality on his verse, less able to shake himself free from the weight of the past as it pressed upon him with the marmoreal perfection of the Latin language. The clusters of poetic commonplaces and modes of expression, the conventional themes, instilled by the processes of education, by school grammars and *florilegia*, all these are liable to circumscribe the poet as he searches for the words of his poem.

But this does not mean that Renaissance Latin poetry could not be original in its subject matter, or in its treatment of themes and ideas. What are its subjects and whence derive its themes and ideas? Are they found too in vernacular poetry? If so, how are they modified as they pass between the learned language and the more popular? Study of sixteenth- and seventeenth-century poetry could profitably proceed along those lines. When we come to the English poets who also essayed to prove themselves in Latin, the interest of their Latin poetry is self-evident. Their Latin poetry is a part of the corpus of their writings. What is its significance, and its relation to their work in English? Can we interpret their English poems in the light of their achievements in Latin? How is our judgment of a poet altered by an awareness of his Latin works? These are some of the questions raised in this volume by discussions of the Latin poetry of six English poets from the sixteenth to the nineteenth centuries – Campion, Herbert, Milton, Crashaw, Bourne, and Landor. These poets exemplify, I believe, the changing fortunes of Anglo-Latin verse throughout these three centuries. In the Elizabethan Age, many Englishmen such as William Gager, Walter Haddon and Christopher Jonson achieved renown as neo-Latin poets, but they wrote either wholly, or else mainly, in the learned language. Thomas Campion is pre-eminent as an Elizabethan valued today for his English poetry, and in his own day as a Latin poet. It was in the seventeenth century more than in any other that English poets famous both in their own day and in our own could still turn as a matter of course to the composition of Latin verses of substantial quality and considerable bulk. The great names of Milton, Herbert and Crashaw will serve as sufficient exemplifications, though Marvell and Cowley could equally bear witness to this.

It is in the eighteenth century that a decline in the importance of Latin for European intellectual life can be observed. It was that century which saw the last editions of many famous Renaissance Latin poets, and witnessed the decline of Latin as the central language of scholarship and science. This decline is also mirrored in the original Latin poetry of the age. 'Latin poetry in all its branches suffered a great falling off in the second half of the century. Hardly any work of importance was produced between Isaac Hawkins Browne's *De animi immortalitate* in 1754 and the appearance of Walter Savage Landor's first Latin poems in 1795. . . . Latin verse was being gradually relegated to the place of an elegant private amusement':[1] so writes Leicester Bradner in his classic *Musae Anglicanae*.

Much elegant Latin verse was indeed written in the eighteenth century; there was still an audience for it in the pages of the *Gentleman's Magazine* and in the numerous anthologies of modern Latin verse then published. Some famous names even, such as Dr Johnson and Thomas Gray, wrote Latin verses, but these are definitely eclipsed by their English writings. Scarcely any of Dr Johnson's Latin poems, which he wrote for his private amusement, were known before his death. Most of Gray's Latin poetry was also published posthumously, and with the exception of a few odes is unremarkable. In this volume, then, the eighteenth century is represented by Vincent Bourne, the most popular Anglo-Latin poet of his day, whose *Poemata* went through numerous editions until 1840, and some of whose best Latin poems were translated by Lamb and Cowper.

Although Latin was declining in importance during the eighteenth century, it was still not quite dead as a literary medium; the last years of the century saw the appearance of the first Latin poems by Walter Savage Landor, who, living well into the latter half of the nineteenth century, dominated all his contemporaries as a writer of Latin poetry of high quality and formidable bulk. Walter Savage Landor, who died not much more than a century ago, is England's last important neo-Latin poet, and a discussion of his poetry appropriately concludes this volume.

J. W. BINNS

Note

1   Leicester Bradner, *Musae Anglicanae. A History of Anglo-Latin Poetry 1500–1925* (New York, 1940), pp. 252–3.

I

The Latin Poetry of Thomas Campion

J. W. Binns

About one-third of Thomas Campion's poetical output is written in Latin. It is customary by and large to ignore this in any assessment of his poetry. Yet a study of his Latin poetry is sufficient to modify the traditional view of Campion as a poet memorable chiefly for his agreeable but minor Elizabethan lyrics. Campion's two longest poems are both in Latin, and in these he forsakes the brief lyric and writes kinds of poetry which he never attempted in English. The Latin elegies are an important part of the corpus of his love poetry, whilst in his numerous epigrams he displays his abilities as a writer of short poems in other than lyric mould. The first publication by Campion of a volume of Latin poetry in 1595, and the second revised and augmented edition of 1619, are important landmarks planted near the beginning and end of his poetical career.

The first collection of poems to be published under Campion's name was the *Poemata* of 1595. This contains the poem *Ad Thamesin* celebrating the defeat of the Spanish Armada, the first 231 lines of the mythological poem *Umbra*, a book of sixteen elegies, principally amatory ones, and 129 epigrams. In the 1619 collection of Latin poems entitled *Epigrammatum Libri II*, the mythological poem *Umbra* was completed, most though not all of the elegies were reprinted with slight revisions and the addition of two new ones, whilst of the 453 epigrams in two books, over 360 appeared for the first time. Thomas Campion's Latin poetry thus falls conveniently into three main types: the elegies, the poems conceived on a more grandiose and extensive pattern, and the epigrams.

In his own day Campion's Latin poetry did not pass unnoticed, and several testimonies survive from the late 1590s onwards to bear witness to the impression he made on his contemporaries. The poet William Vaughan writes in a poem in his *Poematum Libellus* (London, 1598) that the Muses have taken up residence in England, and, praising amongst other poets, both Latin and English, Gager, More, Camden, Spenser, Daniel, Breton, and Drayton, he says of Campion:

> Hic cui cognomen tribuit Campana, volutas
> O Thoma rectis metra ligata modis. (sig. C4r.)

(Here you, O Thomas, to whom Campania herself gives a surname, roll out rhythms bound by strict measures.)

Campion was also praised, along with other English writers of Latin poetry, by Francis Meres in his *Palladis Tamia* (London, 1598): 'these English men being Latine Poets, *Gualter Haddon, Nicholas Car, Gabriel Haruey, Christopher Ocland, Thomas Newton* with his *Leyland, Thomas Watson, Thomas Campion, Brunswerd* and *Willey,* haue attained good report and honorable aduancement in the Latin Empyre.'[1] It is clear from the context of Meres's remarks – he has just been speaking of continental neo-Latin poets who had 'obtained renown and good place among the auncient Latine Poets' – that by his use of the term 'the Latin Empyre', Meres believes that Campion is one of those who merit comparison with the classical Roman poets. Campion's friend Charles Fitzgeffrey praised both his epigrams and elegies in a volume of verse, the *Affaniae,* published at Oxford in 1601:[2]

> Primus apud *Britones* Latiis Epigrammata verbis,
>   More, tuo scripsit nomine notus *Eques*:
> Huic aetate quidem, sed non tamen arte secundus,
>   Cui *Campus* nomen, *Delius* ingenium.

(The first Briton to write epigrams in Latin was that famous knight More, who had the same name as you [i.e. Thomas]. Second to him in point of time, yet not in art, comes the man whose name comes from 'camp' [*lit.* field] but whose talent from Apollo.)

O cuius genio *Romana* Elegia debet
    Quantum *Nasoni* debuit ante suo!
Ille, sed invitus, *Latiis* deduxit ab oris
    In *Scythicos* fines barbaricosque *Getas,*
Te duce caeruleos invisit prima *Britannos*
    Quamque potest urbem dicere iure suam:
(Magnus enim domitor late, dominator et orbis
    Viribus effractis *Cassivelane* tuis
Iulius *Ausonium* populum Latiosque penates
    Victor in hac olim iusserat urbe coli.)
Ergo relegatas *Nasonis* crimine Musas
    In patriam revocas restituisque suis.

(O thou to whose talent Roman elegy is as much indebted as she was previously to her own Ovid! He, albeit unwillingly, left the shores of Italy for the lands of the Scythians and the barbarous Getae. Under your guidance Elegy now visits the blue-dyed Britons for the first time, and the city which she can rightly call her own. (For the great Julius, a conqueror far and wide, and the ruler of the world, when he had broken your power, Cassivellaunus, had once victoriously ordered that the Italian people and the Latin gods should be revered in this city.) Thus you call back to your native land the Muses banished by the crime of Ovid, and restore them to their devotees.)

Campion is in this latter poem seen as an Ovid returned to life, and his Latin elegies do indeed form a substantial portion of his amatory verse. His eighteen elegies are with only two exceptions devoted to erotic themes. In the elegy which introduces the group of elegies contained in the 1595 edition of his poems, which was, however, omitted from the 1619 revision, Campion appeals for a sympathetic audience, and regards himself as the first British writer of elegy:[3]

3

> Ite procul, tetrici, moneo, procul ite severi,
>   Ludit censuras pagina nostra graves,
> Ite senes nisi forte aliquis torpente medulla
>   Carminibus flammas credit inesse meis.
> Aptior ad teneros lusus florentior aetas,
>   Vel iuvenis, vel me docta puella legat.
> Et vatem celebrent Bruti de nomine primum
>   Qui molles elegos et sua furta canat. (1a.1–8)

(Away with you, I say, you harsh and crabbed old men, away with you, my page mocks your stern censures. Away with you, old men, unless perchance some one of you with sluggish marrow believes that there is fire in my poems. A more flourishing age is more suitable for tender dalliance. May either a young man or a learned girl read me, and may they praise me as the first poet of the Britons to compose tender elegies telling of the stratagems of love.)

Campion's use of this topos of Roman love elegy suggests that he regarded his poetry as light-hearted, written for youth and laughter rather than for censorious old age, for the *tetrici* and *severi* of Latin poetry (cf. Martial 11.2.7, Catullus 5.2, Ovid, *Am.* 2.1.3 ff). Campion here makes deliberate use of the vocabulary of Latin amatory poems, *teneros lusus* (cf. Ovid, *Am.* 3.1.27), *docta puella* (cf. *A.A.* 2.281), *sua furta* (cf. *Her.* 18.64).

Campion's amatory elegies delineate various situations in the course of a love affair: falling in love at first sight, the fickleness of a former mistress, the folly of a friend in leaving his mistress in the poet's charge, the desire for hindrances which will add spice and allurement to a love affair, the joys of successful love, a complaint that wealth has more power than beauty to attract women's love, protestations of fidelity, accounts of assignations, advice to a lover. Three different women appear in the love elegies: Sybilla (elegies 1, 8) Caspia (6, 13a), and Mellea (5, 9, 4a). In the other poems the name of the woman involved is not given. But no clear picture emerges of a woman vibrant with individuality. Campion drew much of the inspiration for his verse from Roman amatory poetry, some perhaps from life, but the object of his affections remains shadowy. The force of his mistress's personality, whether real or imaginary, does not impress itself on the verse.

Nonetheless Campion builds up a convincing amatory land-scape: he depicts a world in which the mistress is physically beautiful. Typically she is described as a *lauta puella* (an elegant girl) (5.18); she is *speciosa* (dazzling) (6.31). In a passage of advice to a lover, a range of imaginary charms is sketched:

Quod pulchrum varium est; species non una probatur,
 Nec tabulis eadem conspicienda Venus.
Sive lepos oculis, in vultu seu rosa fulget,
 Compositis membris si decor aptus inest,
Gratia sive pedes, leviter seu brachia motat;
 Undique spectanti retia tendit Amor. (11.5-10)

(Beauty is manifold; it is not just one facet which is ap-proved. We see different representations of Venus in paint-ings. Whether a girl's eyes sparkle with charm, roses gleam in her cheeks, or there's a becoming grace in her shapely limbs, whether she moves her feet daintily, or her arms gently, Love lays his snares on all sides for the beholder.)

The many forms in which the ideal woman of Campion's dreams may manifest herself are adumbrated in 8.39-42:

Candida seu nigra est, mollis seu dura, pudica
 Sive levis, iuvenis sive adeo illa senex;
Qualiscunque datur, modo sit formosa, rogare
 Non metuam, et longa sollicitare prece.

(Whether she is fair or dark, complaisant or unyielding, modest or shameless, young or even quite an old woman – whatever kind of woman comes my way, so long as she's beautiful, I shan't be afraid of approaching her and implor-ing her with a long entreaty.)

There is in this a clear echo of Ovid's stated willingness to fall in love with women of all types in *Am.* 2.4. The joys of Caspia's surrender are also described in physical, tactile terms, which again echo Ovid closely (*Am.* 1.5):

Quas ego, quam cupide vidi tetigique papillas!
 Quam formosa inter brachia molle latus!
Qualia inhaerenti spiravit basia labro!
 Qualia, sed castis non referenda viris! (13a.9-12)

5

(How eagerly did I see and touch those breasts of hers! How soft her side between those shapely arms! What kisses did she breathe with clinging lip! What – ! But chaste men should not be told such things.)

The rewards of love are the *suaves . . . horas, delicias, lusus, basia docta, iocos* (7.3–4) (sweet hours, voluptuousness, dalliance, experienced kisses, lasciviousness).

An antithesis is suggested between the polished cultivation of the town and the boorish rusticity of the country (cf. Tibullus 2.3.1ff):

> Ergo meam ducet, deducet ab urbe puellam
> Cui rutilo sordent ora perusta cane?
> Mellea iamne meo valedicere possit amori,
> Urbeque posthabita vilia rura colet? (9.1–4)

(Will a man whose face is basely burnt by the heat of the summer sun marry my girl, and lead her away from the city? Could Mellea now say farewell to my love, and dwell in the vile countryside, despising the city?)

> Horrida rura virum, sed non metuenda, tenebant;
> Tutum rivali fecit in urbe locum. (8.9–10)

(The uncouth countryside detained your husband, but there was no reason for me to fear it. It made a safe place for his rival in the city.)

A bedchamber is the setting for an assignation (elegies 8 and 10), whilst an idealized vernal or floral landscape provides the backcloth for love in elegies 1 and 4a.

In the revised and augmented 1619 edition of Campion's poems, we have thirteen elegies, of which two, nos 1 and 3, appear for the first time. The other eleven had appeared in the 1595 edition, though a few slight alterations to the text were made in the new edition, whilst five elegies contained in the earlier edition were not reprinted. The number of lines was thus reduced from 578 to 440. The arrangement of the poems in the 1619 edition was considerably different. Thus, of the thirteen elegies in the 1619 edition, nos 1 and 3 were new to the volume, no. 2 in the 1619 edition had previously appeared as no. 8 in the 1595 edition, whilst nos 4–13 of the 1619 edition had appeared as nos 3, 5, 7, 10, 11, 12, 2, 15, 6, and 9 respectively in the earlier edition. Campion probably regrouped the elegies in the later edition so as to bring the poems into a closer thematic relationship. Thus after the new poem beginning:

Ver anni Lunaeque fuit; pars verna diei (1.1)

(It was the Springtime of the year and of the Moon, the vernal part of the day)

(cf. Lucretius 1.10) which, since it describes love at first sight, is an appropriate one for beginning the collection, there follow elegies 2 and 3, not dissimilar in length (32 and 24 lines respectively), each dealing with a similar theme, *La Ronde*, elegy 2 telling of the poet's abandonment by his mistress in favour of Ottalus, whom she will in turn abandon, whilst no. 3 recounts the abandonment of Calvus by Calvus' mistress in favour of the poet.

The final elegy of the 1619 edition concludes with a non-amatory poem addressed to Campion's friend Edward Michelborne consoling him on the death of his sister, a poem which ends on a note of hope. The two preceding poems, nos 11 and 12, form an antithetical pair of almost equal length (18 and 20 lines). Poem 11 opens with a recommendation that love should be shunned:

Qui sapit ignotas timeat spectare puellas

(A wise man should be afraid of looking at unknown girls)

whilst poem 12 concludes with a recommendation that advantage should be taken of the amatory opportunities that present themselves:

Mane rosas si non decerpis, vespere lapsas
Aspicies spinis succubuisse suis. (12.17–18)

(If you don't pluck roses in the morning, you will see them drooping at eventide, sunk down on their thorns.)

Elegy 5 (28 lines) complains of the fickleness of women, who can be bought by any man who chances to be wealthy, and it ends with the ironic complaint:

> verum si olfecerit aurum
> Mulcebit barbam Mellia nostra tuam. (5.27–8)

(If my Mellea smells true gold, she will stroke your beard.)

This poem is immediately matched by elegy 6 (38 lines) which demonstrates the constancy of the lover, elaborating the query of the opening line:

> Caspia, tot poenas meruit patientia nostra?

(Caspia, has my patience deserved such punishment?)

Poems 8 (52 lines) and 10 (48 lines) form a contrasting pair: in poem 8 the lover gains access to the bedchamber of the lady with whom he is in love. Though he fails to take full advantage of the situation, he enjoys the sight of the lady in bed. In poem 10 the situation is reversed; here the lover is in bed waiting for his mistress to join him:

> Adieci porro plumas et lintea struxi
> Mollius ut tenerum poneret illa latus. (10.9–10)

(Moreover I added feathers and piled up linen so that she could rest her delicate side more gently.)

But his solicitude is in vain, since his mistress fails to keep the assignation. The seventh elegy is a protestation of the poet's fidelity to his mistress, the ninth shows the poet as the victim of his mistress's infidelity. The fourth elegy seems to stand alone, set apart by its greater length, 60 lines. It contains within itself, however, the elements of an antithetical situation, in which the lover is dominated by his mistress during the day, to dominate her in turn during the night. The elegy starts with a general maxim,

> Ille miser faciles cui nemo invidit amores,
> Felle metuque nimis qui sine tutus amat.

(He's an unfortunate fellow whose love affair runs smoothly with no one to envy him; who loves in excessive security without any fear and bitterness.)

In itself this echoes an attitude of Ovid:

quod licet et facile est quisquis cupit, arbore frondis
  carpat et e magno flumine potet aquam. (*Am.* 2.19.31–2)

(Whoever desires what is permissible and easily attainable,
let him pluck branches from a tree, and drink water from a
great river.)

Campion follows this maxim with advice to the mistress:

Imperet et iubeat quae se constanter amari
  Expetit: utcunque est, obsequium omne nocet. . . .
Discite, formosae, non indulgere beatis,
  Fletibus assuescat siquis amare velit.
Nec tristes lachrimae, cita nec suspiria desint,
  Audiat et dominae dicta superba tremens. (7–18)

(Let a woman who longs to be loved constantly be imperi-
ous and commanding. All complaisance of whatever kind is
detrimental. . . . Learn, O beautiful girls, not to indulge
your fortunate lovers. If anyone wants to be in love, let
him grow accustomed to tears. Let sad tears and hasty
sighs be his constant companions, let him hear in trembling
the proud commands of his mistress.)

The situation is seen in general terms any lover, any mistress.
The poem develops the theme of servitude to a mistress, seeing
love as a ritualized game. Cruelty helps to keep love strong.

This is Campion's most sensual poem, with its undertones of
sado-masochism. Although the lover is to weep and sigh during
the day, at night he should dominate her, bite her lips, draw
blood from the nipples of her breasts, triumph like a horse in
rich pastureland. But when day returns, he is to be submissive
to his mistress, to help her with her toilette.

Campion seems then to have an interest in exploring certain
amatory themes, in working out the variations of a conventional
situation. He is a commentator on certain aspects of love. Thus
general maxims or *sententiae* abound in his poetry, and many
of the elegies are written to exemplify these maxims, which
frequently occur in the opening lines of the elegy. Poems 4
and 11 simply develop the generalization of their opening
lines already quoted above. Poem 5 illustrates the generalization of its opening couplet:

9

> Prima suis, Fanni, formosis profuit aetas,
> Solaque de facie rustica pugna fuit.

(Fannius, in the first age of men, the handsome reaped the
rewards of their handsomeness, and the only rustic contest
was about beauty.)

General maxims can indeed be found throughout the elegies
(e.g. 6.9–10; 8.43–4; 11.3–4 and 15–16; 12.1–4, 11–12, and
17–20). In particular the poems end on a strong line which
embodies a summarizing conclusion, e.g.:

> Nam perii, et verno quae coepit tempore flamma,
> Iam mihi non ullo frigore ponet hyems. (1.19–20)

(For I am undone, and no winter with its cold will quench
the flame which fired me in the spring.)

> Dum iuvat, et fas est, praesentibus utere; totum
> Incertum est quod erit; quod fuit, invalidum. (12.19–20)

(Take advantage of the present whilst it gives you pleasure
and it's right to do so. The future is entirely uncertain, the
past irrelevant.)

But all the elegies end in an emphatic and pointed, almost
epigrammatic manner, which helps to give the poetry a
detached, ratiocinative tone. The same emphatic endings are
observable in Campion's English lyrics:

> Thinke that thy fortune still doth crie,
> Thou foole, to-morrow thou must die.

> But when we come where comfort is
> She neuer will say no.

> But if she doth of sorrow speake,
> Eu'n from my hart the strings doe breake.
> (poems 2, 3, and 6 of *A Booke of Ayres*)

Campion's mood in his love elegies is one of lightness and
detachment, the result of his easy and graceful style, which
derives above all from Ovid. The mistresses who appear in
Campion's erotic elegies are not placed in any particular
identifiable social or historical setting. There are no allusions

which would enable us to say that they are set in the world of Campion's own day – no reference to ruffs or farthingales – neither is the world recognizably Roman. There is no mention of chariots and games, or the witty social world of Rome. The setting is timeless and placeless, not specific. Nonetheless, the atmosphere of Campion's elegies is that of Ovidian love elegy, somewhat cynical, portraying a love that is concerned with physical beauty and attraction rather than a spiritual and transcendent love. There are, too, many close echoes of Ovid. (The verbal humour of 1.5–6 and 15–16, cf. *Met.* 3.380–92; the personification of Elegy, 13.9–10, cf. *Am.* 3.1.; the desire for rivals in love, 4.1–2 and 57–60, cf. *Am.* 2.19; the advice to beware of women seen at night, under the influence of drink, 9.13–16, cf. *A.A.* 1.243–52; the sensuality of 13a.9–13, cf. *Am.* 1.5.19–22.)

The vocabulary of Love too is drawn from Ovid, e.g. *perii* (1.19; cf. *Her.* 12.33); *flamma* (1.19; cf. *Am.* 2.1.8); *insidiosa* (1.12; cf. *Rem.* 148); *laedor* (1.15; cf. *Her.* 5.102); *speciosa* (2.1; cf. *Met.* 11.133); *calores* (2.3; cf. *A.A.* 1.237); *ignes* (2.5; cf. *Am.* 1.15.27); *regna* (2.14; cf. *Am.* 1.1.13); *levitate* (2.28; cf. *A.A.* 2.429); *ocellis* (3.11; cf. *Am.* 2.19.19); *nec bene sanus* (3.16; cf. *A.A.* 3.713); *Cupidinis arte* (3.17; cf. *Am.* 2.4.30 and 1.11.11); *faciles . . . amores* (4.1; cf. *Her.* 11.29 and *A.A.* 3.27); *amica* (4.3; cf. *A.A.* 1.465); *dominam* (4.5; cf. *Am.* 3.4.43); *docta* (4.10; cf. *A.A.* 2.281); *ussit* (4.11; cf. *Am.* 3.1.20); *callida* 4.13; cf. *Am.* 1.2.6); *formosae* (4.15; cf. *Am.* 1.9.43); *lachrimae* (4.17; cf. *Am.* 1.4.61); *labella* (4.21; cf. *A.A.* 1.667); *delicias* (7.4; cf. *Am.* 3.15.4); *blandus . . . Amor* (8.16; cf. *T.*1.3.49); *Cassibus meis* (8.38; cf. *A.A.* 1.392); *faces* (8.36; cf. *Am.* 1.1.8); *amator* (8.50; cf. *A.A.* 1.722); *fides* (10.3; cf. *Am.* 2.9.50); *improba* (10.4; cf. *Her.* 10.77). The verse-style likewise is indebted more to Ovidian love elegy than to any other Latin poetry. At the end of each elegiac couplet is a strong break which marks the end of a sentence or at least a major pause within the sentence. The structure of the sentences is simple and graceful, with many of the repetitions and exclamations so characteristic of Ovid.

From Ovid too derive the mythological figures whom Campion uses as studied *exempla* in his love elegies – Theseus, Dido, Cephalus and Procris in elegy 7, Thisbe in elegies 10 and 12, Phaedra in elegy 11, and Leander in elegy 12. Campion's most successful use of mythology as an extended *exemplum* is the dramatic citation of Paris in elegy 4 as an illustration of the pleasure to be derived from the successful winning of a woman in the teeth of rivals:

> Quove animo Troiae portas subiisse putatis
> Cum rapta insignem coniuge Priamidem?
> Aurato curru rex, et regina volentes,
> Accurrunt; fratres, ecce, vehuntur equis;
> Et populus circum, iuvenesque, patresque, globantur
> Aemula spectatum multa puella venit. (4.47–52)

(In what spirits do you suppose that the famous son of Priam arrived at the gates of Troy with the wife whom he had abducted? The king and queen hasten gladly in a golden chariot; behold, his brothers ride on horses; the people, young men and old, throng around him; many an envious maiden comes to watch.)

In his English lyrics Campion shows himself to be simple, lucid and graceful. His Latin elegies are longer, more complex, written on a greater scale; in them he shows a gift for exploring a wide range of amatory situations, for analysing the emotions of love, and in certain poems, such as elegies 8 and 10, for creating a vivid and dramatic atmosphere as the setting of the poem. We see in the Latin elegies aspects of Campion as a poet which a consideration only of his English poems would not reveal to us.

In common with most neo-Latin poets, Campion wrote Latin epigrams, which enjoyed an enormous vogue in the sixteenth century. Latin, a terse and laconic language, is ideally suited for the mordant and trenchant qualities of the epigram – suited too for the pedantic and somewhat heavy-handed humour displayed by so many sixteenth-century writers of epigram, including Campion. Campion wrote nearly five hundred epigrams. The 1595 collection of Latin poems, *Poemata*, had contained 129 epigrams; of the two books of epigrams published in the second edition of Campion's poetry in 1619, the first book consisted entirely of 225 new epigrams, whilst of the 228 epigrams in the second book nearly a hundred were reprinted, sometimes with revisions, from the earlier volume.

Campion was interested in the theory of the epigram:

What Epigrams are in Poetrie, the same are Ayres in
musicke, then in their chief perfection when they are short
and well seasoned. (Preface to *A Booke of Ayres*)

He believed that his own collection was unpretentious and
witty:

> At tenues ne tu nimis (optime) despice musas;
> Pondere magna valent, parva lepore iuvant.
>
> (*Epigrams*, 1.1.5–6)

(O best of men, don't be too contemptuous of my trifling
Muses. Great poetry prevails by its grandeur, light-hearted
poetry by its charm.)

He also claimed a didactic purpose for the epigram in its
castigation of human folly:

> Sicut et acre piper mordax epigramma palato
> Non omni gratum est: utile nemo negat.
>
> (*Epigrams*, 1.34.1–2)

(A mordant epigram, like pungent pepper, doesn't please
every palate. But no one denies its utility.)

In another epigram Campion praises his exemplars Catullus
and Martial:

> Cantabat Veneres meras Catullus;
> Quasvis sed quasi silva Martialis
> Miscet materias suis libellis,
> Laudes, stigmata, gratulationes,
> Contemptus, ioca, seria, ima, summa;
> Multis magnus hic est, bene ille cultis. (2.27)

(Catullus composed pure love poetry. But Martial like a
wood houses all sorts of lumber in his little books, praise,
blame, congratulations, scorn, jokes, weighty matters;
he touched the depths and the heights. Martial is a great
man to the many, Catullus to those of refined taste.)

The subject of his epigrams is described as *lusus . . . mollis,
iocus . . . levis* (pleasant mockery, light-hearted joking) (*Epigrams*,
2.2.1). Campion, like Martial, wrote epigrams of one line in

length (*Epigrams*, 1.53, 2.213; cf. Martial 7.98, 8.19). His longest epigram is 59 lines long.[4] The majority are, however, shorter than 16 lines, and many of them are couplets or quatrains.

Sixteenth-century theorists, such as Julius Caesar Scaliger, debated how long an epigram should be. Scaliger believed that 'Breuitas proprium quiddam est. Argutia anima et quasi forma. . . . Breuitatem vero intelligemus, non definitam, nam et monostichon est apud Martialem, et aliquot satis longa, si alia spectes.'[5] ('Brevity is a characteristic of the epigram. Wit is its soul, its form, as it were. . . . We will understand that there is no definition of brevity, for we find a monostich in Martial, and if you look at others, several are quite long.') Scaliger goes on to discuss the versatile nature of the epigram. It can embrace all types of poetry, dramatic, narrative, and mixed, can be written in all metres, and its subject matter can be unlimited.[6]

It would be easy enough to take a superficial view of the epigram, to believe that it is simply a short poem with a sting in the tail which will hardly stand up to discussion. Yet in its long history the epigram has been capable of a surprising degree of development. Originally a poetic inscription (as Scaliger was aware), often on a tomb, in the Alexandrian period the epigram had come to be a brief poem, usually in elegiacs, on a single event, either great or trivial. In the post-Alexandrian period it was not usually intended for funereal inscriptions, and the genre embraced other themes. Epigrams survive which deal with love, wine, works of art, famous men, natural beauties, sketches of women or animals. After the publication by Meleager of an anthology of six centuries of poems in the first century B.C., Philippus of Thessalonica published in A.D. 40 a 'garland' of poets writing after Meleager, in which are found poems which have a 'sting in the tail'. By developing this latter trait Martial made his own contribution to the development of the epigram, which became predominantly satirical.

Epigrams continued to be written after the decline of the antique world, and the introduction of the Planudean and Palatine Anthologies to the Latin West in the sixteenth and seventeenth centuries gave the epigram a new lease of life in the hands of the neo-Latin poets of Europe at that time. In his discussion of 'English Trochaik verse' in *Observations in the Arte of English Poesie* Campion gives examples of twelve English epigrams, mainly amatory and satirical, which make fun of human foibles:

> I haue written diuers light Poems in this kinde, which for the better satisfaction of the reader I thought conuenient here in way of example to publish. In which though sometimes vnder a knowne name I haue shadowed a fain'd conceit, yet it is done without reference or offence to any person, and only to make the stile appeare the more English. (*Works*, ed. Vivian, p. 44)

Campion's Latin epigrams are very varied. We find amongst them poems addressed to the mistresses of the love elegies – Caspia, Mellea, and Sybilla – in the collection which had first appeared in the 1595 *Poemata*. In these the amatory situation is overlaid with irony:

> Anxia dum natura nimis tibi, Mellea, formam
> Finxit, fidem oblita est dare. (*Epigrams*, 2.18)

(Whilst solicitous nature made you excessively beautiful, Mellea, she forgot to give you loyalty.)

In these amatory epigrams it is the negative and sterile aspects of a love affair which are stressed, particularly in the epigrams addressed to Caspia. Thus the poet complains that Caspia holds herself remote from love (2.15), that she is unstable (2.37), that she remains aloof and rejects his advances (2.50), that she is contrary (2.53). In 2.56 the lover is wretched, in 2.66 he bitterly dwells on the punishment in the underworld of the beloved who does not requite the lover's love. In 2.89 the poet complains that he is excluded from Caspia's affections, in 2.92 he longs for one night of love. In 2.109 we are informed that Caspia loves no one, whilst in 2.113 we hear of her *feritas*, savageness. In 2.124 Caspia is stigmatized as an angry woman who repels lovers; she is also constant in hatred (Vivian, p. 342).

Mellea does not appear in any more favourable light. In 2.10 the poet feels an insane jealousy towards her; in 2.12 he tricks her with a kiss. 2.18 is a laconic reflection upon her fickleness, whilst in 2.48 he bids her, 'Circe, in aeternum vale!' ('Enchantress, farewell for ever!') The poet is afraid of Mellea's compliments (2.63); and Mellea loves many men (2.109). The epigrams addressed to women bearing different names from those of the women in the elegies are similarly bitter.

> Qui te formosam negat haud oculos habet; at te
>   Nauci qui pendet, Pasiphyle, cor habet. (*Epigrams*, 2.190)

(The man who says you are not beautiful is blind; but the man who doesn't care two straws for you, Pasiphyle, is discerning.)

That mood of bitter disillusion pervades Campion's amatory epigrams. However, the bulk of his epigrams are written in a low key, drawing attention to some trait of human folly or weakness. They lack the mordant vehemence of satire, the 'sting in the tail' is slight. A good many of them are addressed to unidentifiable individuals who are referred to by such names as Nerva, Eurus, Haedus, Cacculus, Sabellus, Lycus – Roman names, in the manner of Martial, who adopted the same practice of stigmatizing the vice, not the identifiable practitioner of the vice. And so we find poems about the avariciousness of lawyers, the pretentiousness of poets; poems ridiculing quacks, bad singers, cuckolds, false prophets; poems against the vogue for tobacco and against other human frailties or notable peculiarities: the man whose nose makes a loud noise when he speaks (1.117), the man who is indifferent to debt (1.78), the English fashion for wearing too many clothes in the summer (1.144). Many of these seem to be only mildly amusing today, to be low-powered and laboured, lacking the neat and biting conclusion necessary to make them memorable. Campion has toned down the final emphasis characteristic of the epigrams of Martial.

A number of encomiastic epigrams addressed to men of note partake of the qualities of the epigram only in their conclusion. The attribution of praise or blame is, as Scaliger had noted,[7] one of the properties of the epigram. In the epigram praising the achievements of Sir Robert Carey (1.46), the epigrammatic effect lies in the antithesis of the concluding line,

> Qui novit iuvenem, noscet itemque senem.

(Whoever knew the youth will likewise know him in his dotage.)

Likewise in the conclusion of the poem praising Drake's *Golden Hind* (1.94):

> Cuius fama recens tantum te praeterit, Argo,
> Quantum mortalem Delia sphaera ratem.

(The recent fame of this ship excels yours, O Argo, as much as the globe of the sun excels a man-made ship.)

There are finally a number of formal and controlled poems, elegiac rather than 'epigrammatic' in mood, which commemorate the deaths of various famous men, among them Prince Henry (1.96), Walter Devereux (2.9), and Sir Philip Sidney (2.11). Campion thus demonstrated his ability as a writer of epigrams which embrace most of the traditional types and subjects.

In *Umbra*, a work which spans Campion's poetical career, we have his most sustained poetical work. In the 1595 *Poemata*, the first 231 lines appeared, the poem breaking off in mid-sentence after 'Et quid ait' in line 232. The poem was reprinted and completed in the 1619 collection, and part at least of the conclusion must have been written after the marriage in 1613 of Princess Elizabeth to the Count Palatine of the Rhine, to which there is a reference in l. 343.

Umbra is a mythological poem of 404 lines which falls into two almost exactly equal parts. The first section, lines 1–201, tells of the love of Apollo for the nymph Iole, daughter of Cybele. Apollo desires the nymph, but she is unwilling to receive his advances. Apollo drugs Iole to sleep, then rapes her and makes her pregnant. The nymph then begins to suffer the symptoms of pregnancy in ignorance of what they portend. At last she gives birth to a son, Melampus, who is black save for the image of the sun, his father, on his breast. Apollo visits Jupiter to ward off any possible anger on the latter's part. Jupiter laughs at the complaints of Iole's mother, Cybele, whose anger gradually fades away with the passing of time. The second part of the poem centres upon the youth of Melampus. Whilst Melampus is asleep, Morpheus the god of sleep chances upon him, and is entranced by his beauty.

Morpheus tries to attract Melampus' interest by transforming himself into many different shapes, but to no avail. He then decides to make a journey to the underworld, where the shades of the most beautiful women are to be found, in order to fashion for his purposes a composite figure of ideal beauty. He then returns thus disguised to the sleeping Melampus, who welcomes him and falls in love with the vision. But day dawns, and the vision vanishes. Melampus can nowhere find the object of his affections. He wastes away and dies, and his shade wanders in darkness for ever.

Both halves of the poem are thus united by a thematic similarity. Both deal with the love of a god, unrequited at first, until he uses his superhuman powers. Moreover, in both stories the god escapes unpunished, whilst the mortal is ruined. Mythological *epyllia* were popular in England in the late sixteenth century (e.g. Marlowe's *Hero and Leander*, Shakespeare's *Venus and Adonis* and others).

Campion is, however, unusual in that he seems to have invented a story, rather than to have adapted an already existing myth. I am not aware of any previous treatment of the figures of Apollo and Morpheus dealing with the story which Campion relates, although Apollo was of course known from Ovid's *Metamorphoses* as a god addicted to the pursuit of nymphs.

Campion incorporates into his poem much of the machinery of previous philosophical epic. He describes two *loci amoeni*, pleasant and remote places which embody an ideal pastoral landscape. The first of these is the home of the nymphs:

> Est in visceribus terrae nulli obvia vallis,
> Concava, picta rosis, variaque ab imagine florum;
> Fontibus irrorata, et fluminibus lapidosis:
> Mille specus subter latitant, totidemque virenti
> Stant textae myrto casulae, quibus anxia turba
> Nympharum flores pingunt, mireque colorant. (17–22)

(There is a valley hollowed out in the bowels of the earth, which no one can enter, decorated with roses and different types of flowers, watered by fountains and rivers full of stones. Beneath it a thousand grottoes are hidden away; there are the same number of bowers woven from the myrtle in bloom, for which a sedulous band of nymphs adorns the flowers, and decorates them in a wondrous manner.)

The second is the home of Persephone in the second part of the poem:

> Luce sub obscura procul hinc telluris in imo
> Persephones patet atra domus, sed pervia nulli;
> Quam prope secretus, muro circundatus aereo.
> Est hortus, cuius summum provecta cacumen
> Haud superare die potuit Iovis ales in uno.
> Immensis intus spaciis se extendit ab omni
> Parte, nec Elisiis dignatur cedere campis,
> Finibus haud minor, at laetarum errore viarum
> Deliciisque loco longe iucundior omni. (255–63)

(In the dim light, far from here, in the depths of the earth lies the black home of Persephone, accessible to no one. Near is a secret garden, surrounded by a wall of bronze; the bird of Jupiter could not surmount its topmost peak in a day's flight. Inside, the garden extends in all directions, covering an immense area, and disdains to yield to the Elysian fields. It extends over an area just as great, but it is far pleasanter than any other place, both in the wandering of its happy by-ways and in its delights.)

In both instances the inaccessibility of the place described is stressed. In the latter the garden is surrounded by a high wall. Both are *nulli obvia* and *pervia nulli*. Morpheus alone can enter the most exclusive part of the latter when he has performed a curious ritual:

> Non huc fas cuiquam magnum penetrare deorum;
> Soli sed Morpheo, cui nil sua fata negarunt,
> Concessum est, pedibus quamvis incedere lotis. . . .
> Primo fons aditu stat molli fultus arena,
> Intranti. . . .
> Morpheus hac utrumque pedem ter mersit in unda,
> Et toties mistis siccat cum floribus herbis;
> Inde vias licitas terit. (276–88)

(It is not right for any of the great gods to enter this region – only Morpheus, whose destiny has denied him nothing, may enter when he has bathed his feet. . . . On the threshold as you enter there is a fountain resting on the soft sand. . . . Morpheus dipped each foot three times in its waters, and three times dried it with mingled grass and flowers. Then he treads the permitted path.)

In the second part of the poem, Campion envisages an elaborate underworld which owes something to Vergil. His underworld is a feminine one, presided over by Persephone, as the invocation to her at the beginning of the poem makes clear (ll. 1–12). The invocation similarly presents Campion's theory of immortality in the poem – that souls leave the underworld for their sojourn on earth, to return to it on death. But Campion has in mind principally the shades of women. He speaks in Vergilian language (*caelo ostentans* – cf. *Aeneid* 6.869) of Persephone manipulating the *Foemineos . . . manes* (shades of women).

In the high-walled inaccessible garden of which the description has been quoted above dwell the shades of beautiful women, past, present, and still to be born. Most of them rest in a valley, admiring their reflections in water, or weaving flowery garlands. But those who are destined to live in the town rather than in the country are engaged in less rustic pursuits. Finally, a special region situated on a hill is reserved for those who are to be heroines in this world. At the entrance to this region is a fountain where the returning shades wash off impurities contacted in the upper world. In this special region are to be found the shades of famous heroines of classical times, such as Antiope, Helen of Troy and Hippodamia, together with certain contemporary gentlewomen of note, such as the Princess Elizabeth. From these Morpheus fashions his ideally beautiful composite figure with which to enchant Melampus:

> capiunt hae denique formae
> Formarum artificem, nec se iam proripit ultra.
> Gratia, nec venus ulla fugit, congesta sed unam
> Aptat in effigiem. (344–7)

(And then these forms attract the shaper of forms, and he goes no further. None of the grace, none of the loveliness escapes him, in fact he gathers it all together and moulds it into a single figure.)

It may be that Campion is trying to make some sort of statement about beauty. Morpheus creates the shape of an ideally beautiful woman, an amalgam of the charms and beauties of the most beautiful women in the underworld. Zeuxis, the Greek painter, in adorning the walls of the temple of Juno at Croton, had similarly produced a composite of ideal beauty by modelling his portrait of Helen on five beautiful girls[8] – a story often quoted by Renaissance theorists.[9]

Earlier in the poem Campion shows his interest in creation theory. The nymphs paint (externally adorn) flowers for their bowers, and Cybele protects and guides the flowers on the earth above, whilst:

> Forma rosis animos maiores indidit, ausis
> Tollere purpureos vultus, et despicere infra
> Pallentes odio violas, tectasque pudore. (32–5)

> (Beauty supplies the roses with greater spirit, as they dare to uplift their faces brightly coloured and to look down upon the violets beneath them pale with loathing and covered with shame.)

Campion here perpetuates an old tradition common in medieval Latin poetry, that violets are inferior to roses.[10]

Umbra is a strange poem. It contains many elements which suggest that the poem has a serious purpose and an inner meaning – the *loci amoeni*, the interest in the creative powers of Cybele, the impregnation by Apollo, identified with the sun and with light, of Iole, the daughter of Cybele; the birth from this union of the beautiful child, black save for the image of the sun on his breast, Morpheus' journey to the underworld, the mysterious fountain, the fashioning of the vision of ideal feminine beauty, the transformation of Melampus into a shadow. But it is not easy to divine what this meaning is. It is possible that Campion started to write this long poem and then found that his talents lay in other directions, that the writing of large-scale poetry was not for him, and that he quickly abandoned the attempt. Nonetheless he thought highly enough of the poem to print even an incomplete version of it in his 1595 collection of *Poemata*; for the poem does break off at a most inappropriate place in that edition, and the poem is advertised even on the title page as being *Fragmentum Umbrae*.

Campion did anyway complete the poem for the 1619 edition of his poetry. Yet he need not necessarily have had a serious purpose in mind. He might have found in the poem simply an opportunity for colourful description and fluent speeches. Certainly his own statements suggest a simple interpretation of the poem:

> insidias, et furtivos hymenaeos,
> Et Nympham canimus. (14–15)

(I tell of treachery and a stolen marriage, and a Nymph.)

In an *Argumentum* which is prefixed only to the 1595 version of the poem, he simply provides a précis of the narrative. The nearest he comes to suggesting a meaning for the poem is to say that Melampus 'falsa pulchritudinis specie deceptus in miserrimum amorem dilabitur' ('deceived by the false image of beauty slips into a most wretched love'). *Umbra* remains then an enigmatic poem, a decorative *epyllion*.

Campion's other long Latin poem, *Ad Thamesin*, is less lucid and interesting than *Umbra*. It appears only in the 1595 *Poemata*, and Campion probably did not esteem it highly enough to have it reprinted in 1619. An *Argumentum* sums up the ostensible subject of the poem:

> Totum hoc poema gratulationem in se habet ad Thamesin de Hyspanorum fuga, in qua adumbrantur causae quibus adducti Hyspani expeditionem in Angliam fecerint. Eae autem sunt, avaritia, crudelitas, superbia, atque invidia. Deinde facta Apostrophe ad Reginam pastoraliter desinit.

> (This whole poem is a congratulation towards the river Thames on the flight of the Spaniards, in which are outlined the reasons which induced the Spaniards to make an expedition against England. Those reasons are avarice, cruelty, pride, and envy. Then, after an Apostrophe to the Queen, the poem ends in pastoral vein.)

After an address to the *Nympha potens Thamesis* (powerful Nymph of the Thames) the poet explains that Jupiter and Neptune did not tolerate the Spaniards as they followed their cruel banners. Jupiter will protect his Britons, and not allow the rites of the Roman Church to flourish again.

There follows a description of a region sacred to Dis (identified in a marginal note as America) in an inversion of the *locus amoenus* topos, introduced by the traditional words *Est locus* (there is a place). But here all is dark, the abode of Furies and monsters. These Dis urges to summon up anger in their hearts, and then urges Oceanus, the god of the Ocean, to provide a smooth passage for the invading Spanish fleet (ll. 38–61). Oceanus reminds Dis that the latter does not hold sway over the sea, and praises the piety and martial prowess of the Britons. Dis rails against Oceanus, who, frightened, departs to fulfil Dis's request, delighted however at the vengeance which Drake and Frobisher will inflict upon the Spaniards (ll. 91–3). Dis holds council with the Spaniards; Avarice in her brazen tower, Slaughter, and Pride, who are present, are described. The Stygian nymphs sing a mournful, miserable song (ll. 143–5), and then follows an account of the Fountain of Envy. Whoever looks into this fountain sees an image of all that the world contains. In this fountain the Spaniards see a representation of England, its white cliffs, fields, cities, rivers, and fountains, and are consumed with envy. The Spaniards are then entertained by Dis (ll. 201 ff) and depart to launch their invasion of England (ll. 240–1). But the river Thames disturbed the waters of the sea (l. 250) and the Armada was defeated. The poet wishes ruination upon the survivors and the poem concludes (ll. 266–83) with a prayer that Queen Elizabeth should flourish in her prime.

The narrative progress of the poem is certainly interrupted by the static descriptions of the House of Avarice and the Fountain of Envy. England and Elizabeth, rather than the river Thames, as the *Argumentum* had promised, are praised, and the speeches even of Dis are used to reflect credit upon them: thus Dis in his speech to Oceanus reminds him that England has never been conquered (ll. 56–8). Oceanus reinforces this in his speech:

Sunt Angli, sunt Troiana de gente Britanni
Qui pacem, numenque colunt, et templa fatigant. (65–6)

(They are Englishmen, they are Britons of Trojan origin, who worship peace and the Godhead, and weary the temples with their worship.)

In lines 159–62, the Spaniards too praise England:

> longe omnibus eminet una
> Cincta mari tellus, celeberrima rupibus albis,
> Hanc spectant, et agros, urbes, vada, flumina, fontes
> Laudant inviti.[11]

(One land surrounded by the sea far excels all others, a land most renowned for its white cliffs; this do they look upon, and unwillingly praise its fields, its cities, its streams, rivers, and fountains.)

This praise of England is, however, hardly that of 'the whole poem' which the *Argumentum* had promised. It is strange too that *crudelitas* and *superbia*, singled out for mention in the *Argumentum*, are sketched so briefly. Campion remarks that the poem ends *pastoraliter*. The praise of great persons is a feature of Vergilian pastoral – e.g. of Octavian and Pollio in *Eclogues* I and IV – so doubtless Campion is here referring to his apostrophe to Queen Elizabeth which concludes the poem. The whole poem, however, seems to strive for the grandeur of epic, only to be overburdened by its pretension.

Ad Thamesin is a patriotic poem of the type to be written in the immediate aftermath of a great national victory. It presents to us in what may be one of his very first poems (if the poem was indeed written immediately after the defeat of the Armada) the nascent poet making trial of his abilities as a poet, and learning, perhaps, that it was as a writer of shorter poems that his talent could best find expression.

Two conventional poems praising Queen Elizabeth and the Earl of Essex which are to be found only in the 1595 edition of his poems complete the corpus of Campion's Latin poetry.

It must be acknowledged that Campion is not a great writer of Latin poetry. Nonetheless his Latin poetry shows that he is a more versatile poet than he reveals himself to be in the English lyrics for which he is chiefly remembered. In his Latin poetry he demonstrates a competent command of the Latin styles of Vergil, Ovid, and Martial, and displays an interest in mythological and allegorical epic. His most interesting Latin poems are, I believe, his love elegies, in which he develops a range of erotic situations wider than that of his

English poems. Campion will no doubt always be remembered chiefly as the delicate poet of *A Booke of Ayres*, but those who like to explore lesser known Elizabethan literature could well do worse than turn to Thomas Campion's Latin poetry.

Notes

I am grateful to my colleague Mr I. M. LeM. DuQuesnay for reading a draft of this essay and making some helpful comments.

1   Sig. Nn8r.
2   *Affaniae, sive Epigrammatum Libri tres* (Oxford, 1601), sigs F7r. and D5v. Campion is called a *vates* on sig. B6v.
3   Quotations from Thomas Campion are from *Campion's Works*, ed. Percival Vivian (Oxford, 1909, reprinted 1967). I adopt, however, the modern usage of *v* and *u* and transcribe *j* as *i* in quotations from the Latin poems. When referring to elegies which were printed only in the 1595 edition of Campion's poetry (these are given in an appendix by Vivian), I add for convenience of reference the suffix *a* to their number.
4   Appearing only in the 1595 edition of Campion's poetry, it is included in the Appendix to Vivian's edition, pp. 342–3.
5   *Poetics* (Lyon, 1561), iii.cxxvi, p. 170. References are to book, chapter, and page of this edition.
6   *Ibid.*
7   *Ibid.*
8   See Cicero, *De Inventione* ii.i.
9   E.g. by Thomas Nash in *The Anatomie of Absurditie* (see George Gregory Smith, ed., *Elizabethan Critical Essays* (Oxford, 1904), 1.321); by Alberico Gentili in his Oxford, 1593, critical treatise (see my 'Alberico Gentili in defense of poetry and acting', *Studies in the Renaissance* 19 (1972), pp. 231 and 252); by Walter Haddon, *Lucubrationes* (London, 1567), sig. L14v.
10 See, e.g. Venantius Fortunatus, *Carmina* 8.6., ed. F. Leo, *Monumenta Germaniae Historica, Auctores Antiquissimi*, iv.i (Berlin, 1881; reprinted 1961).
11 In l. 160, I read *cincta*, the reading of the 1595 edition, for Vivian's erroneous *cuncta*.

II
The Latin Poetry of George Herbert

W. Hilton Kelliher

George Herbert was in his thirty-fifth year when he lost his mother, the most beloved and dominant personal influence of his life. In the first shock of bereavement he composed a series of poems that celebrate her virtues and lament her death, turning for the occasion not to the native instrument of which also he was an assured master, but to Latin and Greek verse. The intimate lyrics and elegies that make up *Memoriae Matris Sacrum* were completed within a few weeks and at his own death in 1633 remained his only mature poems to have achieved print. To reject the vernacular at such a time of crisis argues not only an appreciation of the splendid opportunities offered by the classical languages for memorial verse but also considerable ease and familiarity with them. As a Westminster schoolboy Herbert must have composed Latin verses by the score before ever he tried his hand at English, and like many other poets of the time first appeared in print in the anthologies that the Universities issued to commemorate royal events.[1] His mature Latin work began during the period of his fellowship at Trinity College, Cambridge, and is chiefly comprised in three sequences and a collection of loosely related pieces; *Musae Responsoriae*, his defence of Anglican ritual, was followed by a series of meditations on Christ's Passion and by the gathering together of some miscellaneous moral reflections under the title of *Lucus*. The freedom with which he circulated these and other Latin epigrams contrasts with a marked reticence about his English lyrics, which are not known to survive in any commonplace copies taken during his lifetime; and how much care he took over his non-vernacular compositions appears from the fact that several occasional pieces, written at about this time, are extant in a number of manuscript versions whose variants indicate authorial revision. Moreover *Passio Discerpta* and *Lucus*, copied in his own beautiful hand, are preceded in the Williams manuscript by a scribal transcript of sixty-nine of the poems that were published after his death as *The Temple*, and the collocation suggests that he acknowledged no significant distinction of medium in his poetry.

The sequence of epigrams that Herbert is thought to have circulated earliest bears an inseparable literary and theological aspect, for *Musae Responsoriae*, despite some flattery of King James to whom it is principally dedicated, is a serious venture into religious apologetics. It was provoked by *Anti-Tami-Cami-Categoria*, a long and vigorous Sapphic ode composed by the Scots Presbyterian minister Andrew Melville (1545–1622) in response to the hostile reaction awakened at Oxford and Cambridge by the Puritan Millenary Petition of April 1603. Melville's poem almost certainly remained unpublished until 1620 when another religious exile on the continent, David Calderwood, appended it to a Latin translation of his own tract, *The Perth Assembly*, for two independent replies originating from the Universities are both datable to this later period. Thomas Atkinson, a Fellow of St John's College, Oxford, dedicated his hendecasyllabic *Melvinus Delirans*[2] to William Laud in terms that set its composition between December 1616 and June 1621. The prefatory epigram that Herbert addressed in *Musae Responsoriae* to the Bishop of Winchester, who may safely be identified as Lancelot Andrewes, must have been written after February 1619, and the very first poem of the sequence proper seems to include a reference to the Latin translation of King James's *Works* that had been presented to Cambridge in May 1620. We may therefore accept as truth the statement made by Walton in the first edition of his *Life of Herbert* that these epigrams were composed 'immediately after Mr. *Herbert* was made *Orator*', in January 1620.

Melville's long ode divides, as Herbert observes in epigram
IV, into three principal sections. The first (ll. 1–64) expresses
the abhorrence felt by Puritans and Presbyterians for certain
ceremonies enjoined by the Anglican Prayer Book; the second
(ll. 65–128) claims support for the reforms urged in the Millenary Petition from leading Protestant theologians of the
previous century; and the last dwells on the wisdom and majesty
of God, contrasted with the senseless pomp and worldly
ambition of prelates. Herbert's reply treats chiefly of the first,
and it is clear that for him the historical fact of the Millenary
Petition was not immediately at issue: in his twelfth epigram
he betrays ignorance of its main objectives, misinterpreting
Melville's verses and writing as if the petitioners took exception
to the churching of women rather than to the custom which
permitted a nurse (Melville's *mulier sacerdos*) to administer
baptism to infants in danger of death. Mention of *Praesulum
fastus* sets him off on a defence of bishops, though episcopacy as
such was not a target for attack in the Petition. The truth is
that he was committed less to a polemic against Calvinist
theology than to an imaginative justification of Anglican
ritual. At his best he transcends the particularities of the
Categoria, and his satire for all its fireworks and wit tends more
to point out absurdities in the Puritan case than to counter
arguments with venom.

Twelve of the forty epigrams in Herbert's sequence, varying
greatly in tone and working for the most part through metaphor
and image, defend specific points of ceremony challenged by
Melville. He complains (xxv) that in stripping the Church
of her forms and even her vestments the Puritans will leave
her naked not merely to her enemies but also before the Lord
whose bride she is. Similar metaphors, traced also in Donne's
English poetry, are elaborated in 'The British Church', and
Herbert follows them in *Musae Responsoriae* with some observations on the peculiar fitness of the alb for the Church of Albion
(xiv) and a lively defence of the Romish biretta against the
skull-cap (xv). When Melville rejects the sign of the cross in
baptism as not laid down in Scripture Herbert recalls (x)
that Tertullian had likened every Christian at the font to a
fish, adding that the natural position of the body in swimming
is cruciform.[3] In the closing verses he insists that however
much a Puritan may dislike symbolism, the cross – that is, the

Redemption – forms the common heritage of Christians. What would most irritate an Anglican, however, was Melville's unflattering comparison of a priest's words at baptism to the noise of a screech owl, and of sacred music to the clash of Phrygian cymbals. This was no gratuitous insult, but resulted partly from a conviction that to address questions to inarticulate infants was a superfluous exercise. Herbert's Alcaics *De Musica Sacra* (xxiii) contain individual stanzas that promise more than the poem as a whole achieves, but epigram xx makes a neat reply to Melville's charges against a set liturgy:

> ... Tu perstrepis tamen; utque turgeat carmen
> Tuum tibi, poeta belle, non mystes,
> Magicos rotatus, & perhorridas Striges,
> Dicteriis mordacibus notans, clamas
> Non convenire precibus ista Divinis.
> O saevus hostis! quam ferociter pugnas!
> Nihilne respondebimus tibi? Fatemur.

(Still you raise a clamour, and to fill out your song – fine poet that you are, though no mystic priest – in bitter phrases you discover magic wheels and hideous screech owls, crying out that such things do not suit with divine worship. Fierce adversary, how savagely you fight! Shall we make you no answer? We admit the proposition.)

Herbert valued the ceremonies current in the English Church since the Reformation not because he felt that they enshrined mystical elements or were in themselves essential to salvation, but being grounded in Scripture, rich in Christian symbolism and instinct with holiness they were such, he believed, as no reasonable worshipper could reject. The emphasis that Herbert placed upon 'reasonable service' is borne out by Walton's illustrations of how the parishioners of Bemerton were instructed in the origins and purposes of Anglican ritual.

Herbert's dislike of 'slovenliness' in worship mingles in this sequence with an equally powerful distrust of the religious condition known in his time as 'enthusiasm'. On the whole his derisive treatment of Puritans is familiar enough from popular tradition and the writings of a score of more or less orthodox satirists of his own and the previous age, among whom it was a commonplace to contrast the humble origins and imperfect education of dissenters with their lofty pretensions. In addressing them as *Cathari* (*katharoi*, 'puritans') Herbert was adopting a term used by and applied to several religious sects of the Middle Ages, amongst whom were numbered the *Tisserants* or *Textores*. In daring to interpret Holy Writ, his weaver is wittily accused (xix) of pretensions to high academic authority:

De Textore Catharo.

Cum piscatores Textor legit esse vocatos,
    Ut sanctum Domini persequerentur opus;
Ille quoque invadit Divinam Flaminis artem,
    Subtegmen reti dignius esse putans,
Et nunc perlongas Scripturae stamine telas
    Torquet, & in Textu Doctor utroque cluet.

(When the weaver reads that fishers were called to carry out the Lord's work he too leaps into the minister's holy office, thinking warp and woof more respectable than nets. Now through the endless yarn of Scripture he weaves his thread and deems himself Doctor both in text and textile.)

A similar technique is found in epigram xi, while the argument of xv turns cleverly on the shape and position of the biretta. The wit and point of such pieces reposes equally in situations imagined or exploited and in pun and word-play, though at times he can poke fairly innocent fun at Melville's Scots accent (xvi, l. 6) or joke with St Ambrose's name (xxxiii, l. 20). If to modern tastes his wit seems to be deployed more readily against the Puritans than in the service of Christianity at large, the worst that he has to say concerns their innovations in worship: he nowhere questions the sincerity of their religion, much less denies them hope of salvation. In the mass they are to him merely *seducti innocentes* (xxxvi), while in the fine hendecasyllables of xxxvii he willingly concedes to Melville, although culpable as a leader, the respect due to an older man, a scholar and a poet. This epigram is a minor masterpiece of ironic compliment, but establishes in its opening paragraph a wry good-humour that was rare in contemporary religious debate:

Atqui te precor unice per ipsam,
Quae scripsit numeros, manum; per omnes
Musarum calices, per & beatos
Sarcasmos quibus artifex triumphas;

Quin per Presbyteros tuos; per urbem
Quam curto nequeo referre versu;
Per charas tibi nobilesque dextras,
Quas subscriptio neutiquam inquinavit;
Per quicquid tibi suaviter probatur;
Ne me carminibus nimis dicacem,
Aut saevum reputes. Amica nostra est
Atque edentula Musa, nec veneno
Splenis perlita contumeliosi.

(So I conjure you most of all by the hand that wrote those
verses; by the drinking-cups of the Muses; and by those
happy strokes of caustic wit that you excel in. More! by
your own Presbyters; by the city that I can't fit into my
narrow verses; by those right hands, so noble and dear to
you, which the Subscription by no means has stained; or
by whatever seems agreeable to you! Don't think me too
bitter or satirical in my epigrams. My Muse is a kindly
creature, not given to biting, nor dyed in the abusive
venom of spleen.)

Behind a playful conjuration that is itself part of the poem's
ironic artifice, Herbert's disclaimer remains ingenuous.

Herbert's opening address to Melville (II) is both tactful and
assured: he borrows and then restores the elder's years as a
duellist returns a defeated adversary's weapon. Yet his confidence that the justice of the cause will make up for his youth
and inexperience in debate cannot altogether excuse occasional
obfuscation. He fails in epigram XVII to prove that the Puritan
dislike of episcopacy was motivated by envy, and his neat conclusion dodges the real issue. In their preference for antitheses
and clear-cut situations, controversial poets are prone to
exaggeration, and even the central image of epigram VIII,
which makes play with a recent invention that Donne had first
introduced into English poetry,[4] ultimately leaves its options
open:

Quisquis tuetur perspicillis Belgicis
    Qua parte tractari solent,
Res ampliantur, sin per adversam videt,
    Minora fiunt omnia:

Tu qui superbos caeteros existimas
(Superbius cum te nihil)
Vertas specillum: nam, prout se res habent,
Vitro minus recte uteris.

(If one looks through Dutch telescopes in the normal way
objects are magnified, but if in the reverse they are all
reduced. You, who think others arrogant – though no one
more so than yourself – should turn the glass round: as
things stand you are using it incorrectly.)

Herbert was perfectly capable of producing a logically con-
clusive argument from a similar image in 'The Elixir', and his
witty application here argues a humorous awareness of both
sides of the case: *solent* is not the same as *debent*. In general the
tone of his epigrams is far from being determined by arrogance
and obfuscation. The close reasoning, though not the economy
of metaphor, to be found in epigrams IX and XII (the latter with
its discreet echoes of Scripture) carries over even into the more
colourful argument of XXVI. At other times Herbert resorts to
popular science and fable (XXII, XXVII) to support or emphasize
his contentions, or else commonsensically reminds Melville
(XIII) that abuse of ceremonies by some need not render them
worthless to all.

Grosart alleged[5] that the two principal faults in the sequence
are a lack of charity and too great a concern with the bride at
the expense of the bridegroom. A certain amount of satire and
witty play is only to be expected in a series of epigrams that sets
out to answer point for point a vigorous plea for reform of
established practices, and it is inevitable that attention should
be focused principally on the temporal church as the immediate
ground of contention, rather than on Christianity at large. By
the common standards of the day Herbert shows not only
restraint but generosity. The language of controversy may
sometimes be what passed current in contemporary verse-
satire but the prejudices behind it are rooted in a firm personal
belief in the aesthetic value of formal worship and its power to
edify; while despite Grosart the tone of the discussion is elevated,
as in Melville's ode, by the presence of elements that are not
polemical or sectarian but affirmative of Christian truths.
Scriptural echoes form an indispensable part of the fabric of

individual poems throughout the sequence, and a persistent and subtle reply to Melville's rejection of ceremony and set liturgies lies in the traditional Christian metaphors that colour not simply Herbert's language but his thinking too. They may be seen in the opening verses of epigram xvii and, with a more expansive force, in xxii:

> Labeculas maculasque nobis objicis:
> Quid? hoccine est mirum? Viatores sumus.
> Quo sanguis est Christi, nisi ut maculas lavet,
> Quas spargit animae corporis propius lutum?

(You taunt us with our blots and blemishes – why so? Are they so surprising? We are travellers. What is Christ's blood for, if not to wash away the spots that the body's neighbour clay sprinkles on the soul?)

Fusion of these elements occurs in epigram xxv, where the argument is resolved by reference to the 'canons of Holy Writ' from which the imagery of the poem itself derives. In this connection Herbert's adaptation of some verses of Horace to serve as the motto for his final hymn *Ad Deum* is not merely a literary pastiche but parody in the serious sense that was sometimes attached to the term in the early seventeenth century. If to modern tastes the hybrid form and unexpected humour of the opening mar a poem that purports to celebrate divine inspiration the conclusion at least is graceful:

> Quem tu, summe Deus, semel
> Scribentem placido rore beaveris,
>   Illum non labor irritus
> Exercet miserum; non dolor unguium
>   Morsus increpat anxios;
> Non maeret calamus; non queritur caput:
>   Sed faecunda poëσεως
> Vis, & vena sacris regnat in artubus;
>   Qualis nescius aggerum
> Exundat fluvio Nilus amabili.
>   O dulcissime Spiritus,
> Sanctos qui gemitus mentibus inseris
>   A Te Turture defluos,
> Quod scribo, & placeo, si placeo, tuum est.

(When you, God of all, have blessed a man in his writing with the gentle dew, no fruitless labour employs the wretch's endeavour, no worry cracks his nails with frenzied gnawing: his pen does not grieve nor his head complain. A fertile and masculine vein of poetry reigns in his pious limbs, as the Nile knowing no breakwaters overflows with its welcome flood. O sweetest Spirit! The Dove from whom these holy sighs sweep down and steal into men's minds! Whatever I write, however I please – if please I do – all is yours.)

The presentation of *Musae Responsoriae* is so managed that various levels of retort to Melville's *Categoria* – witty, discursive, playful, imaginative and satirical – alternate with each other and with more expansive themes. We may fairly claim that Herbert shows the concern of a literary artist to balance the moods of his sequence, for that is partly reflected in the choice and placing of metres. He well knew the various capabilities of the verse-forms perfected by classical epigrammatists (v, ll. 5–6) and it is no accident that except in the case of the staple measure, elegiac couplets, the same metre is never used for two consecutive poems. All this together with the highly personal character of Herbert's defence of Anglicanism make it clear that, despite the formal dress of the sequence, with its flattering dedicatory poems and rather fulsome praise of James in epigram XXXIX, *Musae Responsoriae* was no mere attempt to attract the favourable notice of the Jacobean establishment.

We do not know when the sequence entitled *Passio Discerpta* was composed, though Herbert transcribed it himself into the Williams manuscript, along with the collection of epigrams that he called *Lucus*, not earlier than August 1623. He seems therefore to have regarded them as equal in craftsmanship and character to the English poems which they accompany there. Consequently their omission from the manuscript which he later entrusted to Nicholas Farrer for publication after his death is probably owing less to a lack of confidence in their merits than to a realization that the reader might not find in them so clear 'a picture of the many spiritual Conflicts that have passed betwixt God and my Soul' as in the vernacular poems that we now know as *The Temple*. The anonymity of neo-Latin sacred epigram is inevitable, while among the moral and theological reflections that make up *Lucus* few poems will compete with the English as a record of Herbert's daily communings with God. Moreover his Latin verses, representing for the most part the outcome of a conflict that has been resolved in God's favour, lack the drama and compulsion that we find in his *Temple* poems. The reason is not far to seek. Most of the epigrams pursue a sacred 'wit' that reflects the paradoxes of Christianity and of faith or points out the correspondences that exist in and between the great books of nature and Holy Writ. Such paradoxes and conjunctions, when explored with the full resources afforded by Latin verse for rhetorical emphasis and verbal nuance, may strike us at first as contrived and chill, but to Herbert, as to Crashaw after him, they fulfilled a spiritual and aesthetic need in a manner that was impossible in English poetry.

Passio Discerpta – the epithet capturing at once the violence of the crucifixion and its analytical dissection in Herbert's verses – is a series of meditations upon Christ's sufferings and death, and for the most part follows closely if selectively the events recorded in the Gospels. Unlike Crashaw's *Epigrammatum Sacrorum Liber* (1634), which owes its existence to academic requirements, Herbert's twenty-one poems appear to represent a spontaneous meditation, and may have been composed as part of his Holy Week devotions. In Lactantius' *Carmen de Passione Domini* contemplation of Christ's suffering and sacrifice is recommended as a stimulus to virtue and a shield against the snares of the enemy, but nothing quite like Herbert's sequence is to be found in Anglo-Latin sacred verse before his time. Singleness of subject marks it out from the miscellanies in which Protestant epigrammatists, chary of striking ingenious conceits from Gospel texts, explored Old Testament themes; and although it is probable that Herbert was acquainted with the work of continental Jesuit poets like Jacob Bidermann, whose *Epigrammatum Libri Tres* (Antwerp, 1620) includes pieces on the events of the Passion,[6] they made no such overwhelming impression on his style as they were to do on Crashaw's. In general Herbert cultivates not so much a dramatic presentation heightened by elaborate verbal techniques as the provocative and witty manner lately introduced into Anglo-Latin verse in Campion's secular *Epigrammatum Libri II* (1619) and John Owen's ten books of epigrams on manners and morals (1615).

35

A certain similarity of style may be traced between the eleventh epigram of Herbert's sequence and Owen's *Christus in cruce*,[7] which revolves around the current adage that 'Virtue is found in the middle':

> In medio Christus latronum quando pependit,
>   Aut nunquam, aut Virtus tunc fuit in medio.

(When Christ hung between two thieves, then if ever was virtue in the middle.)

Yet while Owen is here and elsewhere content to rest purely in verbal *pointe* or in wit that is merely surprising, Herbert's epigrams call to mind the deeper meanings of the Redemption. The nature of *Passio Discerpta* could not be guessed from Christ's long lament in 'The Sacrifice', which figures among the English poems of the Williams manuscript, or from Herbert's observation in his prose treatise that 'The Countrey Parson is generally sad, because hee knows nothing but the Crosse of Christ, his mind being defixed on it with those nailes wherewith his Master was.'[8] Although the prevailing tone of the sequence is deadly earnest the instrument of Herbert's gravest reflections is often, here as in *Lucus*, a wit that consists in making fruitful connections between events recorded in the Bible. The existence of such correspondences is noticed in 'The Holy Scriptures (ii)'. Thus in epigram xv he links Christ's plaint that 'the Son of man hath not where to lay his head' with St John's words 'he bowed his head' on the cross:

> Vulpibus antra feris, nidique volucribus adsunt,
>   Quodque suum novit stroma, cubile suum.
> Qui tamen excipiat, Christus caret hospite: tantum
>   In cruce suspendens, unde reclinet, habet.

(Wild 'foxes have holes, and birds of the air have nests'; every creature knows its lair or resting-place. Christ alone lacks a host to take him in; only when hanging on the cross has he anywhere to lay his head.)

Similarly *Lucus* ix suggests that Christ's motive in choosing for his disciple a doctor, St Luke, was to cure the ill effects of the apple that caused the Fall. For Herbert divine providence was inherent not only in the pagan legends that preceded Christ (*Lucus* viii) but also in the seemingly casual implications of everyday acts, and something more than a love of homely image informs *Passio* VIII:

> Ah! quam caederis hinc & inde palmis!
> Sic unguenta solent manu fricari:
> Sic toti medicaris ipse mundo.

(How they smite you from all sides with their palms! Even thus are ointments rubbed in by the hand: even so do you apply your salve to all the world.)

(It will be seen that Hutchinson is mistaken in tracing a correspondence with the notion that 'Pomanders and wood . . . being bruis'd are better sented', from 'The Banquet'.) Like epigram VI, this poem appeals to the awful irony of the Passion, which Herbert sums up with a similar wit in some verses from 'The Thanksgiving': 'Shall thy strokes be my stroking? thorns, my flower? Thy rod, my posie? crosse, my bower?' Elsewhere in the sequence the paradoxes embraced by Herbert's sacred wit include not only familiar topics such as Christ's life-giving death (XVII) but his own characteristic conceit on the earthquake (XVIII) that signalled it.

The metaphors of *Passio Discerpta* bear the stamp of Herbert's character even where they threaten to be most commonplace. His *Pastor* of XIV, ostensibly the biblical Sower or Good Shepherd, turns also into the rustic mower whose fate it is to be mown by his own scythe.[9] In a brief allegory (XVI) the sun is pictured as porter in a household whose master, Christ, must deny his servant what he lacks himself. *Vellum scissum* (XIX), a swift-running poem that accommodates a surprising weight of scriptural detail, opens in mockery of Jewish observances the better to celebrate the Redemption that will substitute glorious realities for the old mystique:

> Excessit tener Orbis ex Ephebis,
> Maturusque suos coquens amores
> Praeflorat sibi nuptias futuras.
> Ubique est Deus, Agnus, Ara, Flamen.

(Our youthful world has come of age, and as adult desires mature savours in anticipation the nuptials yet to come. Everywhere reigns God, Lamb, Altar and Priest.)

The marriage of which Herbert speaks so movingly here expresses in the language of Scripture the intimate bond between Christ and His people which He made by His blood. In the same way the conceits of an epigram *In Coronam spineam* rest partly on Herbert's recollection of St Paul's Epistle to the Ephesians 5:23, 30, and the wit of its two couplets is remarkably complex and allusive. The astonishing assertion of the opening verse seems almost blasphemous until it is recognized as a lament:

> Christe, dolor tibi supplicio, mihi blanda voluptas;
>   Tu spina misere pungeris, ipse Rosa.
> Spicula mutemus: capias Tu serta Rosarum,
>   Qui Caput es, spinas & tua Membra tuas.

(Your suffering in the sacrifice, Lord, is pure joy to me. Sorely are you pierced by the thorn, but I by the rose. Let us exchange these darts: you, who are the head, take the rose-garlands – we, your members, the thorns.)

Here, as in most sacred epigram, an imagery that is neither visual nor merely emblematic serves as the vehicle for the religious statement.

The passionate appeal made by Herbert in epigrams II and XIII to Christ's redeeming blood reflects perhaps a feature of continental Latin sacred epigram that was well known to English readers from Charles Scribani's poem[10] on the statue of the Virgin and Child at Halle, which so offended the elder, as it impressed the younger Crashaw. Herbert seems to echo its sentiments in a verse from *Lucus* XXXIV, *Lac cum sanguine posco devolutum*; and his conceits on the sputum (V) or on Christ's side-wound (IV and *Lucus* XXX), in which grim physical details are made a focus for contemplation of the Passion, certainly conform more to the tastes of his own time than ours. A similar tendency is apparent in English poems like 'The Bag', though in the *Temple* poems sanguinary images usually occur as part of a larger, more complex pattern that modifies them considerably. Yet even when the scourge, with its grisly complement of Christ's flesh, is presented (IX) as a stark moral warning we are relieved to learn that in the last resort Herbert sets greater store by individual conscience. The appearance of typically Jesuit aids to devotion in his epigrams is perhaps less remarkable than the economy of his rhetoric on these occasions, for it is only with epigram vii, in which the mocking of Christ is exposed as mummery in its literal sense, or with *Lucus* iv and xxxv, that he approaches the refinement of diction that was favoured by continental practitioners.

Neo-Latin and vernacular poets of the later Renaissance in imitation of Statius' *Silvae* often used the metaphor of a woodland to describe their collections of occasional verse. The trees of Herbert's *Lucus* are planted characteristically in a sacred grove, and show signs of having been gathered together from the nurture of several years. No single theme or clearly definable structure emerges from them, for besides sacred epigrams on New Testament subjects they include many poems of metaphysical speculation or moral reflection – some of which may have begun life as University exercises – and a number of 'character' satires of the sort that Owen and the Jacobean epigrammatists so readily adapted from Martial. Evidence for dating remains scanty. The sixth epigram could not have been written before the outbreak of the Thirty Years' War in 1618, though the full-scale hostilities that give point to its opening couplet did not develop until 1620. Epigram xxv in the Williams manuscript, a series of uncomplimentary anagrams on the name *Roma*, was originally included in *Musae Responsoriae* though it may have been composed at an even earlier date. That it circulated independently of Herbert's replies to Melville is evident from a contemporary copy that survives among Doctor Birch's collections and from the fact that at some time before or during 1620 the epigram reached Cardinal Maffeo Barberini in Italy. Seven elegiac couplets headed *In maledicum, qui in nomen Romae urbis impie lusit* were published in Barberini's *Poemata* of that year; but in a second edition that appeared shortly after his election as Pope Urban viii in August 1623 the last four couplets were printed correctly as a separate poem.[11] Herbert may have had private notice of these verses, but since he quotes in his manuscript only the first three couplets, and was seemingly acquainted with other poems of Barberini, whom he addresses as Pope, we may assume familiarity with the edition of 1623. Epigram xxviii, moreover, could not have been composed before Bellarmine's death in September 1621. Herbert's ingenious disposition of the offending anagrams in a single poem yields only to Barberini's apt and economic rejoinder – *Invertis nomen, quid tibi dicis?* *Amor* – and his subsequent replies run from a bitter accusation of priestcraft to a compliment on the literary achievements of the Pope whose family was popularly commemorated in the epigram *quod non fecerunt barbari, fecerunt Barberini.* A further squib (x) turns on the supposed assumption by the Papacy of the motto *Nec Deus Nec Homo,* the true origin of which was in fact a distich[12] composed for inscription on a crucifix by Baudri of Bourgueil (1046–1130):

> Nec deus est, nec homo, praesens quam cernis imago,
> Sed deus est et homo, quem sacra figurat imago.

(The image that you see is neither god nor man, but he whom it depicts is both.)

In several fine epigrams dispersed throughout *Lucus* Herbert explores the relationship between soul and body, and the philosophical problem of knowledge; and while none of them could be commended for novelty of thinking they are nevertheless distinguished by his use of metaphor, in the former case to illuminate a familiar dichotomy. When separated from its native virtue by Adam's sin the human organism hardened like coral torn from the sea-bed (I), but the soul in its prison still experiences divine longings and strives to bore through its casing (II):

> Ut tenuis flammae species caelum usque minatur,
> Igniculos legans, manserit ipsa licet;
> Sic mucronatam reddunt suspiria mentem,
> Votaque scintillae sunt animosa meae. . . .

(As a slender jet of flame still shoots towards heaven, sending up sparks though it remains fixed, so sighs blow heavenwards my spear-sharp soul and my fervent prayers are the sparks.)

A ready parallel for the human condition is found in a sun-dial (xxxi), which for its working combines in equal proportion light and shade as man does spirit and flesh. In such a partnership, however, the soul becomes subject to the body's limitations, and man arrives at knowledge both of himself and of the world around chiefly through the five senses which 'bring grist to the mill'. By contrast Herbert asserts that divine beings (xxiv) have immediate apprehension: angels are their own grist and mill. Man's consolation must lie in the Bible as a source of knowledge that takes precedence even over revelation. In *The Country Parson* Herbert wrote that 'wicked men, however learned, do not know the Scriptures, because they feel them not',[13] and his hendecasyllables *In S. Scripturas* (v) attest that Holy Writ operates on his own system like a physical sensation.

> Heu, quis spiritus, igneusque turbo
> Regnat visceribus, measque versat
> Imo pectore cogitationes?
> Nunquid pro foribus sedendo nuper
> Stellam vespere suxerim volantem,
> Haec autem hospitio latere turpi
> Prorsus nescia, cogitat recessum?
> Nunquid mel comedens, apem comedi
> Ipsa cum domina domum vorando?
> Imo, me nec apes, nec astra pungunt:
> Sacratissima Charta, tu fuisti
> Quae cordis latebras sinusque caecos
> Atque omnes peragrata es angiportus
> Et flexus fugientis appetitus.
> Ah, quam docta perambulare calles
> Maeandrosque plicasque, quam perita es!
> Quae vis condidit, ipsa novit aedes.

(Alas, what spirit, what fiery whirlwind reigns within my bowels, turning my thoughts into my inmost heart? Did I, 'as I one evening sat before my cell', swallow a flying star? And is it, all amazed at its lodging in my unworthy breast, seeking a way out? Or did I in tasting honey suck in a bee too, consuming both honeycomb and queen? No; it is neither bee nor star that stings me. Most Holy Scripture, it is you that have penetrated the dark recesses and hiding places of my heart, the retreats of fleeting desire. Ah, how knowing and deft you are at coursing through those meanderings and coils! The power that built the house knows it best!)

As Hutchinson aptly points out, some of the elements in these verses are shared in common with Herbert's English poetry, for *Lucus* is rich in imagery and diction of a strongly personal character. Seldom are Herbert's moral reflections, even when directly inspired by a passage from Seneca's *Moral Letters* (xxiii), so completely denuded of figurative language as epigram xiii. Rapid alternation of metaphors of the briefest and most diverse kinds marks the iambic trimeters (xx) on vainglory. This habit of composition, owing little or nothing to classical models, is often displayed in Herbert's English poems, and it may well be that the yoking of so many disparate elements is feasible only in the context of a highly associative and dramatic vernacular poem like 'The Collar'. His flair for illuminating religious truths by means of homely pictures receives full play in epigram xv, which evokes Martha's housewifely bustling in preparation to receive Christ.

> Christus adest: crebris aedes percurrite scopis,
> Excutite aulaea, & luceat igne focus.
> Omnia purgentur, niteat mihi tota supellex,
> Parcite luminibus, sitque lucerna domus:
> O cessatrices! eccum pulvisculus illic!
> Corde tuo forsan, caetera munda, SOROR.

('Christ is here! Dash through the house with busy brooms! Shake out the hangings and make up a glowing fire in the hearth! All must be thoroughly scoured, I say, and all the furniture shine. No need of torches – the whole house should be a lamp. Lazybones! There's a speck of dust!' 'In your heart perhaps, sister: all else is clean.')

One wonders to what extent the poem entitled *Amor* that immediately follows is intended as a reply to Mary's rebuke. In his eagerness to read all the signs the subject of the verses is described as one entangled in the tail (*crine*) of a comet like a sheep in briars. Such glimpses of humour are rare in *Lucus*, though a happy exception occurs in the rather unlikely context of some verses *In Simonem Magum* (iv) where Herbert writes of a coin *Si sursum iacias, in caput ipsa ruit* – 'if you toss it in the air it falls on its head', or 'comes down heads'.

Surprisingly enough in a collection of miscellaneous verses that were written over a period of years the metres of *Lucus* are not so varied as those of *Musae Responsoriae*. Hendecasyllabics and iambic trimeters, favoured by Martial, make up a third of the total, while elegiac couplets remain the staple measure. Nevertheless the verse shows no sign of undue constraint as Herbert moves from commonplaces to metaphysical speculation, spirited satire or religious rapture, and his *pièce de résistance* is a hexameter poem in which his bitter opposition to war receives vigorous expression in mock-heroics. The casting of *Triumphus Mortis* as a prosopopoeia of Death probably represents a hasty adaptation to the purposes of *Lucus* of an earlier version entitled *Inventa Bellica* that is known to have survived in at least two contemporary manuscripts. In its original form the poem may have been intended to complement the *Inventa Adespota* of the Scot Thomas Reid, who served King James as Latin Secretary from 1618 until his death in 1624, for taken together they illustrate Bacon's aphorism from *Novum Organum* (1620) that the inventions of gunpowder, printing and the mariner's compass changed the world. Whether or not Herbert knew Reid personally, as seems most likely, he must have seen his verses in manuscript, for they were first printed in Thomas Farnaby's *He tis Anthologias Anthologia* (1629). In the Chetham Library transcript,[14] where they follow Herbert's own hexameters, they commemorate as in Farnaby's text the inventions of handwriting and printing; but the version published in Scot's *Delitiae Poetarum Scotorum* (1637) concludes with a further section on the mariner's compass. Resemblances between the two poems are underlined by a verbal parallel that links verses 49–50 of *Inventa Bellica* with Reid's *Deerat adhuc, quam nulla satis mirabitur aetas* . . . (1. 28).

Herbert's mock-heroic affects to trace the development of warfare from its humble beginnings in a rustic holiday that broke out into a brawl, each man seizing whatever crude weapon came nearest to hand, to its refinement by the *doctus homicida* whose ingenuity devised more efficient ways of murdering his fellow men in hand-to-hand combat or by mass extermination. The centre-piece of the poem, a description of the cannon, bears a close resemblance to certain passages in the sixth book of *Paradise Lost*, which it anticipates by some forty years. In particular, Herbert's verses 66–80 are almost paraphrased in Milton's lines 578–94, where the inflated diction similarly reflects a parodic intent; and a common impulse may have come indirectly from the epic fragments on the Gunpowder Plot that schoolboys and undergraduates were often set to compose during James's reign. The heroic cast of the Latin verses is strengthened by the underworld setting which serves to swell them with classical names, while besides the moral disapproval thus conveyed the seeming grandeur of the surface is everywhere undermined by irony. The cannon-ball, or *glans*, is pointedly dissociated from the acorns that our rude forefathers belched over at their meals, yet 'belches' forth clouds as it flies from the barrel, propelled by the gunpowder which Herbert describes as sugar from the tables of Hell. It is the black-clad herald of Pluto, a lead-sealed summons from the Fates. The ironies and literary parodies of the rustic holiday are even more persistent.

> Hic ubi discumbunt per gramina, salsior unus
> Omnia suspendit naso, sociosque lacessit:
> Non fert Ucalegon, atque amentata retorquet
> Dicta ferox: haerent lateri convitia fixo.
> Scinditur in partes vulgus ceu compita: telum
> Ira facit, mundusque ipse est apotheca furoris.
> Liber alit rixas: potantibus omnia bina
> Sunt, praeter vitam: saxis hic sternitur, alter
> Ambustis sudibus: pars vitam in pocula fundunt,
> In patinas alii: furit inconstantia vini
> Sanguine, quem dederat, spolians.

(Now as they recline along the sward a scoffer turns everything to jest and libels his fellows. Ucalegon does not brook this but hurls the winged insults back again, and his censure sticks deep in the other's wounded side. The mob divides like the crossroads: rage supplies weapons and earth itself is the arsenal of their fury. Wine feeds the quarrel, as all things grow double to the drinkers but their lives. One is laid low with stones, another with scorched stakes: some pour out their lives into cups, others into trenchers. Wine's treachery flares out, snatching away the life-blood that it gave.)

Ucalegon's wrath recalls Vergil's *iam proximus ardet Ucalegon* (*Aeneid* 2.312) – a metonym that Herbert mischievously twists to his own purposes. The paragraphs that conclude the poem, sombre and unironic by contrast, attribute the invention of gunpowder to a monk and its monstrous abuse in recent times to a Jesuit. Herbert probably knew that Bellarmine, Mariana and Robert Parsons all supported tyrannicide, but at this point surely had in mind the Gunpowder Plot and Father Henry Garnett. The final verses of *Inventa Bellica*, with their grim reminiscences of Vergil's third eclogue and the first murder in Genesis, were replaced in *Triumphus Mortis* by a blander couplet that merely rounds off the prosopopoeia. Yet the lesson was not lost, for into the speech of welcome that Herbert made to Prince Charles on 8 October 1623 he inserted, some-what boldly in view of the Prince's belligerent designs against Spain, a plea for peace that employs an irony similar to that of *Inventa Bellica*: 'You, a student of philosophy, complain that the bond of body and soul is a hindrance to your meditations: the soldier invades your study and sets you free with his sword.' Herbert's dislike of war and its wastage of lives and creative talents was far from being an academic commonplace: he came after all from a family of warriors, and two of his brothers had died in arms abroad. It is difficult to imagine how, in a poem and a congratulatory address, he might have urged his case more persuasively with equal economy of means.

While the years of Herbert's Fellowship at Trinity saw his three sequences, controversial, meditative and moral, take shape they also witnessed the composition of several Latin poems addressed to older friends. Amongst the epigrams inspired by his admiration for Francis Bacon the most out-standing performance is a set of iambic trimeters composed apparently in the early part of 1621, *post editam ab eo Instaurationem Magnam*, though first printed only in 1637. The fabric of this poem consists of a series of noun-clauses that characterize Bacon's achievements and intellect entirely by means of pithy and sometimes surprising metaphors. This striking technique is also the basis of the English sonnet 'Prayer (1)', but even greater skill was necessary to prevent the Latin verse from degenerating into a monotonous rigmarole. To Herbert in this poem Bacon is – what Epicurus represented to Lucretius – the liberator of mankind from error, who freed the spirit of scientific enquiry and dispelled the Idols of the Tribe. In a bold assertion for one bred under the academic curriculum of those times he proclaims Bacon's complete triumph over

Aristotle and scholasticism. If unlike Donne he shows no uneasiness at the new religious doubts created by the advance of natural philosophy it may be because he had accepted, for the purposes of the poem at least, Bacon's own principle of segregation: 'Sacred Theology ought to be derived from the word and oracles of God, and not from the light of nature, or the dictates of reason'.[15] Nevertheless some of the metaphors that occur towards the end of the poem are taken straight from the Bible. Bacon is Noah's dove, finding certainty only in his own powers of reason; while the mustard-seed recalls Christ's parable (Mark 4:30–2) of the grain that grew into a huge tree in which the fowls of the air took shelter, where it symbolizes the Kingdom of Heaven. This introduces a series of associations that is lacking from the overt scheme of disinterested panegyric, and may perhaps be taken as a discreet reminder that all enquiry ends in God.

Herbert's friendship with John Donne is marked by several Latin epigrams on the device that Donne adopted as his seal at about the time of his ordination in January 1615.[16] In the iambic trimeters 'On the sacred anchor of a fisher of men' Christ's cross grown into an anchor becomes not merely a symbol of hope but a mainstay of religious faith, securing the divine presence longer even than Donne's preaching. The concluding conceit, that through his (waxen) seal Donne gives to earth and water a symbol of their own certainty, is rather overworked. In his own elegiacs on the subject Donne wrote that his baptism was sealed (*impressa*) by the sign of the cross, and it may be that Herbert's *sigillum* and *Unda* were intended to recall the 'shining seal' used metaphorically for baptism. The accompanying elegiac distich on the *sancta catena* presented by this device similarly reveals Herbert's preoccupation at this time with neo-Latin sacred epigram. Two Latin triplets whose authorship should surely not be called into question charmingly illustrate Donne's use of the intaglio in sealing letters to his friends, while commemorating, as Walton noted, his gift of such a ring or pendant seal to Herbert 'not long before his death'.

There is no need to trace the origin of Herbert's meditation *In Natales et Pascha Concurrentes*, composed, if Hutchinson is right, on 3 April 1618, to Donne's English poem 'Upon the Annunciation and Passion falling upon one day. 1608'. The incidence of a birthday on Good Friday would naturally impress a pious soul, and more so one who was familiar with the tradition of sacred epigram. Herbert's verses make excellent use of the opportunities for paradox afforded by the subject, but their real climax is the statement, written at a time when he was 'setting foot into Divinity',[17] that only a life like Christ's is worth living. It is tempting to read the final couplet as an epigraph for *Passio Discerpta*, which, were it not for some suspicion of influence from Jesuit verse published later, might also be dated to 1618.

Memoriae Matris Sacrum, the masterpiece of Herbert's Latin poetry, was composed within four or five weeks of his mother's death early in June 1627, probably at his step-father's house adjacent to the Thames and to Chelsea church where she was buried. On 1 July Donne, who had been unable to officiate at the funeral of his friend and patroness of twenty years' standing, preached at Chelsea *A Sermon of Commemoration of the Lady Danvers*, and in the following week it was entered at Stationers' Hall, together with the *other Commemorations* written by her talented youngest son. While like the sermon these highly personal recollections draw a lifelike picture of the virtues, piety and domestic abilities of Magdalen Danvers, they tell us not a little about Herbert himself, whose circumstances are seldom glimpsed in his poetry. We learn (VII) that on his mother's death he was living contentedly in a small house in the country and (XIX) busying himself with the garden, an occupation which he later continued at Bemerton where he 'made a good garden and walkes'.[18] He seems for some time previously to have forsaken poetry, for he says that nothing less than the urge to commemorate his mother had led him back to it: but this was to be his last venture – *semel scribo, perpetuo ut sileam* (XIX). Perhaps he was speaking here primarily of his Latin poetry, and if so it is doubly fitting that her death should inspire the finest, as it is the briefest, lyric (VIII) that he ever published. The metre is that of Horace's 'Beatus ille' epode.

> Parvam piamque dum lubenter semitam
>   Grandi reaeque praefero,
> Carpsit malignum sydus hanc modestiam
>   Vinumque felle miscuit.
> Hinc fremere totus & minari gestio
>   Ipsis severus orbibus;

Tandem prehensa comiter lacernula
Susurrat aure quispiam,
Haec fuerat olim potio Domini tui.
Gusto proboque Dolium.

(While I pursue a humble and religious path in preference
to the broad and guilty highway an envious star snatches
me from this retiredness, mixing bile with my wine. From
this time all my being burns with rage and bluster:
I lower against the very heavens. At length someone
takes me by the cloak in a friendly way and whispers in
my ear: 'this once was your Lord's bitter draught.' I taste
and approve the vintage.)

Hutchinson's interpretation that he 'has chosen a humble lot
. . . but still finds difficulty in reconciling himself to it'[19] is the
exact opposite of Herbert's cry against the fate that will not
leave him in peaceful obscurity but visits him with new afflic-
tions. Interlocutors, of course, figure often in his English poems,
and in particular this dramatic reversal from acute distress to
meek acceptance of God's will at the bidding of an unmistak-
able *quispiam* finds a parallel in 'The Collar'.

From Walton's biography we know that Magdalen Herbert
watched jealously over the moral as well as the formal education of her sons, and in the fine fourth epigram Herbert pays
tribute to the example of piety that she set him:

Per te nascor in hunc globum
Exemploque tuo nascor in alterum:
Bis tu mater eras mihi,
Ut currat paribus gloria tibiis.

(It was through you that I came into this world, and by
your example I am brought into the next. You were twice
over a mother to me, and your renown goes in double
harness.)

In the previous stanza the turning of his globe is more than a
literary metaphor borrowed from Donne and the sixteenth-
century cartographers, for it suggests that his true 'sphere' is
ceaseless meditation upon his mother's virtues so that he may
take stock of his own position from the perspective thus afforded
him. We must admire the neatness and clarity of the verses

which, by contrast with other pieces in this sequence, speak to
the reader without disguise or artifice, for elsewhere in his
distress and confusion Herbert sees fit to compare himself, in a
popular Renaissance figure, to an inverted tree (xi):[20] his
mother's death sentences him, as the fall of Troy Ulysses, to
wander in search of a home. Sometimes the sad realities of the
situation are conveyed by such transparently literary devices as
sickness and dreams. Yet Herbert was sickly, and the fever of
epigram vi need not be entirely fictional even if he surmises
that his fit of verse was the result of physical prompting – *Mater
inest saliente vena*. When he sees a vision of his mother (vii) we
may infer that the convenient literary artifice was at least
partly inspired by the disruption of his normally delicate state
of health by the blow of her death. The Juno, the Astraea with
whom he compares the pale spectre of his dream, was the noble
lady whose domestic qualities, brilliance of mind and universal
charity he feelingly describes in a poem that alone would have
sufficed to commend her and display his natural talent for
Latin verse (ii):

> . . . Non illa soles terere comptu lubricos,
> Struices superbas atque turritum caput
> Molita, reliquum deinde garriens diem
> (Nam post Babelem linguae adest confusio)
> Quin post modestam, qualis integras decet,
> Substructionem capitis & nimbum brevem,
> Animam recentem rite curavit sacris
> Adorta numen acri & ignea prece.
>   Dein familiam lustrat, & res prandii,
> Horti, colique distributim pensitat.
> Suum cuique tempus & locus datur.
> Inde exiguntur pensa crudo vespere.
> Ratione certa vita constat & domus,
> Prudenter inito quot-diebus calculo.
> Tota renident aede decus & suavitas
> Animo renidentes prius. Sin rarior
> Magnatis appulsu extulit se occasio,
> Surrexit una & illa, seseque extulit:
> Occasione certat, imo & obtinet.
> Proh! quantus imber, quanta labri comitas,
> Lepos severus, Pallas mixta Gratiis;

Loquitur numellas, compedes & retia:
Aut si negotio hora sumenda est, rei
Per angiportus & maeandros labitur,
Ipsos Catones provocans oraculis. . . .

(She did not waste the fleeting hours in efforts to raise a
proud structure of towered hair and then – as confusion of
tongues followed Babel – chatter idly for the rest of the day.
But after arranging her modest tire with a narrow head-
band, as decent ladies do, she duly refreshed her newly-
risen soul with holy rites, addressing God in heartfelt,
fervent prayers. She then surveys her household and, each
in order, takes stock of the state of kitchen, garden and
sewing-parlour. To each duty she allots a proper time and
place, and calls for an end to the work in early evening.
Her life and her house are ordered by a strict procedure
and of both she wisely renders daily account. The grace
and sweetness that brighten all her house fill first her soul.
Yet if a special event occurs, such as the arrival of some
important guest, true to herself she rises with the occasion,
meets and masters it. Ah what ease, what affability of conversation she has! A cheerful gravity, wisdom joined with
charm! Her words are fetters and nets that take one cap-
tive; but when the time comes for business she runs through
the intricacies and implications of the matter, rivalling the
Catos in their judgments.)

This charming passage from one of the finest memorial poems
in Anglo-Latin verse reveals Lady Danvers as the model great
lady of her day, who combines the domestic abilities of a
country housewife with intellectual resources worthy of a
Jacobean society hostess. Herbert emphasizes her restraint in
dress and manners by a jibe from Scripture at ladies of fashion.
The language of the poem is highly charged with moral values,
and in describing his mother's household he never loses sight of
how she kept her own soul in order. Though house-proud, she
values purity of heart more, unmistakably combining in this
Martha and Mary. Her consideration for servants is matched
by her appreciation of the needs of great visitors, whom she
entertains on equal footing and delights with a flow of good
conversation. Walton too wrote of the 'great and harmless wit',

the 'cheerful gravity' and 'obliging behaviour' that won her
the respect and friendship of eminent men. *Loquitur numellas,
compedes & retia*: her words perhaps recall the liquid chains
that according to sacred epigrammatists were wept by
another Magdalen.[21] While from the very first verse the
idiom of the poem is overtly classical its moral tone is set by
the presence of Christian values, expressed through echoes of
Scripture.

Flowers and gardens take pride of place among the imagery
of these commendatory poems. The hint given in epigram IV,
that Magdalen Danvers has exchanged her small plot on earth
for the Gardens of Paradise, is expanded in the conceits of the
succeeding poems, which despite their literary affiliations were
surely brought to mind as Herbert walked that June in his
step-father's gardens at Chelsea. The summer flowers, con-
demned here to follow their mistress to a premature grave, are
reprieved only long enough to shed a tear at evening, for the
poet finds in the flower-beds of Danvers House no garden but a
cemetery – the Greek word for a sleeping-chamber – that both
'recalls' and 'lays up' his mother. Sir John Danvers's Italianate
gardens were famous in their time. Aubrey describes at length
their beds, walks and statuary in his manuscript 'Memoires of
naturall remarques in the Countie of Wilts'.[22] For all their
formal excellence they retained a domestic character that Lady
Danvers loved to foster (II, ll. 18–19), and that is charmingly
captured in an anecdote related by Aubrey: 'Sir John was wont
in fine mornings in the Summer, to brush his Bever-hatt on the
Hysop & Thyme, which did perfume it with its naturall Essence;
and would last a morning or longer.' Similarly in Herbert's
verses it is not the species or the colours of the blossoms that is
significant, but their odours. In the Greek epigram XV his
mother in dying draws after her all the sweet garden scents in a
single trail which he resolves to follow, trusting to his nose.
(He had hoped in epigram III to climb to her by means of a
rope of sunbeams reminiscent of the 'silk twist' of divine
grace in 'The Pearl'.) The flowers of the fifth epigram are
specifically identified with his mother by the pathetic fallacy,
and throughout the sequence their odours represent moral
virtues in the natural state. Herbert emphasizes the point
when he invites (VII) her shade to live with him in his rural
retreat:

Est mihi bis quinis laqueata domuncula tignis
Rure; brevisque hortus, cuius cum vellere florum
Luctatur spacium, qualem tamen eligit aequi
Iudicii dominus, flores ut iunctius halent
Stipati, rudibusque volis impervius hortus
Sit quasi fasciculus crescens, & nidus odorum.
Hic ego tuque erimus, variae suffitibus herbae
Quotidie pasti: tantum verum indue vultum
Affectusque mei similem; nec languida misce
Ora meae memori menti: ne dispare cultu
Pugnaces, teneros florum turbemus odores,
Atque inter reliquos horti crescentia foetus
Nostra etiam paribus marcescant gaudia fatis.

(In the country I have a modest house roofed with ten
crossed beams, and a small garden whose plot wrestles with
a fleece of flowers. It is just such as its owner has carefully
chosen, with flowers compacted so as to breathe a denser
fragrance, that the garden itself, untrodden by common
feet, may resemble a living nosegay, a nest of odours.
Here you and I shall be, nourished daily on the perfumes
of the various plants. This only I ask: wear your true
aspect, the one which delights me, and do not present this
pallid likeness to the mind that still remembers you. For if
we differ over ill-matched appearances we may disturb
the delicate scent of the blossoms, and our flourishing joys
may fade away in equal measure with the other fruits of
the garden.)

Together in this Crashavian *nidus odorum* they are to subsist on a
diet that would be insubstantial fare even in Arcadia, were it
not specifically adapted to the virtuous palate.

The five Greek epigrams of the sequence inevitably share
elements in common with the Latin, especially in their appeal
to flowers, light and tears. Sun and stars (III and XIV) are the
only lodging fit to enshrine Lady Danvers's bright soul, but
her children must seek the obscurity of a moonless night to
weep at her grave by the Thames (XVIII). In the funerary verse
of the age tears were sounded for their secrets until the well of
conceit ran dry, and although Herbert's wit is on the whole
restrained he could not always avoid lachrymose ingenuity (I)

of slight poetic value. His Anacreontics (XVI), almost a drinking-song in reverse, are, however, a modest enough specimen of the genre, while his happiest venture is probably epigram X:

> Nempe huc usque notos tenebricosos
> Et maestum nimio madore Caelum
> Tellurisque Britannicae salivam
> Iniuste satis arguit viator.
> At te commoriente, Magna Mater,
> Recte, quem trahit, aerem repellit
> Cum probro madidum, reumque difflat.
> Nam te nunc Ager, Urbs, & Aula plorant:
> Te nunc Anglia, Scotiaeque binae,
> Quin te Cambria pervetusta deflet,
> Deducens lacrymas prioris aevi
> Ne serae meritis tuis venirent.
> Non est angulus uspiam serenus,
> Nec cingit mare, nunc inundat omnes.

(Until now, it is true, the traveller has censured all too unjustly our darkening South Winds, our skies heavy with undischarged rain, and the damps of British soil. But at your death, noble mother, he is right to expel with a curse the dank air that he breathes, and to spit out the offender. Country, city, and court bewail you now. England, the two Gaelic realms and ancient Wales weep for you, bringing the tears of a former age for fear that they come too late to answer your deserts. Now not a nook of these islands sees fair weather, and the sea no more encompasses but rather floods them all.)

Here Herbert deftly suggests that rain is chiefly the tears of a previous age held in solution in the sky. When he writes that the English climate is guilty (*reum*) of his mother's death he is hinting that her constitution had been, like his own, undermined by 'Rheums and other weaknesses'. But the traveller who on her account expels the miasmal air with a curse is also 'voiding his rheum' (*rheuma*). Opinions may differ as to the propriety of such earthy humour, though elsewhere in the sequence pun and word-play illuminate the situations that inspire them and add a not unwelcome salt to these memorial

53

elegies. In the same spirit Herbert makes the most of his opportunities for indignation (VI) as an artistic contrast to tears and
unstinted eulogy. Stoic ancestry is unflatteringly traced by puns
set in a context (XII) of the Catullan invective for which he had
shown something of a flair since at least *Musae Responsoriae*: the
bones of these callous cynics, says Herbert, are so dry that a
ravening wolfhound could not tear three-farthings' worth of
marrow from them. Elsewhere too his turn of phrase is worthy
of the Roman satirists. His spirited reply to an imaginary critic
in epigram II solves the problem of finding a conclusion that
would not be merely anticlimactic, and this concern with the
tone and force of individual poems is reflected equally in their
careful grouping within the sequence, which tends to emphasize
the virtuosity of his performances. There are few purple
passages in his Latin epigrams, as in his English, for the simple
reason that each was conceived as an integral entity. Here also
the prevailing metaphors of dreams, sickness, flowers and tears
are brilliantly assimilated to Herbert's own situation and his
mother's character so that they acquire a real and independent
meaning beyond the literary conventions to which they appeal.

Memoriae Matris Sacrum illustrates by its highly personal tone
no less than by the Metaphysical spirit that is evident in individual poems how Herbert's mastery of classical idioms was made
to serve his own immediate needs rather than merely to fulfil a
literary ideal. Even in his earliest known Latin pieces, those
written on the death of Prince Henry and in honour of the
Elector Palatine's marriage in 1612 and 1613, he showed some
impatience with conventional tributes, while the nature and
variety of the images that he so readily employed in all his
sequences give his Latin epigrams kinship with contemporary
vernacular verse – and in particular with Donne's – rather than
with Augustan or Silver Latin poetry. What Hallam wrote of
Sannazaro, that the 'unauthorised word, the doubtful idiom,
the modern turn of thought, so common in Latin verse, scarce
ever appear',[23] could not be said of Herbert. With a few exceptions such as the dedicatory verses of *Musae Responsoriae* the
voice of the classical epigrammatists is echoed chiefly in his
satire and invective. His wit is recognizably English and Jacobean, but seldom rests in the verbal play upon which so much
post-Renaissance epigram depends. Everywhere its perspectives take precedence even over the metaphorical language

through which they are expressed, and Hutchinson adds less to our appreciation of lines 23–6 of 'The Church Militant' by likening them on account of their imagery to *Passio* xviii than if he had pointed out their similarity in conception to xx. A wholly contemporary taste for conceited paradox is as pronounced in *Passio* and *Lucus* as in Herbert's only poem of secular love, *Aethiopissa ambit Cestum Diversi Coloris Virum*, a charming *jeu d'esprit* on the wooing of white by black. What distinguishes Herbert's wit from that of Crashaw in similar situations is the real humour that often shows through the literary game.

In metaphor and imagery Herbert's Latin epigrams compare closely with his own vernacular poetry, and a similar line of development may be traced in each. The language of his earlier sequences reveals the same preoccupation as the English poems of the Williams manuscript with astronomy, household matters, law, commerce and warfare; and in its reliance on medicine and botany *Memoriae Matris Sacrum* approaches the manner of the poems added in the Tanner text of *The Temple*. Among Herbert's many references to flowers in his English verse only the rose and the lily are mentioned by name, while the roses of his Latin flourish not in Lady Danvers's flower-beds but in the crown of *Passio* vi. The application to Christ of such traditional emblems in the line '*Roses* and *Lillies* speak thee', from the very early sonnet to his mother, remains implicit much later in a conceit from 'Dulnesse' – 'Thy bloudy death and undeserv'd, makes thee Pure red and white'. The related images of milk and blood are also to be found in *Passio* and *Lucus*, and taken altogether they show Herbert no less sensitive than the widely read Crashaw to the current fashions in religious poetry, native and foreign.

Yet it is not merely their modern spirit and presentation that distinguish Herbert's Latin epigrams from those of their ultimate literary ancestors. Setting aside irregularities of scansion, which partly resulted from contemporary unawareness of the rules of classical versification, his vocabulary is noticeably broader and less selective than that of the Roman poets. This common feature of neo-Latin verse has been attributed to 'the want of tolerable dictionaries; so that the memory was the only test of classical precedent'[24] at a time when a very heterogeneous Latin was the *lingua franca* of Europe in all areas of learning, letters and diplomacy. We must also bear in mind that Christianity and, more recently, scientific discoveries of many kinds had made available to poets fields of experience not open to the ancients, each with its own developing vocabulary. In these circumstances any extension of the language of poetry need not be viewed merely as a lapse from classical purity. It is no more a serious indictment of modern Latin poems that *stroma, latriam* and *crasis* were not used in Augustan verse than that *blasphemando, Scommata, insultus, Magnas* (noun) and *coemeteria* were drawn from the Vulgate or the early Christian writers, though Herbert might easily have avoided words like *gratitudinem* and *certitudinis*.[25] In his poems, as in the prose that he wrote while Public Orator at Cambridge, the character of his Latin varies but at its best may justly be said to achieve a 'clear Masculine, and apt Expression'.[26]

That the literary careers of such fine vernacular poets as Herbert, Crashaw and Marvell were marked by their habit of turning to Latin for poetry of every description cannot be taken merely as a testimony of the high value that was set upon classical imitation in seventeenth-century Cambridge. In all three cases we may fairly claim that the Latin muse was at least as old as the English, and that well into maturity they invoked either with equal relish and assurance. The poetry that they wrote in these media often shares the same perspectives precisely because so much of their neo-Latin verse owes its name to the idiom rather than to the spirit in which it was conceived. It is poetry first of all.

Notes

All quotations from Herbert's poetry and prose are taken from Canon F. E. Hutchinson's edition of the *Works of George Herbert*, Oxford, 1941 (henceforth referred to as *Works*). I have, however, followed modern practice as regards *v* and *u, j* and *i*, and have dropped diacritical accents. Free-verse renderings of all the Latin and Greek verses printed there are to be found in *The Latin Poetry of George Herbert*, translated by Mark McClosky and Paul R. Murphy, Ohio, 1965. Edmund Blunden has published verse-translations of several epigrams in 'George Herbert's Latin poems', *Essays and Studies*, XIX (1934), 29–39.

1   Two sets of Latin verses dedicated to Frederick, Elector Palatine were first published by Leicester Bradner in 'New poems by George Herbert: the Cambridge Latin gratulatory anthology of 1613', *Renaissance News*, XV (1962), 208–11.

2 Autograph presentation-copy to Laud, now British Museum MS. Harley 3496, ff. 79–89.

3 Compare Donne's 'The Crosse', l. 19.

4 'Obsequies to the Lord Harington', ll. 35–8, dating from 1614. The term *perspicillum*, first recorded in 1610, was used by Bacon in *Novum Organum*, 1620, Bk II, 39. See also *Works*, note on p. 602.

5 *The Complete Works of George Herbert*, ed. A. B. Grosart, vol. II, 1874, pp. li–lxiii.

6 See Book I, *passim*. Other collections that Herbert may have known include Bernard van Bauhuysen's *Epigrammatum selectorum libri V*, Antwerp, 1616, and Bauduin Cabilliau's *Epigrammata selecta*, Antwerp, 1620.

7 *Epigrammatum Joannis Owen . . . libri decem*, Leipzig, 1615, Bk III, epigram 121.

8 Chapter XXVII (*Works*, p. 267).

9 Compare a later English poem, Marvell's 'Damon the Mower', l. 80.

10 'Clarus Bonarscius', *Amphitheatrum Honoris*, Antwerp, 1605, pp. 373–4. The poem was translated and its doctrine and diction violently attacked by William Crashaw in *The Jesuites Gospel*, 1610.

11 *Poemata*, Paris, 1620, p. 71: and 2nd edn, Paris, 1623, pp. 60–1. Quotations are taken from the latter.

12 *Les Œuvres Poétiques de Baudri de Bourgueil*, ed. Phyllis Abrahams, Paris, 1926, p. 182, no. 187.

13 'The Country Parson', Chapter IV (*Works*, p. 228).

14 Chetham Library MS. Mun. A.3.48, first printed by G. M. Story, 'George Herbert's *Inventa Bellica*: a new manuscript', *Modern Philology*, LIX (1962), 270–2.

15 *De Augmentis*, Bk. IX (*Works of Francis Bacon*, ed. J. Spedding, vol. I, 1857, p. 830; vol. V, 1858, p. 122).

16 For a full discussion of Herbert's epigrams and Donne's elegiacs on the subject see *The Divine Poems of John Donne*, ed. Helen Gardner, Oxford, 1952, Appendix G, pp. 138–47.

17 Letter III (*Works*, p. 364).

18 John Aubrey's *Brief Lives*, ed. Andrew Clark, Oxford, 1898, vol. I, p. 309.

19 *Works*, p. xxxiii.

20 See A. B. Chambers, '"I was but an inverted tree": notes toward the history of an idea', *Studies in the Renaissance*, VIII (1961), 291–9.

21 For example Bauduin Cabilliau, *Magdalena*, Antwerp, 1625, *passim*.

22 Bodleian MS. Aubrey 2, ff. 53–9.

23 Henry Hallam, *Introduction to the Literature of Europe in the Fifteenth, Sixteenth and Seventeenth Centuries*, vol. I, 1837, p. 596.

24 *Ibid.*, p. 268.

25 See *Passio* xv, xix and *M.M.S.* vi; *Passio* v, vii, xiii, *Lucus* xvii and *M.M.S.* v; *Lucus* xiv and *In Sacram Anchoram*, iambic trimeters.

26 Thomas Tenison, *Baconiana*, 1679, p. 26 (quoted by Joseph Summers, *George Herbert: His Religion and Art*, 1954, p. 97).

III

The Latin Poetry of John Milton[1]

R. W. Condee

John Milton is the greatest English poet to write Latin poetry and his Latin poetry formed an important part of his literary career. In all, he wrote thirty-one poems in Latin and some of them are among the best poetry that he wrote. His career as a Latin poet tends to fall into two periods: first, the early poems written between about 1625 and 1632,[2] and then the later poems, from 'Mansus' (late 1638 or early 1639) to 'Ad Ioannem Rousium' (23 January 1646/7).

Milton's total poetic career ended of course with *Samson Agonistes* and the two great English epics on which much of his fame rests, but he began chiefly as a Latin poet: of the almost 1400 extant lines of poetry that he had written by the time of his twenty-first birthday, over a thousand lines were in Latin, an output of greater length than, for example, Vergil's *Eclogues*. Milton turned away from Latin to English for his poetry only after a deliberate and self-conscious decision: in 1640 he wrote 'Epitaphium Damonis' in Latin, but the poem was concerned in part with this very decision to renounce Latin as the language for his poetry.

Two years later, in *The Reason of Church Government*, he restated his decision to become a poet in English. He said he wished that he 'might perhaps leave something so written to

58

aftertimes, as they should not willingly let it die', and then he went on to discuss the problem of language:[3]

> For which cause, and not only for that I knew it would be hard to arrive at the second rank among the Latines, I apply'd myselfe to that resolution which *Ariosto* follow'd against the perswasions of *Bembo*, to fix all the industry and art I could unite to the adorning of my native tongue.

In fact, however, in 1646, Milton wrote a Latin poem to John Rouse, Librarian at Oxford University, and two trivial Latin epigrams (in 1651 and 1654) which were included in tracts[4] attacking his political opponent Salmasius. It is these which were literally his last poems in Latin.

Milton's earliest extant Latin verses are three poems of little interest – 'Carmina Elegiaca', an untitled fragment in the lesser asclepiad, and a twelve-line fable on the peasant and the landlord. None of these was published in Milton's 1645 collection of poems.

'Elegia Prima' is Milton's first work in either English or Latin which can be seriously discussed as a poem. It is the first of Milton's seven elegies (Milton uses 'elegia' to describe the verse form, not the subject of the poem), and probably the first poem of a youthful *annus mirabilis*: in 1626 he wrote between six and eleven Latin poems (precise dating is difficult), perhaps more than in any other year of his life. Of the 1626 poems, 'Elegia Prima' is beyond question the best.

Nominally the poem is a verse letter 'ad Carolum Diodatum'. Charles Diodati (1609?–38) was a close friend of Milton; the first and sixth elegies and the fourth sonnet (in Italian) are addressed to him, and Milton's last long poem in Latin, 'Epitaphium Damonis', is a lament for Diodati's death.

Diodati, 'Elegia Prima' says, is in Chester, while Milton is in London, 'rusticated' temporarily from Cambridge University. The cause of Milton's suspension is not now clear and the poem does not explain. The poem falls into three sections: a short introduction addressing Diodati in Chester; a long middle section expatiating on Milton's joy in books, the theatre, the shady London walks, and above everything else the pretty girls of London; and then a short conclusion announcing his regretful return to Cambridge.

Like all Milton's early Latin poetry, 'Elegia Prima' depends heavily on Ovid; the tags of phrases from the *Amoers*, the *Metamorphoses*, the *Epistulae ex Ponto*, and the *Tristia* mark almost every line of the poem. In this kind of recurrent verbal borrowing from standard Latin authors Milton resembles most Renaissance Latin poets.

But 'Elegia Prima' uses Ovid more cleverly than merely as a source for pat phrases: it poses a parallel, or more properly a cross-relation, between Milton's exile from Cambridge and Ovid's exile from Rome. As every seventeenth-century school-boy knew, Ovid had been exiled from Rome to Tomis, on the shores of the Black Sea, in A.D. 8 by Augustus Caesar for offences not now known; Ovid spent the remaining ten years of his life there, writing the *Epistulae ex Ponto* and the *Tristia* to his friends in Rome, begging them to intercede for his return.

But Milton's fate he tells Diodati, is not so harsh as Ovid's:

> O utinam vates nunquam graviora tulisset
>   Ille Tomitano flebilis exul agro,
> Non tunc Ionio quicquam cessisset Homero
>   Neve foret victo laus tibi prima Maro. (21–4)

(Ah! If only that poet who was once a tearful exile in the land of Tomis had never had to put up with anything worse than this: then he would have been a match for Ionian Homer, and you, Virgil, outdone, would not enjoy the supreme glory.)[5]

This passage not only brings Ovid explicitly into Milton's poem, it echoes Ovid's complaint (*Tristia* 1.1.47–8) that not even Homer could write under the conditions at Tomis. Cambridge University, Milton implies (13–16), is as hostile to poetry as Tomis; but unlike Ovid, Milton is writing about the place from which, not to which, he has been exiled.

London supplies the exiled Milton with what residence at a university should:

> Tempora nam licet hic placidis dare libera Musis,
>   Et totum rapiunt me mea vita libri. (25–6)

(For here I can devote my leisure hours to the mild Muses: here books, which are my life, quite carry me away.)

This is an inverted echo from Ovid, who in his exile lamented the absence of things which Milton had in exile. Ovid writes,

Non hic librorum, per quos inviter alarque
    copia: pro libris arcus at arma sonant. (*Tristia* 3.14.37–8)

(Not here have I an abundance of books to stimulate and nourish me: in their stead is the rattle of bows and arms.)[6]

Part of Milton's central section is concerned with his enjoyment of comedy and tragedy while in London. The 'sinuosi pompa theatri' which delights Milton in London is the subject of pitiful dreams for Ovid in Tomis. In a mournful elegy on the belated coming of spring to Tomis, Ovid remembered the Roman games, and he could almost hear the applause of the crowded theatres.[7]

For Milton the landscape of Cambridge is repellent (11–14), and Milton's revulsion is a counterpart of Ovid's complaint against the barren Pontic landscape, with no apples bending the branches, no grapes or even vines, a treeless plain whose typical vegetation is wormwood.[8] Even the swamps of Tomis[9] are reflected in Milton's sneers at the marshy banks of the Cam (11, 89). For Milton, in this poem, there is nothing good about Cambridge University, from which he has been exiled, and nothing bad about London, just as for Ovid there was nothing good about Tomis, to which he had been exiled, and nothing bad (in the *Tristia* and the *Epistulae*) about Rome.

Essentially, 'Elegia Prima' centres on Milton's youthful contempt for Cambridge; it is a conscious insult fashioned with neat irony out of the learned tradition which a university should have embodied and at which, Milton felt, it had utterly failed. But 'Elegia Prima' also looks forward to 'L'Allegro' and 'Il Penseroso', with their similar lists of sensuous delights.[10] It is not as good a poem as either of the Companion Pieces, partly because it lacks their vividness, partly because its structure tends to ramble.

But 'Elegia Prima' does manage a climax which is appealingly rousing in an adolescent way. After considering the shortcomings of Cambridge, Milton sees the height of London's attraction enter – its beautiful girls. And here the seventeen-year-old Milton manages a fusion of erotic chauvinism which has a charm that is perhaps different from what he intended:

Ah quoties dignae stupui miracula formae
  Quae possit senium vel reparare Iovis;
Ah quoties vidi superantia lumina gemmas,
  Atque faces quotquot volvit uterque polus. (53–6)

(Ah, how often have I been struck dumb by the miraculous
shapeliness of a figure which might well make even old
Jove young again! Ah, how often have I seen eyes brighter
than jewels, brighter than all the stars which wheel round
the poles.)

These girls are not only beautiful, they are British!

Cedite laudatae toties Heroides olim,
  Et quaecunque vagum cepit amica Iovem, . . .
Gloria virginibus debetur prima Britannis,
  Extera sat tibi sit foemina posse sequi. (63–4, 71–2)

(Admit defeat, you heroines so often praised; admit defeat,
all you girls who have caught the eye of inconstant Jove. . . .
The first prize goes to the British girls: be content, foreign
woman, to take second place!)

But then the poem comes back to earth. Milton has mastered
considerable learning, but he is only seventeen years old and
not the master of his fate. Unlike Ovid, Milton's exile comes
to a quick, albeit involuntary end:

Stat quoque iuncosas Cami remeare paludes,
  Atque iterum raucae murmur adire Scholae.
Interea fidi parvum cape munus amici,
  Paucaque in alternos verba coacta modos. (89–92)

(I am to return to the Cam's reedy marshes and face the
uproar of the noisy University again. Meanwhile accept
this little gift from a loyal friend – one or two words forced
into elegiac metre.)

The temporary colleague and counterpart of Publius Ovidius
Naso will now go back to his seat in class at Cambridge.

James Burnett, Lord Monboddo, called 'Elegia Prima' the
equal of anything by Ovid or Tibullus, and various critics
have praised the facility and autochthonous character of
Milton's Latin. Rand says that Milton's Latin elegiacs 'breathe

a spirit of Horace and Ovid'.[11] Keightley on the other hand objects to Milton's grammatical errors, false quantities, and deviations from classical usage[12] (Keightley also collected the 'incongruities' of Vergil). But analysis of the linguistic quality of Milton's Latin in the poems is necessarily outside the scope of this type of essay.

Milton probably wrote at least five other Latin poems in 1626, making this one of the most productive years, so far as we can tell, of his career. He wrote four epicedia: 'In Obitum Procancellarii Medici' (for Dr John Gostlin), 'Elegia Secunda' (for Richard Ridding, the University Beadle), 'Elegia Tertia' (for Lancelot Andrews, Bishop of Winchester), and 'In Obitum Praesulis Eliensis' (for Nicholas Felton, Bishop of Ely). In addition, he wrote 'In Quintum Novembris', on the Gunpowder Plot, probably in 1626; Milton also wrote three other brief and unimportant poems (totalling only thirty lines) on the Gunpowder Plot, but their dates are unknown. The best that can be said for these early epicedia is that they are not unpromising for a seventeen- or eighteen-year-old, but it would have been reckless, on the basis of these poems of late 1626, to predict the great poems which were to follow.

Most of these poems are badly overfreighted with classical learning and, unlike the clever manipulation of Ovid in 'Elegia Prima', the learning serves no purpose. The epicedion for Gostlin introduces Iapetus, Nessus, Hercules, Hector, Athene, Sarpedon, Jove, Patroclus, Achilles, Hecate, Circe, Medea, Machaon, Philyn, Chiron, Aesculapius, Apollo, Persephone, and Aeacus – all in a forty-eight line poem. Poor Gostlin, the dead vice-chancellor, is almost crowded out of his own epicedion.

'Elegia Secunda', commemorating the death of the University Beadle, is no better. We know from other sources that the beadle concerned was Richard Ridding. But it is symptomatic of the faceless impersonality of the poem that, if the poem were undated, we should have no way of telling from the poem itself that the beadle being lamented was Richard Ridding; it might have been any other recently deceased holder of the office.

In 'Elegia Tertia' Milton suppresses his weakness for Greco-Roman mythology and centres the poem on the death of Bishop Andrewes. The poem resembles 'Lycidas' and 'Epitaphium Damonis' in its transition from initial grief to ultimate consolation in the knowledge that Andrewes rests happily in Heaven. But 'Elegia Tertia' is interesting in part because it tries and fails to manage this transition with the sure sense of progression that characterizes poems like 'Lycidas' and 'Epitaphium Damonis'. The two later poems, each in a quite different way, create a poetic dialectic which carries each poem, sometimes in a circuitous fashion, to a conclusion which is inherent, although perhaps not obvious, in the opening. We shall examine Milton's mature method more closely when we come to 'Epitaphium Damonis'.

'Elegia Tertia', however, progresses not by means of its inherent structure but by a fortuitous leap from grief to consolation: night falls, sleep comes, the poet dreams, and the dream, luckily, is of Andrewes in the company of the saints. And then, with the poet's awakening, the poem stops.[13]

'In Quintum Novembris', probably written in this same productive year, is 226 lines – Milton's longest poem so far. It contains four large 'movements': first, the aerial flight of Satan, with his survey of western Europe and the happy British Isles, and his passage across the Alps to Rome; second, his survey of Rome, the procession of priests and the Pope, and the Pope's retirement to sleep. Satan visits the Pope in sleep and suggests to him a conspiracy to subjugate England. The third 'movement' consists of the Pope's meeting with the College of Cardinals to hatch the Gunpowder Plot, and the fourth 'movement' concludes the poem with Fama spreading the story of the plot, with the result that Satan is defeated and England saved.[14]

No-one has claimed 'In Quintum Novembris' as one of Milton's great poems, although Landor thought it 'a wonderful work for a boy of seventeen',[15] and Rand found in it 'greater poise and firmness than the little epic on the *Gnat* which Virgil wrote at sixteen'.[16]

Its chief interest for the modern reader lies in its foreshadowing of *Paradise Lost*. Satan in 'In Quintum Novembris' is a brief but not incompetent sketch for the gigantic figure of *Paradise Lost*. Both poems use many of the epic conventions – the adventurous journey, the council (of Cardinals in 'In Quintum Novembris', of devils in *Paradise Lost*), the rousing speech to the indolent follower, the supernatural being in disguise, and so on.

But 'In Quintum Novembris' is marred by several flaws. Perhaps the most important is the poorly managed conclusion: for the first 169 lines the poem has an enthusiastic if melodramatic drive; suddenly at line 170 Fama appears and twenty-three lines of the poem are devoted to describing her. Then within thirty-three lines she saves England by revealing the fact of the conspiracy. After such elaborate preparations for England's downfall we might justifiably expect more heroic efforts would be needed to save her. A Satan who would be foiled by these last thirty-three lines of the poem doesn't resemble the 'ferus ignifluo regnans Acheronte tyrannus,/ Eumenidum pater' 'the fierce tyrant who controls Acheron's flaming currents, the tyrant who is father to the Furies' (7–8), who dominates the beginning of the poem. One suspects that the seventeen-year-old poet tired after 150 or so lines and simply finished off the poem as quickly as he could.

On 6 October 1626, Nicholas Felton, Bishop of Ely, died, and Milton memorialized the event with 'In Obitum Praesulis Eliensis', in alternating iambic trimeters and dimeters. But the poem has little to distinguish it beyond its slight biographical interest.

'Elegia Quarta', a verse letter to Thomas Young, Milton's former tutor, was probably written during the next year, 1627. Young was an ardent Presbyterian later famous as the 'TY' of 'Smectymnuus', an acronym for the five Presbyterian authors of a tract attacking episcopacy in 1641.

'Elegia Quarta' is a pleasant poem by a schoolboy to his former teacher, but it would not be notable if it were not by John Milton. As a poem by Milton it has two interesting aspects: first, in some ways it looks ahead to another panegyric, 'Mansus' (1638–9), and secondly it anticipates another poem to a revered elder, 'Ad Patrem' (1631–2? 1637?).

As often in his early poems, Milton crowds aboard almost all the Greeks and Romans he can think of – Aeolus, Doris, Medea, Triptolemus, Jove, and countless others. Young is dearer to him than Socrates was to Alcibiades, dearer than Aristotle to Alexander the Great. It is interesting to compare the hackneyed use of *synkrisis*[17] in this early poem with Milton's later, subtler use of it in 'Mansus', where it serves a more complex poetic function.

But the poem loses its stiffness as Milton expresses concern for Young's safety (71 ff). He becomes surprisingly paternal towards this divine who was twenty years his senior:

> At tu sume animos, nec spes cadat anxia curis
>   Nec tua concutiat decolor ossa metus. (105–6)

(But take heart. Do not let anxieties quench your hope, even if they make you uneasy, and do not allow pale fear to send shudders through your limbs.)

And he concludes with the encouraging air not of a pupil but of a reassuring adviser:

> Nec dubites quandoque frui melioribus annis,
>   Atque iterum patrios posse videre lares. (125–6)

(Do not doubt that some day you will enjoy happier times and be able to see your home again.)

'Elegia Septima' is numbered as the last of Milton's elegies but it seems to have been written prior to 'Elegia Quinta'. It records an erotic episode in which he sneers at the power of Cupid, and Cupid retaliates by causing him to fall in love, in vain, with a beautiful girl he chances to see, and she passes by, never to appear again. He now knows the full power of Cupid. He vows sacrifices on the altar of Cupid and prays that next time his love will be successful.

This is a minor conventional poem on a minor theme, but Milton handles it with dexterity; he makes fun of himself not only by setting forth his foolhardy scorn for Cupid early in the poem, but also by the quasi-heroic quality of his mock-serious invocation to the god at the end:

> Iam tuus O certe est mihi formidabilis arcus,
>   Nate dea, iaculis nec minus igne potens:
> Et tua fumabunt nostris altaria donis, [18]
>   Solus et in superis tu mihi summus eris. (95–8)

(Child of the goddess, you may be sure that I dread your bow now: you are mighty with your arrows, and no less so with your fire. Your altars shall smoke with my offerings, and you alone shall be supreme to me among the gods.)

These passages manage the poem's *persona* with considerably more skill than most of the early poems – far better than the second or third elegies, for example, where the speaker is a conventional mourner, undistinguished in either his grief or his consolation.

At some time between 1628 and 1632 Milton wrote two hexameter poems, 'Natura non pati Senium' ('That Nature does not suffer from old age') and 'De Idea Platonica quemadmodum Aristoteles intellexit' ('Of the Platonic Ideal Form as understood by Aristotle'), which seem to have been University exercises. They are of little significance in Milton's poetic career.

'Elegia Quinta', on the other hand, is one of Milton's greatest short poems in either English or Latin and certainly the best poem he had written up to this time, when he was twenty years old. It succeeds so well because it is a direct, full-blooded, celebration of fertility in a skilful, well-integrated poem. It rejoices in the return of spring to the land, in the sunshine, in sexual love. The gods embrace, the human lovers woo, and the earth itself feels sexual desire:

> Sic Tellus lasciva suos suspirat amores
> Matris in exemplum caetera turba ruunt. (95–6)

(This is the way lascivious Earth breathes out her passion, and all the other creatures are quick to follow their mother's example.)

An important factor in making the poem the exuberant creation that it is lies in its purely celebratory mood: it arrives at no decision and draws no moral; it urges nothing on the reader, not even 'carpe diem'. The closing lines simply wish for an eternal or at least a long-lasting spring.

While the Greco-Roman deities are present as in most of Milton's poems, the poem controls them: it is the deities who serve the poem by giving shape to the natural forces of fertility, rather than, as in some of the earlier poems (e.g. 'Elegia Secunda'), the deities usurping almost the whole poem.

'Elegia Quinta' is also a stronger poem structurally than any of its predecessors. It achieves this structural integrity in part by refusing to attempt the problem which causes difficulty in the earlier poems. 'Elegia Quinta' is in the main a static poem, while most of the earlier poems attempted a progression which they were unable to bring off. 'Elegia Quinta' attempts no progression and therefore fails at none. In this it resembles the Nativity Ode, probably written the following December, which – for all its complexities in other respects – is likewise a static poem. As A. S. P. Woodhouse puts it, '[The Ode] is in the nature of a simple affirmation, with no problem stated or implied and no emotional tension to be resolved.'[19] 'Elegia Quinta' anticipates the Ode in this respect.

This is not to say that 'Elegia Quinta' is an amorphous outpouring. Milton begins with the announcement that spring and his own creative powers are returning. Apollo, the sun-god, the leader of the Muses, lifts the poet to the heavens; the spring's gift to Milton is song and Milton's gift to the spring is therefore this song. Spring brings the nightingale, and the nightingale and the poet will join in song (25–8).

The rest of the poem is their mutual song, and it is constructed out of these ideas and images of fertility, creativity, and the passionate confluence of poet and nightingale, man and nature, earth and sun, god and goddess, nymph and Pan, man and woman. Thus the plunge of Phoebus the sun into Tethys the sea causes the renewed Earth to cry out in a jealous passion which contagiously arouses mankind:

Cur te, inquit, cursu languentem Phoebe diurno
    Hesperiis recipit caerula mater aquis? . . .
Sic Tellus lasciva suos suspirat amores;
    Matris in exemplum caetera turba ruunt.
Nunc etenim toto currit vagus orbe Cupido,
    Languentesque fovet solis ab igne faces. (81–2, 95–8)

('Phoebus, why should the sky-blue mother take you into her western waves when you are exhausted by your daily journey?' . . . This is the way lascivious Earth breathes out her passion, and all the other creatures are quick to follow their mother's example. For now wandering Cupid speeds through the whole world and renews his dying torch in the flames of the sun.)

The poem uses Earth, Tellus, not only as a personification of fertility and sexuality, but also as the appropriate and joyful place for sexuality. Phoebus, plunging into the sea and thereby arousing the jealousy of Earth, is 'clivoso fessus Olympo' ('tired out by heaven's steep path', 79), and while Jupiter has his sexual pleasures on Olympus (117–18), it is in the woods and fields of Earth that the gods find their greatest pleasure.

The conclusion of the poem is more than a prayer for eternal spring; it is a celebration of the fertility and sexuality in which the poem is steeped:

> Et sua quisque diu sibi numina lucus habeto,
>   Nec vos arborea dii precor ite domo.
> Te referant miseris te Iupiter aurea terris
> Saecla, quid ad nimbos aspera tela redis?
>   Tu saltem lente rapidos age Phoebe iugales
>   Qua potes, et sensim tempora veris eant.
> Brumaque productas tarde ferat hispida noctes,
>   Ingruat et nostro serior umbra polo. (133–40)

(Long may each grove have its own particular deities: do not leave your homes among the trees, gods, I beseech you. May the golden age bring you back, Jove, to this wretched world! Why go back to your cruel weapons in the clouds? At any rate, Phoebus, drive your swift team as slowly as you can, and let the passing of the springtime be gradual. May rough winter be tardy in bringing us his dreary nights, and may it be late in the day when shadows assail our sky.)

In view of the fact that Milton, prior to his twenty-first birthday, was primarily a Latin poet – he had written nineteen Latin poems totalling over a thousand lines and only three poems in English totalling barely two hundred lines – it is not surprising that his first solid achievement as a poet, 'Elegia Quinta', was a Latin poem.

Later that year, 1629, Milton wrote his sixth Latin elegy, 'Ad Carolum Diodatum Ruri Commorantem' ('To Charles Diodati staying in the country'). At the same time he was writing the Nativity Ode. Diodati had written Milton a verse letter apologizing that poetry had fled from him because of the feasts and wine of the Christmas season. Milton answers in 'Elegia Sexta' that he himself writes from an empty stomach, but that Diodati's high living should be no deterrent. The lack of good wine in Tomis caused Ovid to write bad verse. The elegiac poet needs music, wine, love, and grand banquets to produce his verse. The epic poet, on the other hand, must live a pure, chaste life, drinking only water and eating herbs as he sings of wars and heroes; this was the way of life of Tiresias, Linus, and Homer. 'But if you will know what I am doing', Milton continues,

> Paciferum canimus caelesti semine regem,
> Faustaque sacratis saecula pacta libris. (81–2)

(I am writing a poem about the king who was born of heavenly seed and who brought peace to men. I am writing about the blessed age promised in Holy Scripture.)

That is, he is in the process of writing the Nativity Ode.

A ten-line epilogue, in elegiac distichs, follows the seventh elegy in both editions of Milton's poems (1645 and 1673) printed in his lifetime. The epilogue seems to be a retraction –

> Haec ego mente olim laeva, studioque supino
> Nequitiae posui vana trophaea meae. (1–2)

(These lines are the trifling memorials of my levity which, with a warped mind and a base spirit, I once raised.)

And in the remaining eight lines Milton promises to give up erotic poetry. The epilogue raises some minor scholarly problems[20] but it has little poetic value. Bateson calls it 'perhaps the most repellent product of that social vacuum to which Milton consigned himself in reaction against Cambridge'.[21]

'Ad Patrem' was written perhaps in Milton's last year at Cambridge.[22] Apparently the elder Milton objected to his son's writing poetry, or perhaps to his devotion of so much of himself to his poetry. 'Ad Patrem' is addressed to the old man in justification of his son's poetic career. In his justification Milton deprecates the poems he has written up to now, but praises the power of poetry, reminds his father of his father's own success as a composer of music, and expresses his deep and humble thanks for all that his father has done for him. He closes with the hope that his poem to his father will help to bring immortality to the old man.

Milton builds his poem and his justification out of two chief elements: a deprecation of his own poetry up to now ('tenues sonos' – 'trivial songs'), and an exaltation of the ideal of poetry, which is loved by the gods and has the power to bind the underworld; kings have honoured poets and poets have preserved in song the deeds of heroes. Thus the poem is moving to a resolution whereby Milton's predicted future glory as a poet will both change his father's opinion and fulfil the potentialities of his 'tenues sonos'. There is a need at this point in 'Ad Patrem' for the kind of structural progression that Milton will manage magnificently in 'Lycidas' and 'Epitaphium Damonis'.

But this developmental structure does not occur in 'Ad Patrem', and three quite different faults cause Milton's difficulties here. The first of these faults is inherent in the crucial passage where he predicts his ultimate crowning with laurel and ivy:

> Iamque nec obscurus populo miscebor inerti,
> Vitabuntque oculos vestigia nostra profanos.
> Este procul vigiles curae, procul este, querelae,
> Invidiaeque acies transverso tortilis hirquo,
> Saeva nec anguiferos extende Calumnia rictus;
> In me triste nihil, faedissima turba, potestis,
> Nec vestri sum iuris ego; securaque tutus
> Pectora, vipereo gradiar sublimis ab ictu. (103–10)

(Now I shall no longer mix with the brainless mob: my steps will shun the sight of common eyes. Away with you, sleep-destroying worries, away with you, complaints, and the squinting eye of envy with its crooked goatish look. Do not stretch your snaky jaws at me, cruel calumny. Your whole filthy gang can do me no harm: I am not within your power. I shall stride on in safety with an unwounded heart, lifted high above your viperous sting.)

Something similar to the earlier passage (17–40) on the supernatural power of poetry might have lifted the poem to the climax it needed here, but unfortunately Milton raises us up to his vision of glory while looking over his shoulder: he speaks of himself as 'nec obscurus', as no longer mingling with the 'populo inerti', and the repeated negations deflate his climax rather than exalt it. Milton appears in the scene not so much as triumphing in what he strives for, but as renouncing what he wants to seclude himself from.

A second fault, one which also prevents the climactic lines concerning Milton's being wreathed with laurel and ivy from being an effective climax, is the haphazard arrangement of some of the previous parts of the poem. 'Ad Patrem' begins (1–16) with the hope that his muse will rise with bold wings, pointing to these two central conflicts of the poem – his clash with his father and the difference between the potential and the actual worth of his poetry.

But the poem immediately leaps (17–40) to a pronouncement of the divine nature of poetry, of its power over the gods, and thence to an Olympian/Heavenly vision of an eternity in which men, crowned with gold, will sing sweet songs echoing to the vault of the stars. The poem's rapturous praise of 'immortale melos et inenarrabile carmen' (37) rises to a peak which takes on the manner of a solution to the poem's conflicts. But this passage is not a resolution and Milton still has three-quarters of his poem left to be developed. And indeed the rest of the poem tends to wander anticlimactically to lower emotional pitches and to less exalted matters.

On leaving the Heavenly Realms the poem moves (41–55) to the banquets of ancient kings, where bards sang of heroic subjects. This is of course relevant to Milton's justification of poetry, but one wonders why it follows, at a lower level in almost all senses, the lofty passage preceding it. Again, the section on his father's permitting him to escape careers in business or law (67–76), and the following passage (77–92) on his father's encouragement of his linguistic and philosophical studies are logical parts of the poem. But it is difficult to see any structural reasons for their position here in the poem.

The next section (93–110) is the passage we have already discussed as occupying a climactic position in the poem without actually being climactic. The section begins, however, by dismissing the folly of seeking for gold (93–4), and this leads only to an awkward reversion to the subject of his father's generosity:

> Quae potuit maiora pater tribuisse, vel ipse
> Iupiter, excepto, donasset ut omnia, coelo?
> Non potiora dedit, quamvis et tuta fuissent,
> Publica qui iuveni commisit lumina nato,
> Atque Hyperionos currus, et fraena diei,
> Et circum undantem radiata luce tiaram. (95–100)

(What greater treasures could have been given by a father, or by Jove himself for that matter, even if he had given everything, unless he had included heaven as well? That father who trusted his young son with the universal light of the world and the chariot of Hyperion, with the reins of day and the diadem which radiates waves of light, gave (even had those gifts been safe) no better gifts than my father's.)

The reference to Phaëthon, destroyed by his father Hyperion's gift, takes the poem in quite the wrong direction, as Milton's 'quamvis et tuta fuissent' ('even had those gifts been safe') indicates. Then the poem lurches suddenly from Hyperion and Phaëthon to a statement of its resolution:

> Ergo ego iam doctae pars quamlibet ima catervae
> Victrices hederas inter, laurosque sedebo. (101–2)

(Therefore I, who already have a place, though a very low one, in the ranks of the learned, shall one day sit among those who wear the ivy and the laurels of victory.)

One wonders where Milton's 'ergo' came from. The laurel and ivy are reasonable resolutions of the early references to 'tenues sonos' and 'exiguum opus'. But the intervening parts of the poem have not led us on to such a triumph in the way that, a few years later, 'Lycidas' and 'Epitaphium Damonis' will proceed by means of inexorable poetic logic to their beatific visions. 'Ad Patrem' simply wanders from its discussion of alternative careers to Hyperion and his son, to Milton's father's generosity – and then, baldly, 'ergo': Milton will become the great poet that he has not yet been.

A third difficulty in 'Ad Patrem' lies in the lines which conclude the poem.

> Et vos, O nostri, iuvenilia carmina, lusus,
> Si modo perpetuos sperare audebitis annos,
> Et domini superesse rogo, lucemque tueri,
> Nec spisso rapient oblivia nigra sub Orco,
> Forsitan has laudes, decantatumque parentis
> Nomen, ad exemplum, sero servabitis aevo. (115–20)

(And you, my youthful poems, my pastimes, if only you are bold enough to hope for immortality, to hope that

73

you will survive your master's funeral pyre and keep your eyes upon the light, then perhaps, if dark oblivion does not after all plunge you down beneath the dense crowds of the underworld, you may preserve this eulogy and my father's name, which has been the subject of my verse, as an example for a far-off age.)

Rather than carrying the poem forward, as do the concluding lines of 'Lycidas' and 'Epitaphium Damonis', this conclusion lets 'Ad Patrem' fall back into the conflicts from which it began: 'nostri, iuvenilia carmina, lusus' ('my youthful poems, my pastimes', 115) simply echoes 'tenues sonos' (4) and 'exiguum opus' (7). And what ought to be a resolution to the poem merely reaffirms the difference between Milton's own poetry and the ideal poetry of which the middle of the poem (17–40) spoke so fervently. This leaves Milton's hope that his verses will make his father immortal a feeble thing both logically and poetically.

But 'Ad Patrem' represents an advance in poetic technique for Milton in many ways. Written in dactylic hexameters rather than in the elegiac distichs of most of his early poems, it begins to develop rhythmic patterns which give Milton more freedom and syntactical flexibility: where the elegiac distichs tended to constrict him into short sentences to fit the couplets, the flowing hexameters of 'Ad Patrem' permit the development of a kind of verse paragraph not found in the elegies. And this more fluid verse form will be an invaluable instrument for Milton in 'Mansus' and 'Epitaphium Damonis'.

The great strength of 'Ad Patrem', however, lies in the *personae* which Milton projects for his father and himself. The interplay of the two *personae* must have presented Milton with some difficult poetic problems – problems which he solved with greater skill than he had heretofore shown. In no other poem, before or after, does Milton adopt a posture of such humility. This poem is 'exiguum opus' ('this little offering'), 'charta ista' ('this sheet of paper'); his gratitude to his father is 'arida' because his words are futile, and he concludes, as we have seen, by deprecating his work as 'my youthful poems, my pastimes'. He uses the honorific 'donum' (8, 10, 112)[23] for his father's gifts to him, while his own possible repayments are merely 'munera' (8) and 'factis' (112). Yet his humility never becomes obsequious, as it so easily might.

This is because of the great skill Milton uses in handling the figure of his father in the poem. The aesthetic problem here is a difficult one: the poem must make the elder Milton an attractive figure (the biographical considerations here are obvious and need not delay us) in part because the poet's own *persona* depends on that of his father: the two *personae* emerge through their interactions. If the elder Milton appears as merely a grumpy old man, the younger Milton will appear, in trying to appease and persuade him, as either comic or servile. Yet an inevitable and central element of the poem is the clash between the young poet's lofty concept of poetry and the old man's deprecation of it. Milton solves this aesthetic problem essentially by the use of two ideas – by repeated praise of the old man's 'dona', and by skilfully stressing the old man's accomplishments as a musician and therefore also as a protégé of Phoebus:

> Nunc tibi quid mirum, si me genuisse poetam
> Contigerit, caro si tam prope sanguine iuncti
> Cognatas artes, studiumque affine sequamur:
> Ipse volens Phoebus se dispertire duobus,
> Altera dona mihi, dedit altera dona parenti,
> Dividuumque Deum genitorque puerque tenemus. (61–6)

(No wonder, then, that you should have the good luck to beget me, a poet, or that we who are so closely related by ties of affection and blood should cultivate sister arts and have kindred interests. Phoebus, wishing to share himself between the two of us, gave one lot of gifts to me and the other to my father, with the result that father and son have each one half a god.)

Instead of refuting his father, Milton includes him, and the old man appears not as a dominating, insensitive boor (a role into which the poem could easily have pushed him), but simply as mistaken about the artistic bond which actually unites them.

Thus Milton's address to his father establishes the old man as generous, permissive, and a lover of learning who is in part responsible for his son's knowledge of Greek, Latin, Hebrew,

75

and philosophy. By showing his father as a man of breadth and depth, Milton makes his own self-deprecation appear in the poem as appropriate, attractive, and free from any traces of fawning subservience. This diffident and humble Milton of 'Ad Patrem', who occurs nowhere else in his poetry, is a charming person because the poem very skilfully makes him so.

If we accept 1631–2 as a probable date for 'Ad Patrem', there is then a hiatus in Milton's career as a Latin poet until 1638 (*Comus* and 'Lycidas', in English, appeared in the intervening years). In late April or early May of 1638 Milton left England on the traditional grand tour of the continent. This tour began his closing period as a Latin poet. He wrote four brief Latin poems ('Ad Salsillum' and three poems 'Ad Leonoram'), and the long poem 'Mansus', to his host in Naples, Giovanni Battista Manso. 'Ad Salsillum' (to a fellow-poet, Giovanni Salzilli) and three poems to Leonora Baroni are trivial and need not delay us.

While in Italy Milton visited Naples, where he met Giovanni Battista Manso, Marquis of Villa (1560?–1645), who had been a patron of both Tasso and Marino, and apparently was as hospitable to the young English Protestant poet as possible. In response to Manso's kindness Milton wrote a poem of 100 hexameters to the old man, presumably late in 1638 or early in 1639. The poem is a panegyric, making use of the conventional rhetorical topoi that had come down through centuries of stylized adulation. But Milton, now thirty years old, is a mature poet; not only the Latin poems already discussed, but such great English poems as the Nativity Ode, 'L'Allegro', 'Il Penseroso', and *Comus* have already been written. And the year before, in 1637, he wrote 'Lycidas', which Marjorie Hope Nicolson calls 'the most perfect long short poem in the English language'. In fact, Milton's career as a Latin poet was drawing to an end.

As we might expect, 'Mansus' is a considerably more complex and better poem than his earlier tributes to Andrewes, Felton, Young, or even 'Ad Patrem'. Like the other great poems of his maturity, 'Mansus' is in an important sense a conventional poem: it returns again and again to the traditions of its genre, the panegyric or encomium. But, like 'Lycidas', 'Epitaphium Damonis', *Paradise Lost,* and *Paradise Regained,* it also self-consciously breaks with the tradition and establishes itself as a unique poem by the interrelations between itself and the panegyric tradition. Further, 'Mansus', like the other poems of Milton's maturity, transcends its literal occasion or theme. It enlarges to a contemplation of death, of the rewards of life, and in the end it creates not merely a panegyric of Manso but a poem celebrating the essential harmony of the universe.

'Mansus' resembles 'Lycidas' and 'Epitaphium Damonis' in beginning with a brief prose preface which explains who Manso is, and Milton's use of the panegyric tradition begins here: Manso is 'one of the most famous gentlemen of Italy, not only because of his reputation for intellectual ability but also because of his devotion to literature and his courage in war'. The topos of excellence in both war and peace goes back in the panegyric tradition hundreds of years in countless poems.[24] Appended to Manso's own collected poems, *Poesie Nomiche*, were more than a hundred poems in his praise by his friends, and time and again his friends praised him for his prowess 'nella militia e nella dottrina'.[25]

In the panegyric tradition, the extent of the subject's fame is an incessant topos,[26] and it is on this theme that Milton begins the actual poem:

> Haec quoque Manse tuae meditantur carmina laudi
> Pierides, tibi Manse choro notissime Phoebi,
> Quandoquidem ille alium haud aequo est dignatus honore,
> Post Galli cineres, et Maecenatis Hetrusci. (1–4)

(Manso, the Muses are singing this song, too, in your praise, yes, yours, Manso, Phoebus' choir knows all about you, because since Gallus and Etruscan Maecenas died Phoebus has hardly thought anyone so worthy of honour as you.)

The main reason for praising Manso, Milton tells us, is his friendship and helpfulness to poets – specifically to Tasso, to Marino, and now to Milton himself. Then he compares Manso with the centaur Chiron in a long metaphor which is central to the poem:

> Dicetur tum sponte tuos habitasse penates
> Cynthius, et famulas venisse ad limina musas:
> At non sponte domum tamen idem, et regis adivit
> Rura Pheretiadae coelo fugitivus Apollo;

77

Ille licet magnum Alciden susceperat hospes;
Tantum ubi clamosos placuit vitare bubulcos,
Nobile mansueti cessit Chironis in antrum,
Irriguos inter saltus frondosaque tecta
Peneium prope rivum: ibi saepe sub ilice nigra
Ad citharae strepitum blanda prece victus amici
Exilii duros lenibat voce labores.
Tum neque ripa suo, barathro nec fixa sub imo,
Saxa stetere loco, nutat Trachinia rupes,
Nec sentit solitas, immania pondera, silvas,
Emotaeque suis properant de collibus orni,
Mulcenturque novo maculosi carmine lynces. (54–69)

(Men will say that, of his own free will, Apollo dwelt in
your house, and that the Muses came like servants to your
doors. Yet that same Apollo, when he was a fugitive from
heaven, came unwillingly to King Admetus' farm, although Admetus had been host to mighty Hercules. When
he wanted to get away from the bawling ploughmen
Apollo could, at any rate, retreat to gentle Chiron's
famous cave, among the moist woodland pastures and
leafy shades beside the river Peneus. There often, beneath
a dark oak tree, he would yield to his friend's flattering
persuasion and, singing to the music of his lute, would
soothe the hardships of exile. Then neither the river banks,
nor the boulders lodged in the quarry's depths stayed in
their places: the Trachinian cliff nodded to the tune,
and no longer felt its huge and familiar burden of forest
trees; the mountain ashes were moved and came hurrying
down their slopes, and spotted lynxes grew tame as they
listened to the strange music.)

Milton is using *synkrisis* much as he did in 'Elegia Quarta',
to Thomas Young. A very common type of *synkrisis* is that
which concerns the relation of the giver (the poet) to the
receiver (the patron being praised), the two becoming metaphorically the poet/host and the patron/guest. In such a
comparison the lowly poet/host appears as one or another of
the humbler figures of Greek legend who received a god or
hero into his home – Icarus, Molorchus, or Chiron, honoured
at the visit of Apollo, Bacchus, Jove, Hercules, or Achilles.[27]

But Milton has reversed the metaphor: instead of comparing the noble patron/guest with Apollo or Hercules, and the humble poet/host with Chiron or Molorchus, it is Milton, the poet, who is the guest, who is like Apollo or Hercules. And in Milton's poem, the poet/guest graciously expresses his appreciation for the hospitality of patron/hosts like Manso and Chiron. Milton even goes so far as to link Manso's very name to Chiron's with a pun:

Nobile mansueti cessit Chironis in antrum

(. . . retreat to gentle Chiron's famous cave . . .)

This air of majestically praising Manso for being such a good assistant to poets boldly pervades much of the poem. Milton establishes a clear class-distinction: of primary importance are the poets – Homer, Vergil, Horace, Tasso, Marino, and Milton; of secondary importance are those who help the poets by patronage or by preserving their fame – Gallus, Maecenas, Herodotus, and Manso.

Then Milton suddenly departs from his praise of Manso to discuss his own plans for poetry:

O mihi si mea sors talem concedat amicum
Phoebaeos decorasse viros qui tam bene norit,
Si quando indigenas revocabo in carmina reges,
Arturumque etiam sub terris bella moventem;
Aut dicam invictae sociali foedere mensae,
Magnanimos heroas, et (O modo spiritus ad sit)
Frangam Saxonicas Britonum sub Marte phalanges. (78–84)

(O may it be my good luck to find such a friend, who knows so well how to honour Phoebus' followers, if ever I bring back to life in my songs the kings of my native land and Arthur, who set wars raging even under the earth, or tell of the great-hearted heroes of the round table, which their fellowship made invincible, and – if only the inspiration would come – smash the Saxon phalanxes beneath the impact of the British charge.)

E. M. W. Tillyard, who thought that 'Mansus' was 'the best of all Milton's Latin poems (the *Epitaphium Damonis* included)', said of this passage, 'There is great power in the crash of *frangam* after the hushed parenthesis of *O modo spiritus*

79

adsit.'[28] And Landor in his *Imaginary Conversations* called the line 'a glorious verse' and had Southey object only in that it overrated the early Britons: '"Was the whole nation [of Britons] ever worth this noble verse of Milton? It seems to come sounding over the Aegean Sea and not to have been modulated on the low country of the Tiber."'[29]

As we have seen, Milton builds into his panegyric a significant reversal of an important part of the panegyric tradition – for Milton it is the function, almost the duty, of patrons to honour poets, rather than the function or duty of the poets to honour their patrons. And this artful dissonance between Milton's 'Mansus' and the tradition derives its force not only from the reversed metaphor of Chiron, Apollo, and other mythological figures, but also from the closing vision (85–100); where Milton's predecessors in the tradition had visions of their patrons smiling down from Heaven on poor mortals such as the poet, Milton, with what Bradner calls 'Marlovean' exuberance,[30] envisages himself smiling down with satisfaction at the assistance of patrons like Manso. It would be difficult to defend the tone of these closing lines, and especially the last line, where Milton is so enraptured by his own apotheosis that he bursts into applause for himself. But the passage does have important connections with the panegyric tradition and with the happy relations of poet and patron, which is at the heart of the poem.

This closing vision resembles the visions which concluded several of Milton's epicedia – most importantly, 'Lycidas', written the year before, and 'Epitaphium Damonis' the next year (1639). In these other two poems the world of mortals is tainted; Lycidas received no proper reward here below and death came too soon; Damon's death also, from a purely human point of view, was senseless, and, until the closing vision, it was in many ways worse than that of the animals. Each poem progresses from the polluted natural world to the Christian supernatural community which resolves the earlier dilemma by surmounting and abandoning the natural world.

'Mansus' represents the natural world as having its own logic, rewards, and happiness. The result of Manso's help to Tasso is 'felix concordia'. The 'pia officia' of Manso continue after Tasso's death and it is important that they should. On the other hand, in 'Lycidas' the question '. . . What boots it with uncessant care/To tend the homely slighted shepherd's trade?' (64–5) implies (at this point in the poem and in the natural world) a quite different answer.

'Mansus' presents a different world-view also from that in 'Epitaphium Damonis' where the 'certa praemia' (36) for Damon leave the world's essential dilemma unsolved and insoluble except by supernatural means. But in 'Mansus' the picture of human society is one of harmony and happiness. Manso's acts bring satisfaction to Marino not only while Marino is alive but even when he is dead. Therefore Milton is confident of his own happiness after death partly because of the hope for the support of patrons like Manso who will preserve his fame.

In the large view, Milton's poem, then, finds its integrity not merely in the theme of praise for Manso, but more importantly in its embodiment of a universe united by mutual trust, respect, and affection, transcending human mortality. And in so doing, it becomes what it speaks of: it helps to transmit the continuity of the historic community of panegyric poems through the traditions of its generic ancestors just as the old man has carried on the customs of his spiritual ancestors, Herodotus, Gallus, and Maecenas.

In the summer of 1638, while Milton was making his way across the continent to Italy, Charles Diodati died in London. We do not know with certainty when Milton learned of his friend's death – perhaps in Italy that autumn, almost certainly by the time he returned to Geneva, where he visited Giovanni Diodati, the theologian, Charles's uncle.

Milton returned to London probably in the summer of 1639 and apparently soon after this wrote his last Latin poem of any length and seriousness. It is appropriate that it should have been an epicedion for Charles Diodati, close friend of his childhood and youth, recipient of two of the verse letters, and companion to whom the fourth sonnet (in Italian) was addressed.

'Epitaphium Damonis', like 'Lycidas' written eighteen months earlier, is a pastoral poem, invoking nymphs and Sicilian shepherds, and depending heavily on the pastoral tradition handed down from Moschus, Bion, Theocritus, and Vergil. Like Theocritus' first idyll and Vergil's eighth eclogue, Milton's poem uses a refrain. Like Vergil's fifth eclogue and like his own 'Lycidas', Milton's poem for Diodati comes to a vision of his dead friend enjoying a deserved happiness in the next world.

But 'Epitaphium Damonis' is no more docilely pastoral than 'Mansus' was inertly panegyric; it begins in pastoralism and quickly develops a restlessness with its pastoral metaphor. It then uses this restlessness as a dynamic force to lift the poem out of its pastoralism into a hymn of joy at the vision of Diodati in Heaven. Thus the pastoralism of 'Epitaphium Damonis' is not merely the poetic language by which the poem states its grief; it is also the instrument for imparting to the poem its upward surge from despair to the ecstatic knowledge that Diodati dwells in the presence of God.

This technique of using a poetic tradition not merely as a passive container for the poem but as an active metaphor is one which we have already seen operating in 'Mansus'. And perhaps one can see the first gleams of this mode of using a poetic tradition as early as 'Elegia Prima', written thirteen years earlier, where Milton played off his own rustication against Ovid's *Tristia* and *Epistulae ex Ponto* to fashion his poetic insult to Cambridge University. Certainly one can see the full flowering of the technique in *Paradise Lost*, where the tale of Adam's fall and subsequent education is 'not less but more heroic' than the adventure of Achilles, Odysseus, and Aeneas.

An important means in 'Epitaphium Damonis' for effecting this upward thrust from sorrow to consolation – an aesthetic problem which 'Elegia Tertia', for example, could not handle – is the refrain of the poem:

Ite domum impasti, domino iam non vacat, agni.

(Go home unfed, lambs, your shepherd has no time for you now.)

This refrain derives from two different lines in Vergil's eclogues (7.44 and 10.77). But the refrain in 'Epitaphium Damonis' does more than give a pastoral Vergilian flavour to the poem; the refrain modulates in its meanings as it recurs, taking on new colourings from the developing context of the poem. Thus at its first occurrence at line 18 the refrain rests wholly within its pastoral genus: the shepherd Damon, a conventional pastoral name, is dead; his fellow shepherd Thyrsis mourns him and brushes away the distracting sheep. But by line 180, when the refrain recurs for the last time, the poem has moved both generically and emotionally to a stage where it is no longer pastoral and no longer sorrowful; it is ready for its resolution both poetically and philosophically, and when the resolution emerges (198 ff) we get a significantly modified vestige of the refrain:

> Ite procul lacrymae, purum colit aethera Damon. (203)

> (Away with you, tears. Damon dwells now in the pure ether.)

And the poem concludes, having risen out of its pastoral genus and beyond its initial grief, in part by means of this recurrence in developing contexts of the very line which helped establish the pastoralism.

'Epitaphium Damonis' centres, of course, on ideas of companionship, love, death, and loneliness. Milton strikes this chord in the prose *Argumentum* preceding the poem – 'Thyrsis . . . suamque solitudinem hoc carmine deplorat'. After the ritual invocation to the muses of Sicily in the opening lines, which helps to establish the pastoral genus, the poem suddenly bursts forth with a depth of emotion:

> Tum vero amissum tum denique sentit amicum,
> Coepit et immensum sic exonerare dolorem. (16–17)

> (Then, then at last, he felt the loss of his friend and began to ease his huge burden of pain with these words.)

And the refrain enters for the first time in a context of deep grief:

> Ite domum impasti, domino iam non vacat, agni.

The poem resumes its pastoral metaphors but then again becomes personal and direct in its sorrow:

> Pectora cui credam? quis me lenire docebit
> Mordaces curas, quis longam fallere noctem
> Dulcibus alloquiis, grato cum sibilat igni
> Molle pyrum, et nucibus strepitat focus, at malus auster
> Miscet cuncta foris, et desuper intonat ulmo.
> Ite domum impasti, domino iam non vacat, agni. (45–50)

(To whom shall I open my heart? Who will teach me to calm eating cares or to beguile the long night with pleasant chatter while soft pears hiss before the cheery blaze and the hearth crackles with nuts, and while the cruel south wind throws everything into confusion out of doors and thunders through the tops of the elm. 'Go home unfed, lambs, your shepherd has no time for you now.')

The movement in these early lines from ritual pastoralism to some of the most personal passages in all Milton's poetry keeps 'Epitaphium Damonis' both generically pastoral and at the same time emotionally vibrant and human:

At iam solus agros, iam pascua solus oberro,
Sicubi ramosae densantur vallibus umbrae,
Hic serum expecto, supra caput imber et Eurus
Triste sonant, fractaeque agitata crepuscula silvae.
    Ite domum impasti, domino iam non vacat, agni. (58–62)

(But now I wander all alone through fields and pastures. I wait for evening in valleys where the shadows of branches are thick and black: over my head the rain and the southeast wind make mournful sounds in the restless twilight of the windswept wood. 'Go home unfed, lambs, your shepherd has no time for you now.')

In this passage, however, Milton is not so overcome by personal feelings that he cannot write one of his most skilfully onomatopoetic lines –

    Triste sonant, fractaeque agitata crepuscula silvae.

The line has further implications to which we shall return later.

Milton skilfully uses Vergil's eclogues as a delicate instrument throughout the 'Epitaphium'. Where his early Latin poems almost capsized with their cargo of unnecessary Greco-Roman figures, here the figures serve a subtle and vital function in the poem. For example, Milton writes:

Tityrus ad corylos vocat, Alphesiboeus ad ornos,
Ad salices Aegon, ad flumina pulcher Amyntas,
Hic gelidi fontes, hic illita gramina musco,
Hic Zephyri, hic placidas interstrepit arbutus undas;
Ista canunt surdo, frutices ego nactus abibam.
    Ite domum impasti, domino iam non vacat, agni. (69–74)

(Tityrus is calling me to the hazels, Alphesiboeus to the ash-trees, Aegon to the willows, lovely Amyntas to the streams: 'Here are cool fountains! Here is turf covered with moss! Here are soft breezes! Here the wild strawberry tree mingles its murmurs with the mild streams. They sing to deaf ears.' I managed to reach the thickets and escape from them. 'Go home unfed, lambs, your shepherd has no time for you now.')

Tityrus and the others are of course old inhabitants of the pastoral genus since at least the time of Theocritus. And their call to Thyrsis echoes Vergil's tenth eclogue:

> Hic gelidi fontes, hic mollia prata, Lycori,
> hic nemus; hic ipso tecum consumerer aevo. (10.42–3)

(Here are cold springs, Lycoris, here soft meadows, here woodland; here, with thee, times alone would wear me away.)[31]

Milton has Thyrsis respond to this Vergilian echo with

> Ista canunt surdo, frutices ego nactus abibam.
> Ite domum impasti . . .

(They sing to deaf ears. I managed to reach the thickets and escape from them. Go home unfed, lambs . . .)

And this is not merely Milton's *persona* Thyrsis rejecting Tityrus; it is also the poem generically moving away from pastoralism. Thus the refrain, although verbally unchanged, is modulating from being a metaphorical sign-post that this is a pastoral poem into expressing a literal rejection of pastoralism. The poem is saying that pastoralism is not adequate – it is Diodati who is dead, and old rituals have no power on such an occasion.

The poem now (113 ff) becomes quite autobiographical as it tells of the trip to Italy, of Milton's cordial reception there, and of his thoughts of Damon while abroad. He remembers intending to tell Damon of his own literary plans:

> Ipse etiam nam nescio quid mihi grande sonabat
> Fistula, ab undecima iam lux est altera nocte,
> Et tum forte novis admoram labra cicutis,
> Dissiluere tamen rupta compage, nec ultra

> Ferre graves potuere sonos, dubito quoque ne sim
> Turgidulus, tamen et referam, vos cedite silvae.
> Ite domum impasti, domino iam non vacat, agni.
> Ipse ego Dardanias Rutupina per aequora puppes
> Dicam, et Pandrasidos regum vetus Inogeniae,
> Brennumque Arviragumque duces. . . . (155–64)

(And I – for my pipe was sounding some lofty strain,
I know not what, eleven nights and a day ago, and I had
by chance set my lips to a new set of pipes, when their
fastening broke and they fell apart: they could bear the
grave notes no longer – I am afraid that I am being swollen-
headed, but still, I will tell of that strain. Give place, woods.
'Go home unfed, lambs, your shepherd has no time for
you now.' I shall tell of Trojan keels ploughing the sea
off the Kentish coast, and of the ancient kingdom of
Inogene, daughter of Pandrasus, of the chieftain Brennus
and Arviragus. . . .)

And he continues in this outline of his ideas for the Arthurian
epic which he had mentioned in 'Mansus' (80–4).

But simultaneously the poem is continuing its generic
development. The phrase 'vos cedite silvae' (160) resonates
with the whole poem; most obviously the phrase relates to
Milton's plans to move from pastoral poetry to epic. But it
does so by paraphrasing Vergil's 'concedite silvae', which is
Vergil's farewell to pastoral poetry, in his last eclogue. So also
this is Milton's farewell to pastoral poetry before the beginning
of his great epic – and indeed, although the great epic was on
Adam unparadised and not on King Arthur, still only the
occasional 'Ad Ioannem Rousium', some sonnets, and the epigrams on Salmasius intervene between 'Epitaphium Damonis'
and the publication of *Paradise Lost*.

Further, 'silvae' were of course not only the 'forests' of the
pastoral scene; ever since Statius wrote his 'Silvae' in the
first century A.D., 'silvae' were also 'sketches', 'improvisations',
or 'minor poems'. 'Silvae' were not necessarily trivial; one of
Statius' best 'silvae' is his 'Epicedion in Patrem Suum' (5.3).
But they were lesser poems than his epic *Thebaid* or *Achilleid*.

This meaning also underlines line 61 of 'Epitaphium
Damonis' – 'fractaeque agitata crepuscula silvae'. This is not

merely onomatopoetic pastoralism: for Milton, twilight, 'crepuscula', had come for the worn-out time of 'silvae'. By now Milton had written his seven Latin elegies and eleven poems in Greek and Latin which he called, in the 1645 publication of his poems, 'Sylvarum Liber'. Thus the phrase 'vos cedite silvae' at line 160 in this last poem of Milton's 'Sylvarum Liber' summons the poet to his life work of writing the great English epic, 'doctrinal to the nation'. And now, when the refrain 'Ite domum impasti . . .' recurs at line 161, it resonates with meanings quite beyond those of its first occurrence in line 18: he is brushing away 'silvae' for 'heroic song'.

Milton continues in this high pitch of excitement, indicating that he is writing Latin poetry for the last time, and bids Latin poetry farewell as he turns to a career as an English poet:

> . . . O mihi tum si vita supersit,
> Tu procul annosa pendebis fistula pinu
> Multum oblita mihi, aut patriis mutata camoenis
> Brittonicum strides . . . (168–71)

(O, if I have any time left to live, you, my pastoral pipe, will hang far away on the branch of some old pine tree, utterly forgotten by me, or else, transformed by my native muses, you will whistle a British tune.)

He will be content if he is known only in Britain:

> Si me flava comas legat Usa, et potor Alauni,
> Vorticibusque frequens Abra, et nemus omne Treantae,
> Et Thamesis meus ante omnes, et fusca metallis
> Tamara, et extremis me discant Orcades undis.
> Ite domum impasti, domino iam non vacat, agni. (175–9)

(If only yellow-haired Usa reads my poems, and he who drinks from the Alan, and Humber, full of whirling eddies, and every grove of Trent, and above all my native Thames and the Tamar, stained with metals, and if the Orkneys among their distant waves will learn my song. 'Go home unfed, lambs, your shepherd has no time for you now.')

Here the refrain has become a farewell to Latin verse for the English poetic career ahead, and it is of course by means of this refrain that the generic thrust, from the lowly pastoral beginning[32] to the plans for heroic English poetry in the future, has been managed.

This already complex poem now moves into even more intricate patterns: Milton's projected work of art, his epic, leads him to tell of two other works of art, the twin cups, given him in Naples by Manso.[33] The cups are engraved with various images, mainly resurrection symbols. Most significant of the engravings is the figure of Amor on the cups, scattering his arrows aloft 'Hinc mentes ardere sacrae, formaeque deorum' ('kindle holy minds and the forms of the gods themselves', 197).

Amor is of course the neo-Platonic figure of Love, by whose 'divine splendour', Ficino tells us, 'the Soul is inflamed . . . glowing in the beautiful person as in a mirror, secretly lifted up as by a hook in order to become God'.[34]

Amor serves a complex function in 'Epitaphium Damonis'. First and simplest, he is the figure on the cups which Thyrsis received from Mansus; secondly, as lines 197 ff tell us, Amor, the neo-Platonic force of Love, enkindles the 'mentes sacrae' such as Damon, making possible for Damon the Heavenly union which the closing section describes. And Amor, operating by means of the physical beauty of the cups, lifts Thyrsis's eyes to the metaphysical eternal beauty of his final vision.

At last this extremely complex poem achieves its goal, the vision of the transfigured Damon in Heaven, where Love is eternal. Appropriately, artfully, and inevitably, the last vestiges of pastoralism drop away; up to now Diodati has been clothed in the pastoral name of Damon. But in line 210 he casts aside his shepherd garments to assume his true (in several senses) name, his 'divino nomine', Diodatus, the gift of God, even though 'silvisque vocabere Damon' (211) – 'silvis' again being a play on words. Now the earthly dilemma of love and death, of the need for companionship that is not merely gregariousness, finds its solution in the true and eternal Love of the celestial marriage feast, Bacchic in its ecstasy and divine in its dedication.

As for Thyrsis, what he achieves, as the intricate structure of the poem reaches its culmination, is a solace for the agony of his loneliness, a glimpse of divine and eternal Love – and also (and this is part of the poem too) the creation of this pastoral epicedion which evolves into a hymn celebrating the eternal joy of his friend; this work of art which, like the cups of Mansus, both embodies the vision of bliss and lifts him up to perceive it.

'Epitaphium Damonis' is both the high point and, as Milton saw it then, the end of his career as a Latin poet. Shortly after 'Epitaphium Damonis' Milton began work on the great English poem which ultimately emerged as *Paradise Lost*.

One Latin poem and two inconsequential epigrams attacking his political opponent Salmasius conclude Milton's Latin poetry. The two epigrams (1651 and 1654) are routine polemics, but 'Ad Ioannem Rousium' is a poem of considerable merit. It was written, Milton says, on 23 January 1646 (i.e. 1647). Milton had sent a copy of his *Poems*, just printed, to Rouse, the Librarian of Oxford University. The volume was lost or stolen and Rouse asked for another copy. Milton sent a second copy and included the manuscript of this poem, written for the occasion.

In spite of its having been put together presumably in a very short time, it is a graceful, skilful poem. It addresses the lost volume of poems and wonders where it has wandered:

> Seu quis te teneat specus,
> Seu qua te latebra, forsan unde vili
> Callo tereris institoris insulsi,
> Laetare felix, en iterum tibi
> Spes nova fulget posse profundam
> Fugere Lethen. . . . (40–5)

(Though now you lie in some ditch or on some hidden shelf from which, perhaps, you are taken and thumbed over by a blockheaded bookseller with calloused, grimy hands – cheer up, lucky little book! See, here is a gleam of hope for you – hope that you will be able to escape from the depths of Lethe.)

Rouse will preserve it:

> Tum livore sepulto
> Si quid meremur sana posteritas sciet
> Roüsio favente. (85–7)

(Then, when spite and malice are buried in the past, posterity with its balanced judgment will know – thanks to Rouse – what, if anything, I have deserved.)

Tillyard thought the poem to Rouse 'one of the greater Latin poems, less serious than *Mansus* and the *Epitaphium Damonis*, but in completeness of achievement worthy to rank with them'.[35] He remarks that the poem gives a charming picture of the more amiable Milton, 'of whom we see but too little during the years of the Commonwealth' – Milton as a modest, graceful, witty, and pleasant man.

After 'Ad Ioannem Rousium' there was no more Latin poetry worth mentioning; the dedication to English poetry which he had announced in 'Epitaphium Damonis' was in effect, and *Samson Agonistes*, *Paradise Lost*, and *Paradise Regained* were the results. There was a moment in 1653, after his blindness, when he might have produced one more Latin poem: Oliver Cromwell's portrait was to be sent to Queen Christina of Sweden and a Latin poem was to accompany it. But the poem came to be written not by Milton, Cromwell's Secretary for Foreign Tongues, but by his assistant Andrew Marvell. Perhaps it was because Milton, now blind, could not honestly write of the portrait; or perhaps because for him Latin was no longer the language for his poetry.

Although Milton's final decision was to renounce Latin poetry and 'to be an interpreter & relater of the best and sagest things among mine own Citizens throughout this Iland in the mother dialect',[36] still in 1673, the year before he died, he supervised a new, enlarged edition of *Poems, &c. upon Several Occasions by Mr. John Milton: Both English and Latin*, including all the youthful Latin epicedia, the praise of the king and the bishops, the mature Latin poems of the 1630s, and he concluded the volume with the first public appearance of his deft 'Ad Ioannem Rousium'. John Milton gave up his brilliant career as a Latin poet to produce his English masterpieces, *Samson Agonistes*, *Paradise Lost*, and *Paradise Regained*. But touchingly, humanly, and rightly, his pride in his Latin poems survived until his death.

Notes

1 I am indebted to the Pennsylvania State University for research grants and to Glasgow University for its cordial assistance in supplying much of the material for this study.

2 The dating and sequence of Milton's Latin poems is taken from *A*

Variorum Commentary on the Poems of John Milton, ed. M. Y. Hughes, I, *The Latin and Greek Poems*, ed. Douglas Bush (London: Routledge & Kegan Paul, 1970, and New York: Columbia University Press, 1970). Bush's datings are reasonable and a further enquiry into the problems of dating would not be appropriate to this essay.

3   *The Reason of Church Government. The Works of John Milton*, ed. Frank Patterson (New York, Columbia University Press, 1933), III, p. 236. All quotations from Milton's prose are from this edition.

4   *Defensio Pro Populo Anglicano* and *Defensio Secunda*.

5   *The Poems of John Milton*, ed. John Carey and Alastair Fowler (London: Longmans, 1968), p. 23. All quotations and translations of Milton's poetry are taken from this edition, by kind permission of Messrs. Longman and Dr Carey and Professor Fowler.

6   Trans. by Arthur Leslie Wheeler in the Loeb Classical Library edition.

7   *Tristia* 3.12.23–4; *Epistulae ex Ponto* 1.8.35–6.

8   *Tristia* 3.10.71–8; 3.12.13–16. *Epistulae* 1.3.49–52; 3.1.13; 3.8.13–16.

9   *Epistulae* 2.7.74; 4.10.61–2.

10 See the discussion in James Holly Hanford, 'The youth of Milton', *Studies in Shakespeare, Milton, and Donne* (New York: Macmillan, 1925), p. 110.

11 'Milton in rustication', *Studies in Philology*, 19 (1922), p. 109.

12 *The Poems of Milton*, ed. Thomas Keightley (London: Chapman & Hall, 1859).

13 The last line of 'Elegia Tertia', 'Talia contingant somnia saepe mihi ['May I often be lucky enough to have dreams like this!'] is a most un-Miltonic howler. It echoes a line from Ovid's *Amores* (1.5.26). But while Milton's vision is of the saintly Bishop of Winchester in Heaven, Ovid's was of Corinna in the nude.

14 See Macon Cheek, 'Milton's "In Quintum Novembris": an epic foreshadowing', *Studies in Philology*, 54 (1957), p. 175.

15 'Southey and Landor', *The Complete Works of Walter Savage Landor*, ed. T. Earle Welby (London: Chapman & Hall, 1927), v, p. 328.

16 'Milton in rustication', p. 122.

17 Aristotle, *Rhetoric* 1.9.1368 a, urges the use of *synkrisis*, that is, the comparing of one's subject to a great figure in history or mythology.

18 This is a common epic phrase; cf. Lucretius 6.752; *Aeneid* 5.54 and 11.50.

19 'Milton's pastoral monodies', *Studies in Honour of Gilbert Norwood* (University of Toronto Press, 1952), p. 262. See also Woodhouse, 'Notes on Milton's early development', *University of Toronto Quarterly*, 13 (1943–4), p. 77.

20 For a summary of the arguments as to whether the epilogue applies only to 'Elegia Septima' or to all seven elegies, see Bush, pp. 129–30.

21 F. W. Bateson, *English Poetry: A Critical Introduction* (New York: Barnes & Noble, 1966), p. 113.

22 The date of this poem is the least certain of the important Latin poems but this essay is not the place to weigh the arguments. See Woodhouse, 'Notes', p. 84 and Bush, pp. 232–40.

23 Milton throughout his Latin poetry tends to follow the common but not

invariable Roman practice of using 'donum' for gifts to or from gods or superior people, and 'munus' for less honoured rewards. See *A Concordance of the Latin, Greek, and Italian Poems of John Milton*, comp. Lane Cooper (Halle: Niemeyer, 1923), pp. 44–5, 104.

24 See, e.g. Lucan (?), 'Laus Pisonis'; Pseudo-Tibullus, 'Ad Messallam'; Mantuan, 'In Robertum Sanseverinatem Panegyricum Carmen'.

25 I am grateful to Dr Alfred Triolo for his help with these Italian poems.

26 See, e.g. 'Ad Messallam', 31–8; George Buchanan, 'Ad Carolum V', 7–18.

27 See, e.g. 'Ad Messallam', 7–13; Sidonius Apollinaris, 'Praefatio Panegyrici Dicti Anthemio Augusto bis Consuli', 15–20; 'Ad Carolum V', 24–8

28 E. M. W. Tillyard, *Milton* (London: Chatto & Windus, 1946), pp. 90–1.

29 Landor, p. 330.

30 Leicester Bradner, *Musae Anglicanae: A History of Anglo-Latin Poetry 1500–1925* (New York: Modern Language Association, 1940), p. 114.

31 Trans. by H. Rushton Fairclough in the Loeb Classical Library edition.

32 In the hierarchy of poetic genera it was a Renaissance commonplace that the pastoral was at the bottom and either tragedy or epic at the top. See, e.g. Sir Philip Sidney, *Defence of Poesie*, ed. Albert Feuillerat (Cambridge University Press, 1923), pp. 22, 25.

33 There is a long scholarly dispute, irrelevant here, as to whether Manso gave Milton actual cups. See my 'The structure of Milton's "Epitaphium Damonis"', *Studies in Philology*, 62 (1965), pp. 591–2 and n. 62, for a brief summary.

34 Marsilio Ficino, *Opera Omnia* (Basle, 1561), p. 306, quoted in Paul O. Kristeller, *The Philosophy of Marsilio Ficino*, trans. Virginia Conant (New York: Columbia University Press, 1943), p. 267.

35 Tillyard, p. 172

36 *The Reason of Church Government*, p. 236.

IV
Richard Crashaw's
Epigrammata Sacra

Kenneth J. Larsen

While Richard Crashaw's most notable contribution to English poetry has been his mastery of the baroque form, about which critics and readers have remained divided, his original reputation was built on his Latin poetry. In this field critics have not been unkind, some opinion regarding him as 'the greatest writer of the conventional sacred epigram in England'. Indeed Austin Warren, the original biographer and critic of Crashaw, sees his genius in a wider context:[1]

> Distinguished of style they are: the best Latin epigrams written by an Englishman. Nor will a diligent search through the neglected volumes of Renaissance Neo-Latinity discover any master of whom Crashaw is not peer.

Son of a noted Puritan divine, William Crashaw, Richard had been educated at Charterhouse after the death of his parents. David Lloyd tells us that his poetry was nurtured there: 'the essays Mr. *Brooks* . . . imposed upon him, on the Epistles and Gospels, at School, were the ground of that Divine Fancy, so famous in *Pembroke-hall*.'[2] The poetry, in which he was coached at Charterhouse, and which was publicly screened at Pembroke College, Cambridge, was the Latin

epigram. In this genre Crashaw served his poetic apprentice-
ship and built his original reputation. Other Latin poetry,
which he was to write, was principally of an occasional and
dedicatory nature, by invitation and of little variety.

Crashaw was accepted for Pembroke Hall on 6 July 1631,
under the tutelage of Mr Tourney, and on 2 October was
elected to a Watt Scholarship, his Charterhouse epigrams and
early Pembroke epigrams no doubt forming the basis of his
election. His compositions during his tenure of the scholarship
were subsequently published as the *Epigrammatum Sacrorum
Liber* by the University Press in 1634. The book is carefully
produced, which suggests that it may have been proof-read by
Crashaw himself. Further epigrams also exist in manuscript
form, an additional sixty-three epigrams being in the possession
of the Bodleian Library in a collection of poems transcribed
and bequeathed by Archbishop Sancroft, a contemporary of
Crashaw at Cambridge.[3]

The corpus of epigrams, in its original and subsequent
editions, immediately impresses as massive, without any hint
of internal order.[4] As such, the epigrams have remained un-
attractive and impenetrable, allowing of little work except in
general terms; any comparative analysis was certainly impossible and any religious or poetic development hardly discernible. Fortunately this position no longer prevails and a reading
of the Book of Common Prayer allows the epigrams to be seen
in sequence; this in turn makes analysis and comparison possible. Some short description of this process, worked out partly
by Austin Warren and Sister M. S. Milhaupt, is necessary.[5]

Besides the custom of writing on topics from the Epistles and
Gospels at Charterhouse, Crashaw had been obliged to write,
on the Sundays of his final year, Latin and Greek epigrams
'upon any part of the Second Lesson appointed for that day,
for the Master of the Hospital, or any stranger to view and
examine'. This practice he was to continue as Watt Scholar.
Matthew Wren has provided the detailed conditions for the
scholarship in his statutes of the Watt Foundation:[6]

> To make verses. 4 Hexam. Pentam. Latin as many Greeks
> of ye same matter at Circumcision, Epiphany, Purification,
> Annunciation, Easter, Ascension, Pentecost, Trinity Sun,
> All Sts, Xtmas, Good friday. 2 greeke 2 Latin e'ry Sunday

other holy day. Written wth theire owne hand, set on ye skreene before dinner. The argument of ye verses to be taken out of some pt of ye Scriptures yt day read. To have $7^s \, 5^d$ a yeare payd by quart's for verses.

The scriptures 'that day read' would include the Epistle and Gospel from the Communion Service, the first lessons from morning and evening prayer (generally Old Testament selections) and the second lessons from the same (New Testament selections).[7] Some of Crashaw's epigrams can be traced to the Sunday Gospels of the 1631–4 period, yet the key to the dating of the majority lies with the second lesson at morning prayer.

The Anglican reformers of the sixteenth century had reduced the medieval office of the traditional eight hours to a simple two-hour office of morning and evening prayer. The scripture lessons of these liturgies are the clue to any regular chronological sequence in Crashaw's epigrams.

The Church Year, as in the Book of Common Prayer, has three cycles, the *ferial*, the *temporal* and the *festive*. The *ferial* cycle, providing lessons for morning and evening prayer, and following the actual calendar year, is the basic cycle. The *temporal* cycle is that which follows the church's liturgical seasons, Advent, Christmas, Epiphany, Lent, Easter, Pentecost and Time after Trinity. The major liturgical feasts of this cycle had both an Epistle and a Gospel and special lessons for morning and evening prayer. The ordinary Sundays had their own Epistle and Gospel but took their lessons for morning and evening prayer from the *ferial* cycle. The *festive* cycle comprises those Feast Days, such as All Saints (1 November) or St Peter (29 June), which are not attached to the church's liturgical seasons, and which fall on the same date each year. These feast days were generally provided with an Epistle and Gospel and special lessons for morning and evening prayer, which took precedence over the *ferial* lessons.

The scriptural selections used on a particular day can, therefore, derive from several sources: from the Epistle or Gospel of the day, from the two lessons at morning prayer and the two lessons at evening prayer. In fact Crashaw seems to have used only the Epistle and Gospel and the second lesson at morning prayer as sources for his epigrams, although on one occasion he uses the first lesson at evening prayer. Moreover, the reason why critics have failed to detect any topical pattern in Crashaw's epigrams is that the Epistles and Gospels themselves did not follow any scriptural sequence, but were chosen in so far as they conformed to the particular temporal season, be it Advent, Epiphany, Lent, etc. The Epistles and Gospels of the *festive* cycle were chosen in so far as they conformed to the particular feast. But the second lesson at morning prayer for the *ferial* cycle was always a chapter of one of the Gospels or the Acts of the Apostles, and these chapters ran continuously throughout the year falling on the same day each year. So the second lesson for morning prayer on 2 January was Matthew, Chapter 1, on 3 January, Matthew, Chapter 2, on 4 January, Matthew, Chapter 3 and so on until all four Gospels and the Acts of the Apostles were exhausted. Matthew started again with Chapter 1 on 3 May, and a third cycle started on 31 August.

The dovetailing of these three cycles, *temporal*, *festive* and *ferial*, is of great importance for it allows a definite date to be ascribed to nearly all of Crashaw's epigrams. Obviously the Epistle and Gospel for each Sunday and feast day is the same for every year, but the second lesson at morning prayer depends on the date, and so varies for each Sunday depending on which date the Sunday falls. If the epigrams were to follow only the Epistles and Gospels of the Sundays and feast days, the occasions of the epigrams could be established but not the date or year. Since the second lessons have been used, the day and year can be well established as well, because a particular date, or its corresponding chapter, will fall on a Sunday only once in six or seven years. If one starts to correlate Crashaw's epigrams with the feasts and Sundays of his time at Pembroke Hall, the epigrams' scriptural headings coincide exactly with either a Gospel or a second lesson for morning prayer of the same period: the epigrams commence on the feast of St Bartholomew, 24 August 1631, and conclude with an epigram for Whit Sunday, 17 May 1635.

Crashaw's epigrams, once dated, reveal a chronological sequence in their original and published form in the *Epigrammata Sacra*, although an epigram is sometimes slightly displaced and the first eighteen epigrams resist definite appointment. A table of epigrams and dates can be calculated with the scriptural references, which head each epigram, coinciding with the scriptural reading of the day. An example of a section of the table extracted for April 1632, under the titles *Scriptural Heading of Epigram, Liturgical Source of Epigram, Liturgical Reading, Feast Day,* and *Date* would read:[8]

Scriptural Heading of Epigram	Liturgical Source of Epigram	Liturgical Reading	Feast Day	Date
Act. 5.	II Matins	Acts 5	1st Sunday after Easter	Sun. 8 Apr. 1632
Luc. 24.39	Gospel	Luke 24.36–49	Easter Tuesday	Tues. 3 Apr. 1632
Act.12.	II Matins	Acts 12	2nd Sunday after Easter	Sun.15 Apr. 1632
Act. 19.12	II Matins	Acts 19	3rd Sunday after Easter	Sun. 22 Apr. 1632
Joann. 15	Gospel	John 15.1–12	Saint Mark	Wed.25Apr.1632
Act. 26.28	II Matins	Acts 26	4th Sunday after Easter	Sun. 29 Apr. 1632

This chronological order remains consistent not only for the series of epigrams in the printed edition of *Epigrammata Sacra*, but also for the further epigrams of the Bodleian Tanner MS. Indeed, the two series dovetail. The printed epigrams close with a sequence leading up to the Feast of the Ascension, 1634, the final epigram being composed 'In die Ascensionis Dominicae'. Although, as in *Epigrammata Sacra*, the first few epigrams of the Tanner MS. lack any cohesion, a new sequence starts with 'In Atheniensem Merum' and 'Abscessum Christi queruntur discipuli',[9] the first being occasioned by the second lesson at morning prayer for the 2nd Sunday after Easter, 20 April 1634, the second by the Gospel for the Sunday after the Ascension, 18 May 1634. The epigrams in the Tanner MS. retain their order until Whit Sunday, 1635.

This appointment of dates reveals Crashaw's epigrams as individual and related units, in contrast, indeed, with their original format, which had allowed only a haphazard and somewhat speculative selection of parallels, principally with continental sources. The key to Crashaw's epigrams lies within the Anglican liturgy, which background, furthermore, both partially explains the description of Crashaw as 'the other *Herbert* of our Church' and suggests his father's influence: his schooling and his inherited love of the traditional liturgy. But more pertinently, because the same scriptural topics recur regularly in the four yearly cycles of the liturgy between 1631 and 1635, the development of Crashaw's religious thought during his formative years at Pembroke College becomes patent: while his epigrams have commonly been accepted as betraying little hint of doctrinal polemic, a more subtle degree of movement towards the High Church attitudes, which characterized his later work, is revealed.

The Church of England in the first half of the seventeenth century had seen a gradual polarization of doctrine and life. Within the shifting sands of religious jargon and practices, positions hardened and bitter controversy ensued between Puritan and High Churchman, the latter faction united under the leadership of William Laud, Archbishop of Canterbury. The Puritan felt reformed purity of doctrine threatened by the Laudian; the Laudian, heavily reliant on the plank of 'traditional church', feared the total destruction of the Church as a national heritage. The Puritan based his theology of salvation strictly on the Reformation maxim of faith alone; central to Laudian theology was the primacy which must be given to charity or its everyday application, good works. This controversy of precedence allowed of an easy contemporary yardstick, by which a man's orthodoxy or heterodoxy could be gauged. It is also reflected in Crashaw's epigrams: the early epigrams concern themselves primarily with eliciting from the Gospel incidents a strengthening of faith; those of the later years concentrate on the motive of love.

Crashaw's early position cannot be disassociated from the influence of his father, who, among Puritan apologists, upheld a considerable and orthodox reputation. Although William Crashawe died when Richard was thirteen or fourteen, he was, for the most part, in sole charge of his son and prescribed where and how his son was to be educated after his death. As a conscientious father and solicitous author of children's primers, his views can scarcely have failed to leave their imprint. The father promoted himself as a forthright defender of Reformation orthodoxy and in his commentary, *Romish Forgeries and Falsifications*, a vindication against Rome of the theologian Ferus, his principal concern is to prove the precedence of faith over charity: 'charitie springs *out of faith*, and not faith out of charitie'.[10]

In Calvinist theology Christ had completely vindicated man's sinfulness; no merit could be attributed to man. William Crashaw attacked Rome because Catholics ascribed man's salvation to himself: 'Let no man ascribe anything at all to himself; but all his meriting to Christ, who is made to us of God righteousnesse and redemption.'[11] Within Christ's total and extrinsic justification, man's active faculties were directed inwardly, towards the conviction that he had been saved by Christ and the attribution of all to Christ. Good works, derivative of the virtue of charity, could never imply co-operation in redemption, but served rather to bear witness to a deeper belief in a justification already objectively assured.

As such, the virtue of faith assumed the dominant role in the scheme of salvation and there arose a natural interest, perhaps a preoccupation with the question of personal salvation. Man's salvific duty to strengthen his faith in Christ's justification was underpinned by the safeguard that 'a man elected, justified and sanctified, cannot fall from the state of grace and be damned', where 'grace' intended that state of objective justification. Human preoccupation could be allayed by the realization that feelings of doubt derived from 'a relique of corrupt nature' and that man's interior disposition could never affect his objective state: 'the feeling of grace may, but saving grace it selfe cannot be extinguisht or utterly lost'.[12]

Yet in human terms the strengthening of faith as an interior disposition remained the everyday duty of common man. Thus belief in Christ's total justification not only maintained a whole theology of salvation, but its own maintenance was the essence of man's conduct. As such it took precedence over all other virtues, including charity; as William Crashaw succinctly states: 'We hold and teach that charitie is not onely after faith, but proceeds from and out of faith.'[13]

By mid-1634, however, Crashaw's religion had so moved, that he deliberately chose to align himself within Laudian ranks by contributing prefatory verses to Robert Shelford's masterly Laudian polemic, *Five Pious and Learned Discourses*,[14] which endorsed the precedence of love and good works:[15]

> These learned leaves shall vindicate to thee
> Thy holyest, humblest, handmaid Charitie.

Crashaw's theme and imagery draw extensively upon Shelford's chapter 'A Sermon preferring Holy Charity before Faith, Hope and Knowledge', which, because of its uncompromising stand, aroused particular Puritan ire. As did Crashaw in his verses, Shelford attacked Calvin directly for perverting scripture, which states categorically: '*Now abideth faith, hope, and charitie, but the greatest of these is charitie.* He saith not, *shall be,* as Calvin and Beza offer to evacuate the Apostles comparison & commendation; but *is* now.'[16] Shelford's presentation of the Laudian concept of salvation is orthodox: man's salvation derives principally from the virtue of charity, which takes precedence over faith:[17]

> Faith converts the minde to God; but it is love and charitie that converts the heart and will to God, which is the greatest and last conversion, because we never seek any thing untill we desire it. Our conversion therefore is begun in the minde by faith: but this conversion is but half a conversion, yea, it is no conversion of the whole man, except the love of the heart, where lieth the greatest apprehension, do second and follow it. . . . Wherefore I conclude, that, for as much as charitie is the nearest and immediate cause of our conversion, of our seeking and finding God, therefore this is the most precious grace of God for our good, and is the greatest mean and instrument of our justification; because justification and conversion to God is all one.

If man were to be saved by faith alone, Shelford asks 'what need I care how I live? no sinne can hurt me as long as I beleeve'; prayer and all good life are already stillborn. Rather man must co-operate in his redemption, and the more he co-operates, the more the good works he performs because of charity, the higher his prize in heaven. Without charity, faith and works are dead because charity informs all virtues and all actions: 'where no works are, there is no charitie; and where no charitie is, there faith and works and all is dead . . . without charitie works are dead, as well as faith, and knowledge, and other graces.'[18] In Laudian terms, love, not faith, is constituted salvific grace, which inspires all: 'where there is charitie, that is to say, a divine love to God and all goodnesse, there all things are alive, and every grace working to salvation'.[19]

Crashaw, in his prefatory verses, also employed the virtue of charity to justify the Laudian revival in liturgy and insistence on church beauty. To the Puritan these liturgical extras were both Romish and dangerous, detracting from Christ's total justification, and distracting man from his primary inward effort. Two of the first three epigrams that Crashaw composed at Pembroke display this earlier Puritan attitude towards church decorum. Of the two men in the 'Pharisaeus & Publicanus', the Pharisee might possess the exterior temple, but the Publican finds his God, rightly, in his interior faith:

> Ecce hic peccator timidus petit advena templum;
> Quodque audet solum, pectora moesta ferit.
> Fide miser; pulsaque fores has fortiter: illo
> Invenies *templo* tu *propriore* Deum. (Martin, *Poems*, p. 17)

(Look, this faint-hearted sinner and stranger approaches the temple; he dares only to strike his sorrowful breast. Take heart, wretch; knock boldly on these doors; in that closer temple you will find your God.)

In the first epigram in *Epigrammata Sacra* the same lesson is drawn with the further implication that the externals of the church, the high altar and the sanctuary, are to be censured:

> En duo Templum adeunt (diversis mentibus ambo:)
> Ille procul trepido lumine signat humum:
> It gravis hic, & in alta ferox penetralia tendit.
> Plus habet hic *templi*; plus habet ille *Dei*.
> (Martin, *Poems*, p. 15)

(Here two men approach the temple (each of a different mind). The first, from a distance, scores the ground with worried eye; the second, self-important and arrogant, goes on and walks towards the high sanctuary. He has more of the temple; the first has more of God.)

God exists, Crashaw seems to say, more in the heart of man than in a presence in a sanctuary.

A Christian's conversion and subsequent interior disposition should be buttressed by corresponding symptoms of repentance for sins, which assure him of his right to heaven. Writing on the feast of All Saints, 1 November 1631, Crashaw points out that the elect have attained heaven because of their tears of repentance:

> Undique Pax effusa piis volet aurea pennis,
> Frons bona dum signo est quaeque notata suo.
> Ah quid in hoc opus est signis aliunde petendis?
> Frons bona sat lacrymis quaeque notata suis.
> (Martin, *Poems*, p. 23)

(Let golden Peace, deployed on sacred wings, fly far and wide – until every good forehead is marked by his sign. Ah, but why must signs be sought elsewhere? The forehead of the good man is clearly marked by its own tears.)

Similarly in Crashaw's epigram written on 18 September 1632, one can detect, in his portrayal of the harshness of everyday experience, an inevitable Puritan joylessness:

> I Miser, inque tuas rape non tua tempora curas:
> Et nondum natis perge perire malis.
> Mi querulis satis una dies, satis angitur horis:
> Una dies lacrymis mi satis uda suis.
> Non mihi venturos vacat expectare dolores:
> Nolo ego, nolo *hodie crastinus esse miser*.
>
> (Martin, *Poems*, p. 20)

(Go on pessimist, add to your worries times not yet yours; continue to die of evils not yet born. For me one day full of choking hours is sufficient: one day wet with its own tears is enough. I have no time to anticipate coming sorrows: and I certainly have no desire that unhappy tomorrow should be here today.)

These earthly cares find traditional release in death, of which Crashaw treats in his early epigrams without any suggestion of the mystic tone employed in his later poetry. Death is a release presented within the interplay of life and death and the Christian paradox of Christ's death and man's life.

In 1631, also, we find the two epigrams which have a distinct anti-papal bias. The first of these, written on 24 August, impugns the Pope for his petrine claims:

> O Petri umbra potens! quae non miracula praestat?
> Nunc quoque, Papa, tuum sustinet illa decus.
>
> (Martin, *Poems*, p. 19)

(O powerful shade of Peter! What miracles do you not effect? Now, O Pope, it also underpins your glory.)

Similarly William Crashaw's writings about the Gunpowder Plot find an echo in his son's epigram for 5 November 1631, a feast introduced into the Book of Common Prayer in 1611. That Crashaw did not find it necessary to compose an epigram on the same day in succeeding years can perhaps be considered a mark of his religious development. Crashaw sees the day in its liturgical setting:

> Quam bene dispositis annus dat currere festis!
> Post *Omnes Sanctos, Omne Scelus sequitur.*
>
> (Martin, *Poems*, p. 23)

(How fit our well-rank'd Feasts doe follow,/All mischiefe comes after *All Hallow.*)

As outlined above, however, the main movement discernible within the epigrams is the shift of emphasis from the virtue of faith to the virtue of love. The following list, compiled from the references where faith or love is the explicit lesson of an epigram, provides a convincing outline of Crashaw's development:

Faith	9 Oct. 1631	Faith	2 June 1633
Faith	20 Nov. 1631	Love	10 June 1633
Faith	21 Dec. 1631	Faith	18 Oct. 1633
Faith	16 Jan. 1632	Love	27 Dec. 1633
Faith	22 Jan. 1632	Faith	26 Jan. 1634
Faith	5 Feb. 1632	Faith	25 Mar. 1634
Faith	12 Feb. 1632	Love	4 Apr. 1634
Faith	11 Mar. 1632	Love	8 Apr. 1634
Faith	3 Apr. 1632	Love	11 May 1634
Faith	27 May 1632	Love	15 May 1634
Faith	17 June 1632	Love	24 Aug. 1634
Faith	3 Sep. 1632	Faith	7 Sep. 1634
Faith	14 Oct. 1632	Love	14 Sep. 1634
Faith	21 Dec. 1632	Love	28 Sep. 1634
Faith	4 Feb. 1633	Love	26 Oct. 1634
Faith	3 Mar. 1633	Love	16 Nov. 1634
Faith	22 Apr. 1633	Love	23 Nov. 1634
Love	25 Apr. 1633	Love	1 Jan. 1635
Faith } Love }	28 Apr. 1633	Love	11 Jan. 1635

Faith, in this outline, is the strikingly dominant virtue in the first two years. During late 1633 and early 1634 a period of uncertainty prevails, while a sustained emphasis on love emerges in April and May 1634.

The miracles, which Crashaw chooses as topics for his early

epigrams, serve as occasions by which faith is confirmed. Crashaw wonders at the general inability of the Jews to believe in Christ after the many miracles he had performed; he wrote on 21 November 1631,

> Non tibi, Christe, fidem tua tot miracula praestant:
> (O verbi, o dextrae dulcia regna tuae!)
> Non praestant? neque te post tot miracula credunt?
> Mirac'lum, qui non credidit, ipse fuit.
>
> (Martin, *Poems*, p. 22)

(So many of your miracles, Christ, fail to prompt faith (O sweet authority of your word and hand!) Fail to prompt? They still do not believe after so many miracles? The real miracle is the one who does not believe.)

Individual miracles are also employed to reinforce man's faith. The cure of the blind man, for example, implies not only a physical cure, but also a cure of faith; Crashaw wrote on Sunday, 12 February 1632:

> Iam, credo, *Nemo est, sicut Tu*, Christe, *loquutus*:
> Auribus? immo *oculis*, Christe, loquutus eras.
>
> (Martin, *Poems*, p. 26)

(Now I believe, for no one has ever spoken as you have spoken, O Christ. Spoken to the ears? Quite the reverse; you have spoken, O Christ, to the eyes.)

Similarly the following year:

> *At video*; fideique oculis te nunc quoque figo:
> Est mihi, quae nunquam est non oculata, fides.
>
> (Martin, *Poems*, p. 40)

(But I do see; I now fix you with the eyes of faith: I have a faith, which is never unseeing.)

The withered hand cured by Christ, Crashaw suggests, should prove a helping hand to the man's faith:

> Quae nec in externos modo dextera profuit usus,
> Certe erit illa tuae jam *manus* & *fidei*.
>
> (Martin, *Poems*, p. 43)

(That right hand, which was no use at all outside itself, will certainly now be a hand to your faith.)

The Canaanite woman is upheld as the epitome of faith, a model to all Christians, and Crashaw presents the cure of the leper in exemplary terms: the same faith which prompted his cure in Christ will also uphold man:

> Credo quod ista potes, velles modo: sed quia credo,
> Christe, quod ista potest, credo quod ista voles.
>
> (Martin, *Poems*, p. 54)

(I believe that you can do this, should you so wish; but because I believe, O Christ, that you can, I believe that you will.)

As an interior condition, the 'feeling of grace' is realized by a deep sense of repentance. One of the earliest epigrams, that composed on 11 September 1631, condemns the lepers for failing to undergo an internal healing:

> Dum linquunt Christum (ah morbus!) sanantur euntes:
> Ipse etiam *morbus* sic medicina fuit.
> At sani Christum (mens ah malesana!) relinquunt:
> Ipsa etiam morbus sic *medicina* fuit.
>
> (Martin, *Poems*, p. 20)

(In leaving Christ (such a disease) those departing are healed: the disease is then construed as the medicine. Healed (but with hearts unhealed) they leave Christ: the medicine is here construed as the disease.)

In a similar epigram, that of 6 March 1632, Crashaw claims that, in fact, their leprosy was not cured, it merely changed its seat. Now the lepers have contracted an internal leprosy, a lack of faith:

> Non abit, at sedes tantum mutavit in illis;
> Et lepra, quae fuerat corpore, mente sedet.
>
> (Martin, *Poems*, p. 28)

(Their disease did not depart but merely changed its seat; and the leprosy, which was in the body, now sits in the mind.)

Early epigrams concerned with Christ's passion in its traditional detail are frequently so construed as to occasion deeper
feelings of personal belief. Writing on Septuagesima Sunday,
5 February 1632, Crashaw concedes that Christ's word has
often fallen on bramble thorns and failed to arouse faith;
nevertheless he himself believes Christ's word because the
bramble thorns also crowned Christ the Word:

> Credo quidem: nam sic spinas ah scilicet inter
> Ipse Deus Verbum tu quoque (Christe) cadis.
>> (Martin, *Poems*, p. 25)

(I certainly believe: for even as you fall among those thorns,
O Christ, you are both God and the Word.)

As late as Easter Monday, 1633, he still defines the Resurrection
in terms of faith:

> Scilicet & tellus *dubitat* tremebunda: sed ipsum hoc,
> Quod tellus dubitat, vos dubitare vetat.
>> (Martin, *Poems*, p. 42)

(Surely even the earth is trembling and shaking: but this
in itself – the earth shaking – should prevent your
doubting.)

In detail, Christ's wounds are interpreted as sources of faith:
the interplay between wounds and faith forms the base for
Crashaw's epigram on Easter Tuesday, 1632:

> En me, & signa mei, quondam mea vulnera! certe,
> Vos nisi credetis, vulnera sunt & adhuc.
> O nunc ergo fidem sanent mea vulnera vestram:
> O mea nunc sanet vulnera vestra fides.
>> (Martin, *Poems*, p. 29)

(Look at me, and these signs of me that were once my
wounds! Surely unless you have faith, these are wounds
even now. So now let my wounds repair your faith: so now
let your faith repair my wounds.)

Similarly St Thomas's lack of faith is linked initially with
Christ's wounds, then further projected as cause of the whole
passion:

Impius ergo iterum clavos? iterum impius hastam?
Et totum digitus triste revolvet opus?
Tune igitur Christum (Thoma) quo *vivere* credas,
Tu Christum faceres (ah truculente!) *mori*?

(Martin, *Poems*, p. 36)

(So, will a godless finger relive the nails? or the spear? the whole sad affair? You, Thomas, that you might believe that Christ is living, would you heartlessly make Christ die?)

Crashaw also holds out the New Testament saints as inspirations of faith. St Peter walking on the water, sinks as his faith weakens:

Petre, cades, o, si dubitas: o fide: nec ipsum
(Petre) negat fidis aequor habere fidem.

(Martin, *Poems*, p. 18)

(Peter, you will sink if you doubt; have faith: even the sea, Peter, is prepared to keep faith with those who believe.)

St Luke is considered as a model for Crashaw's own faith:

'Quippe ego in exemplum fidei dum te mihi pono'

(Martin, *Poems*, p. 49)

(Indeed I accept you as a model for my faith.)

The martyrdom of St Stephen reduces the traditional meaning of 'witness' to a specific witness of faith; although Stephen can bear the pain of the stones, he finds insupportable the hearts of stone of the unbelieving Jews:

Ista [saxa] potest tolerare; potest nescire: sed illi,
Quae sunt in vestro pectore, saxa nocent.

(Martin, *Poems*, p. 24)

(He can bear the stones; he can ignore them; but the stones which hurt him are those in your hearts.)

Crashaw's attitude towards the Virgin betrays none of his later High Church adulation; the Virgin's Annunciation is the result of faith, to carry Christ is reward for her faith. Love does not intrude, neither her love for God, nor the motherly love for a son:

107

Miraris (quid enim faceres?) sed & haec quoque credis:
Haec uteri credis dulcia monstra tui.
En fidei, Regina, tuae dignissima merces!
Fida Dei fueras filia; *mater eris.*

(Martin, *Poems*, p. 35)

(You wonder at this (what else could you do?) but yet
you also believe: you believe in the sweet wonders in your
womb. Here is the most appropriate reward for your faith,
O Queen; you were the faithful daughter of God, you will
be his mother.)

Nor, in the Christmas epigram of 1631, is there any trace of
love. The Virgin's faith prompts prayer to the God in her
womb, but no notion of intercession is included:

Quam bene sub tecto tibi concipiuntur eodem
Vota, & (vota cui concipienda) Deus!
Quod nubes alia, & tanti super atria coeli
Quaerunt, invenient hoc tua vota domi.

(Martin, *Poems*, p. 23)

(How well under the same roof are both prayers conceived
and he to whom prayers must be conceived – God! What
so many seek above the clouds and the courts of heaven,
your prayers will find under your own roof.)

The Eucharist, too, is couched in terms of faith. The miracle
of the loaves, traditionally considered as prefiguring the
institution of the Eucharist, feeds not only the people's hunger
but also their faith. Crashaw writes on 11 March 1632:

Ecce vagi venit unda cibi; venit indole sacra
Fortis, & in dentes fertilis innumeros.
Quando erat invictae tam sancta licentia coenae?
Illa *famem* populi pascit, & illa *fidem.*

(Martin, *Poems*, p. 26)

(Behold a source of abundant food; it comes to many
mouths, of sacred nature, strong and rich. When was there
ever such sacred bounty of peerless meal? It feeds the
people's hunger – and their faith.)

Christ as the Bread is a recurring theme. He eats with sinners but he himself is the food:

> Istis cum Christus conviva adjungitur, istis
> O non conviva est Christus, at *ipse cibus*.
>
> (Martin, *Poems*, p. 46)

(When Christ, their guest, dines with them, Christ is not their guest but the food itself.)

As late as 4 August 1633, Crashaw still sees the Eucharist primarily as stimulating faith:

> Vescere pane tuo: sed & (hospes) vescere Christo:
> Est panis pani scilicet ille tuo.
> Tunc pane hoc CHRISTI recte satur (hospes) abibis,
> Panem ipsum CHRISTUM si magis esurias.
>
> (Martin, *Poems*, p. 47)

(Eat your bread, guest, but eat Christ too: for Christ, as Bread, is your bread. Then, guest, full of this bread of Christ, you will leave graciously, only if you are still hungrier for Christ as Bread.)

But in late 1632 and 1633 the specific stress on faith begins to yield to an interest in the wider implications of salvation itself. On 30 November 1632, while treating of the fish caught by St Andrew, he explains how man must be caught to be saved:

> Non potuisse capi, vobis spes una salutis:
> Una salus nobis est, potuisse capi.
>
> (Martin, *Poems*, p. 35)

(To escape capture is your one hope of safety; for us only one salvation exists: to have been able to be caught.)

The man with the withered hand is told in 1633 to seize his salvation with it. Similarly, on 26 May 1633, in response to Christ's claim that he had come to conquer the world, Crashaw asks that the world overwhelm Christ so that he himself might be saved:

> Si tu, dux meus, ipse jaces, spes ulla salutis?
> Immo, ni jaceas tu, mihi nulla salus.
>
> (Martin, *Poems*, p. 44)

(If you yourself, my leader, are overthrown, is there any hope of salvation? Indeed unless you are overthrown, for me there is no salvation.)

The anti-papal bias also seems to have faded in 1632. Writing on 8 April, there is no hint of the irony contained in his first epigram on St Peter:

> Umbra dabit tua posse meum me cernere solem;
> Et mea lux umbrae sic erit umbra tuae.
>
> (Martin, Poems, p. 29)

(Your shadow will enable me to see my sun; and so my light will be your shadow's shadow.)

In 1633 a distinct pro-papal bias appears in his treatment of St Peter's keys, traditionally held in Rome; on the feast of St Peter, 29 June, he writes, with overtones of Matthew 16.29:

> Et Petro *claves* jam liquet esse suas.
> Dices, Sponte patent: Petri ergo hoc scilicet ipsum
> Est clavis, Petro clave quod haud opus est.
>
> (Martin, Poems, p. 46)

(Peter's keys already belong to him. You say the doors open of their own accord: Peter's key then consists in this, that he has no need of a key.)

The epigram of the first Sunday after Easter, 1633, symbolically marks the half-way point in the development of Crashaw's thought. Treating of the wounds of Christ, which remained after his Resurrection, it combines the sentiments of both faith and love. As such, it affords an interesting comparison with the lessons of faith drawn in the earlier epigrams on Christ's wounds and the feelings of love conjured up in the later epigrams:

> His oculis (nec adhuc clausis coiere fenestris)
> Invigilans nobis est tuus usus amor.
> His oculis nos cernit amor tuus: his & amorem
> (Christe) tuum gaudet cernere nostra fides.
>
> (Martin, Poems, p. 43)

(With these eyes (not yet joined as closed windows) your

love watches over us. With these eyes your love sees us: and with these our faith rejoices to see your love, O Christ.)

During the remainder of 1633 and in early 1634 Crashaw appears to have undergone a period of uncertainty. Faith has certainly become less emphatic but the salvific motive of love has yet to emerge fully. This hesitancy was paralleled and no doubt induced by the Laudian theology and Laudian practices being increasingly preferred at Pembroke. Heading this movement was John Tourney, Crashaw's tutor, to whom Crashaw wrote a dedicatory poem in *Epigrammata Sacra*, and who, in March 1634, became the centre of a *cause célèbre*, when he was arraigned in Cambridge for delivering a sermon, in which he impugned the doctrine of salvation by faith alone. On 9 February, he had stated that faith must be reinforced with love and good works, for:[20]

> first it workes with Love in ye doeing of oʳ works and then it Cooperateth unto ye encrease of Justification with oʳ workes being done, soe you have ye quallification of faith, & the manner of its working, first it must be working & soe it is not Fides mortua. 2ly it doth but cooperate & soe it is ... not ye onely cause soe faith alone being insufficient it brings us unto ye second generall, The necessity and efficacy of good workes.

Later in his act for Bachelor of Divinity, Tourney defended the thesis that the 'fulfilling of ye lawe was possible to a Christian in this life'.[21]

While Tourney was required to retract these statements in consistory, the backing he received from other members of his college suggests wide support. Mr Novell, another Fellow of Pembroke, was accused by the Puritans for teaching that saving faith also included hope and charity, and Dr Duncon, in a speech in the Commencement House, defended the thesis that 'Bona opera sunt efficaciter necessaria ad salutem. The drift of this discourse was to make good ye perfection of workes by ye concurrence of them in ye matter of Justification.' The Vice-Chancellor Dr Laney is accused, in a similar passage, of adhering to the same doctrine.[22] In promoting the virtue of love and the value of good works, the Laudian, in the eyes of the Puritan, reduced the power of saving faith; he himself argued that good works merited God's love and grace, that faith alone was not sufficient to attain salvation, and that preference must be given to love.

The sounds of controversy seldom allow a neutral position and Crashaw's close personal involvement with Tourney, Duncon and Laney finally sees him preferring a Laudian position. In nearly all the epigrams he wrote during this critical period, March and April 1634, he is concerned to illustrate Christ's own love for man and to foster that love in man himself.

Earlier in 1631 the generic 'Cum tot signa edidisset, non credebant in eum' was interpreted to arouse feelings of faith, but on 24 August 1634 the same topic is read as an occasion of Christ's love spurned:

> Quanta amor ille tuus se cunque levaverit ala,
> Quo tua cunque opere effloruit alta manus;
> Mundus adest, contraque tonat.
>
> (Martin, *Poems*, p. 359)

(Whatever heights your love might reach, however much your hand might show forth your work, the world persists and thunders against you.)

Crashaw marvels that anyone could watch Christ, see his miracles, and yet not love him:

> Vidit? & odit adhuc? Ah, te non vidit, Jesu.
> Non vidit te, qui vidit, & odit adhuc.
> Non vidit, te non vidit (dulcissime rerum)
> In te qui vidit quid, quod amare neget.
>
> (Martin, *Poems*, p. 362)

(He saw and yet he hated? Ah, he did not see you, Jesus. He who saw you and yet hated you, did not see you. He who saw anything in you he could refuse to love didn't see you (sweetest of things), he didn't.)

Comparisons of two other pairs of epigrams also provide evidence of Crashaw's different approach. Treating of the Centurion on 22 January 1632, Crashaw had wondered at such high faith contained in a human heart:

In tua tecta Deus veniet: tuus haud sinit illud
Et pudor, atque humili in pectore celsa fides.
(Martin, *Poems*, p. 25)

(Under your roof God will come: yet your modesty will
scarcely allow it, nor will your lofty faith concealed in
your humble heart.)

But in 1634 the centurion provides an opportunity to portray
Christ's love and its healing power:

Ille ut eat tecum, in natique, tuique salutem?
Qui petis; ah nescis (credo) quod Ales Amor.
(Martin, *Poems*, p. 361)

(You ask that he might accompany you to save both your
son and yourself. You who ask don't realize (I feel) that
Love is winged.)

In an earlier epigram the Canaanite woman is considered the
epitome of faith:

Quicquid Amazoniis dedit olim fama puellis,
    Credite: *Amazoniam* cernimus ecce *fidem*.
Foemina, tam fortis fidei? iam credo fidem esse
    Plus quam grammatice *foeminei generis*.
(Martin, *Poems*, p. 55)

(Anything fame once gave to the Amazon maidens,
believe: we see here Amazonian faith. Can a woman be of
so strong a faith? Now I believe that faith is feminine in
more ways than just in grammar.)

On 14 September 1634, Crashaw again treats of the Canaanite
woman. Christ wills strength to the woman that she will find
strength, yet through Christ the classical harshness of love is
softened:

Atque in te vires sentit, amatque suas,
Usque adeo haud tuus hic ferus est, neque ferreus hostis!
Usque adeo est miles non truculentus Amor!
(Martin, *Poems*, p. 360)

(He feels and loves his strength in you, to such a degree

that this enemy of yours is scarcely harsh or cruel, to such a degree that Love remains a soldier, though not a savage one.)

In the twin miracles of the men cured of the fever and the dropsy, Crashaw sees, on 28 September 1634, a reciprocal sign of love:

> Haec vice fraterna quam se miracula tangunt,
>   Atque per alternum fida iuvamen amant!
>
> (Martin, *Poems*, p. 360)

(How closely these miracles are related by a fraternal link, and how faithfully they reflect their love through mutual help.)

Christ is Love personified in the episode of the woman, who was cured by touching the hem of Christ's garment. Crashaw, prompted obviously by a picture, wrote on 16 November 1634:

> Falleris. & nudum male ponis (Pictor) Amorem:
>   Non nudum facis hunc, cum sine veste facis.
> Nonne hic est (dum sic digito patet ille fideli)
>   Tunc, cum vestitus, tunc quoque nudus amor?
>
> (Martin, *Poems*, p. 363)

(You are wrong, Painter, and you wrongly depict naked Love: you do not paint him naked when you paint him without clothes. When Christ is so laid bare by a believing finger, then, even though clothed, isn't he then naked Love?)

Christ as Love now mediates between God and man. In the epigram for the feast of the Purification, 1634, he is the Lamb, the 'conciliator', who is offered to God according to full merit:

> Donum hoc est, hoc est; quod scilicet audeat ipso
>   Esse Deo dignum: scilicet *ipse Deus*.
>
> (Martin, *Poems*, p. 54)

(This, this is the gift, that he dares to be worthy of God himself: He himself is God.)

On 11 May 1634, he is seen as the love which tempers the severity of God with man:

Ergo roga: *Ipse roga*: tibi scilicet ille roganti
Esse nequit durus, nec solet esse, Pater.

(Martin, *Poems*, p. 63)

(You ask, you yourself ask, for the Father cannot be hard
on you, if you ask; Nor is he ever.)

Earlier, in an epigram written on 21 December 1631, the
wounds of Christ remaining after the Resurrection confirmed
St Thomas's faith:

Vulnera, *ne dubites*, vis tangere nostra: sed eheu,
Vulnera, *dum dubitas*, tu graviora facis.

(Martin, *Poems*, p. 16)

(You wish to touch my wounds to overcome your doubt:
but alas you make my wounds more serious, when you
doubt.)

On 8 April 1634, these wounds bear witness to Christ's love; as
weapons of love, they have superseded the old, classical
weapons of the bow, quiver and arrows:

Arma vides; arcus, pharetramque, levesque sagittas,
    Et quocunque fuit nomine miles Amor.
His fuit usus Amor: sed & haec fuit ipse; suumque
    Et jaculum, & jaculis ipse pharetra suis.
Nunc splendent tantum, & deterso pulvere belli
    E memori pendent nomina magna tholo.
Tempus erit tamen, haec irae quando arma, pharetramque
    Et sobolem pharetrae spicula tradet Amor.

(Martin, *Poems*, p. 59)

(You see arms; bow, quiver, light arrows – anything by
which Love is called soldier. Love used these: yet was these
also; itself its own arrow and its own quiver of arrows.
Now they shine brightly, and with the dust of battle shaken
off, they hang up their reputations in the temple of memories. There will be a time however when this Love will
hand over to anger the arms, the quiver and its fruit, the
arrow-tips.)

Christ's blood, shed on Good Friday, is no longer a source of
faith but a witness to Christ's love, which in turn should
promote love in the beholder.

> ... atque ecce est *Vinum* illud *amoris*:
> Unde ego sim tantis, unde ego par cyathis?
> (Martin, *Poems*, p. 58)

(Here is the very wine of love. How can I be worthy of such cups?)

Similarly the events of Christ's public life provoke feelings of love. The Ascension of 1634 emphasizes that the love of Christ remains after his departure:

> Usque etiam nostros Te (Christe) tenemus amores?
> (Martin, *Poems*, p. 64)

(Do we continue to retain your love, Christ?)

The Last Supper also affirms Christ's love; just as the dying swan, sweeter in its last notes, lives on in the melody of its dying song, so Christ,

> Ut tu inter strepitus odii, & tua funera, Jesu,
> Totus amor liquido totus amore sonas.
> (Martin, *Poems*, p. 353)

(Just as you, between shouts of hate and your death, Jesus, love entire, sing forth in pure love.)

The Circumcision is interpreted as the original manifestation of Christ's blood and Christ's love. In 1635 even Christ's fear is lovable:

> Dat Marti vultus, quos sibi mallet Amor.
> Deliciae irarum! torvi, tenera agmina, risus!
> Blande furor! terror dulcis! amande metus!
> (Martin, *Poems*, p. 366)

(He gives Mars glances, all the better for love. Delights of anger; tender troops; grim smiles; charming fury; sweet terror; lovable fear!)

Christ lost in the temple is the personification of love; the Blessed Virgin is told not to complain, not to fear, for '*Non est hic fugitivus Amor*' (Martin, *Poems*, p. 367). (This is no fugitive Love.)

Crashaw's final epigram, that for Whit Sunday, 1635, completes the swing to Laudianism. The first epigram in *Epigrammata Sacra* had preferred an interior presence of God to the presence of God in the sanctuary. This last epigram, with its liturgical undertones, presents a High Church position. Crashaw denigrates the fiery Puritan preacher who insistently calls for repentance. He sees his own prayers as incense, a Laudian institution, which the Puritans abhorred. His final plea is for a mystical heart of fire, but a tongue of sweetness:

> Absint, qui ficto simulant pia pectora vultu,
> Ignea quos luteo pectore lingua beat.
> Hoc potius mea vota rogant, mea thura petessunt,
> Ut mihi sit mea mens ignea, lingua luti.
>
> (Martin, *Poems*, p. 368)

(Keep away you who affect pious hearts with deceitful faces, who are blessed with a fiery tongue and earthly heart. My prayers ask, my incense seeks this rather, that I might have a soul of fire and a tongue of earth.)

This religious development, now outlined, together with the original dating, reveals both the English setting of Crashaw's epigram and the disjunctive reaction between continental or native, to which all his poetry has been subject. Both the Latin epigrams, which have been measured in terms of continental antecedents, the epigrammatists Franciscus Remundus, Bernardus Bauhusius and Jacob Bidermann, and also his more mature English poetry, which has been valued within the continental context of Counter Reformation themes and Teresian imagery, have thereby been distorted. While the influences and imagery are indisputably present in both cases, to focus attention exclusively on stylistic and outward marks is to ignore his poetry's native setting and Laudian spirit and to see Crashaw for what he has become – a continental poet writing in English. Nothing could be farther from the truth. That he was an English poet writing in an English tradition can best be adjudged by the defence even he himself felt forced to write in the dedicatory verses of *Epigrammata Sacra*. As such, the Latin epigrams reflect the interpretative mishap incurred by all his later poetry.

Crashaw points to the source of his poetic spirit in his defence of Benjamin Laney, Master of Pembroke: 'Enimvero

Epigramma sacrum tuus ille vultus vel est, vel quid sit docet;
ubi nimirum amabili diluitur severum, & sanctum suavi
demulcetur' (Martin, *Poems*, p. 7).

> (Truthfully your very spirit is a sacred epigram, or teaches
> what it should be: where the severe is tempered by love
> and the holy mellowed by sweetness.)

The controlling forces of a sacred epigram, Crashaw suggests,
must be sweetness and love, and after May 1634, when this
dedication was written, he adheres to his announced resolution
to treat no longer of any but sacred love. Venus and the blind
Cupid, the loves of classical and secular poetry are now
renounced, and Crashaw subscribes entirely to a new love, a
Christian love of another Mother and Child, marked by love
for one another.[23]

Crashaw's subsequent poetry, both the Latin but principally
the mature English, is the literal outcome of this firming of
ideals. Little poetry that he wrote after 1634 can be placed on
the altar of the pagan muse. Yet his resolution is both firmly
planted in his English religion and is wrought to further it: the
spirit of his poetry will contrive to promote the religious substance, on which the epigrams are built:

> Neque sane hoc scriptionis genere (modo partes suas satis
> praestiterit) quid esse potuit otio Theologico accommo-
> datius, quo nimirum res ipsa Theologica Poetica amoeni-
> tate delinita majestatem suam venustate commendat.
>
> (Martin, *Poems*, p. 7)

> (Nor more assuredly than in this kind of writing (providing
> its functions are properly discharged) can theological
> leisure be better employed; for in it the very substance of
> theology is presented with poetic grace and its great value
> offset by beauty.)

More specifically, Crashaw in his preface not only rejects
Jesuit and continental claims about himself and the substance
of his poetry, and thus confirms his loyalty and adherence to his
mother church and its doctrine, but also frames his theology
within the tradition of the Church of England and appeals to
his countrymen, whose eyes are turned towards Geneva, not
to despise the traditional values of the English Church.

Nor can the shift in emphasis to the virtue of love in Crashaw's epigrams be construed as merely realizing the potentialities of his baroque models for sacred purposes. Crashaw himself is at pains to deny this and his conversion at Pembroke was far more fundamental involving a change in his own being towards a more traditional religion. The epigrams are illustrative of this conversion; the setting which inspired them explains it. At this critical juncture he also fixed his poetic principles and ideals, of which his English poetry was the manifest product. Thus in Crashaw there arose a twofold influence: a vehicle of continental imagery, but a substance of religious love embedded in an English setting. Unfortunately the critical reaction, which has misconstrued his Latin epigrams as continental, has similarly clouded and misjudged his later English poetry.

Notes

1 Austin Warren, *Richard Crashaw, A Study in Baroque Sensibility* (Baton Rouge, 1939), p. 89.
2 David Lloyd, *Memoires of the Lives, Actions, Sufferings & Deaths of those Noble, Reverend, and Excellent Personages* . . . (London, 1668), p. 618.
3 Cf. Bodleian Tanner MS. 465, fols 7r–22v.
4 Cf. Alexander Grosart (ed.), *Complete Works of Richard Crashaw* (London, 1872), II, p. 168: 'The Epigrams seem to have been composed and written down on the spur of the moment as a subject struck him, and hence there is the same absence of arrangement.'
5 Sister M. S. Milhaupt, 'The Latin Epigrams of Richard Crashaw', unpublished doctoral thesis (University of Michigan, 1963). I am indebted to Austin Warren and Sister Milhaupt for the following account. Austin Warren discovered that some of the epigrams seemed to follow the sequence of Sunday Gospels during the period 1631–4; Sister Milhaupt posited the principle that many others were based on the second lesson at morning prayer and calculated dates for the great majority of the remainder. Unfortunately, however, she has used the wrong edition of the Book of Common Prayer (1627), for the 1629 edition, which incorporates a number of different Gospel selections, is the edition to which Crashaw adheres. As well she has failed sometimes to recognize that Crashaw has entitled his epigrams with a biblical quotation parallel to the actual Gospel selection. Finally the alternatives, of which her calculations allow, are mutually exclusive and a definite sequence can be established.
6 Cf. Warren, *Richard Crashaw*, pp. 215–16.
7 Although Crashaw was free to choose any part of the scripture read on the Sunday he invariably composed an epigram on a New Testament

selection. Austin Warren has interpreted Crashaw's choice as a mark of his Laudianism, but this penchant for New Testament passages would seem more attributable to his Charterhouse training, for his High Church beliefs did not develop until two years after his entrance to Pembroke College.

8 The relevant epigrams are to be found on pages 29–30 of L. C. Martin (ed.), *The Poems of Richard Crashaw* (2nd ed., Oxford, 1957). 'II Matins' refers to the second lesson at morning prayer.

9 Cf. Martin, *Poems*, p. 356.

10 W. Crashaw, *Falsificationum Romanarum et Catholicarum Restitutionem. Romish Forgeries and Falsifications* (London, 1606), p. 128.

11 *Ibid.*, p. 141.

12 *Ibid.*, p. 84.

13 *Ibid.*, p. 23.

14 Robert Shelford, *Five Pious and Learned Discourses* (Cambridge, 1635).

15 Martin, *Poems*, p. 138.

16 R. Shelford, *op. cit.*, p. 100.

17 *Ibid.*, p. 107.

18 *Ibid.*, p. 102.

19 *Ibid.*, p. 102.

20 British Museum Harley MS. 7019, fol. 53.

21 *Ibid.*, fol. 66.

22 *Ibid.*, fols 66 and 65.

23 Cf. Martin, *Poems*, 'Lectori', p. 13, ll. 83–91.

V
The Latin Poetry of Vincent Bourne

Mark Storey

Nobody who had read Vincent Bourne's poems would want
to talk in terms of genius unjustly neglected. Bourne nonetheless
occupies a unique place in a rather odd corner of English
literature, a place worth examining both for what it tells us
about neoclassicism, and for the sake of the poetry itself.
When we put Bourne beside Prior and Gay, for example
(poets often invoked in this connection), he may seem rather
dull; but there is a vein of poetry that runs through his work,
that of an occasionally inspired craftsman who is yet an
amateur and who doesn't much care what the world thinks of
him, or whether the world cares what he thinks of it. This
fine disregard for posterity is an engaging quality, and it lends
to much of his verse a light-hearted abandon not found in
many neo-Latin writers of the eighteenth century. But even
then it is hardly the audacious wit of a Prior that lurks in this
shabby schoolmaster's work. The humour is quiet and sub-
dued, slightly mocking, as he sits at his desk, away from all
the world, pointing only a small finger of scorn at what he
sees outside. His is a world of books and philosophers, of wry
melancholic thoughts: but it is also one of stark observation,
of affectionate reminiscence, as he mulls over former relation-
ships, apostrophizing in a gently elegiac tone acquaintances

dead or dying. Bourne writes because he wants to: moral motives are there, but not censoriously. He knows only a few are going to read him, and realizing that grand gestures would be futile, he avoids them. There is a logic (even ruthless) about his work in that everything inessential is thrown away, as he sticks to his particular last, eschewing the long, tediously philosophical poems so popular amongst his contemporary neo-Latinists; he makes his points with economy and deliberation. Although it is the apparent lack of positive qualities in his modest output that most disturbs an attentive reader, the corollary – an unpretentious honesty and directness – has its own rewards. There is no one quite like Vincent Bourne.

For most people, Vincent Bourne might as well not have existed. In spite of William Cowper's love of the man as a man, and in spite of his odd personal anecdotes about his Latin master at Westminster, Bourne remains a nebulous figure, with only a few salient biographical facts surviving to fill out the picture. Born in 1695, he went from Westminster School to Trinity College, Cambridge, where he was elected a Fellow in 1720. He returned to Westminster as an usher, and became (through the help of a former pupil of the school, the Duke of Newcastle) Housekeeper Sergeant at Arms to the House of Commons. He married, had two children, and died on 2 December 1747, leaving his possessions to his widow, Lucia. Two letters to the Duke of Newcastle survive in the British Museum, suggesting Bourne's servility for the sake of his own position or that of his son;[1] but they tell us little about the man who writes Latin verse. Just as his own epitaph makes no comment on his poetry, so his poetry makes little explicit comment on his life.[2] Bourne must survive, if at all, because of what he wrote.

His reputation is in itself curious and oddly instructive. Few Latin masters can have achieved fame on the strength of their pupils' recommendations, yet that is virtually all the eighteenth century left by way of critical judgment, before Charles Lamb confirmed Cowper's opinion. (Publication history, however, reveals that Bourne was being read: editions of his work appeared in 1734, 1735, 1743 (with additional poems – the last before his death), 1750, 1764, 1772, 1808, 1826 and 1840.[3]) Cowper preferred Bourne to Tibullus, Propertius and Ausonius, and thought him 'not at all inferior' to Ovid: but we must assume that Cowper's affection for him as a man influenced his critical judgment.[4] He draws an endearing portrait of this indolent, slovenly, almost disgusting fellow, who was not even a very good teacher. His critical remarks are rather equivocal, in that Bourne's 'harmlessness' rather diminishes the originality of humour which Cowper applauds; and we might wonder about the virtue of being 'animated by the spirit' of a magpie. On the other hand, Cowper refuses to rely solely on a commendation of style: the classical elegance which he rightly admires is not an empty exercise, but the proper vehicle for his thought.

Lamb was another poet generous in his praise of Bourne; again, his lively response suggests reasons for fostering this poet. For Lamb, Bourne's value was seen in terms of the feebleness of present-day verse: his poems 'fix upon *something*; they ally themselves to common objects; their good nature is a Catholicon, sanative of coxcombry, of heartlessness, and of fastidiousness'.[5] Lamb was moved to translate a number of poems, with a certain amount of flair and liveliness. He seemed to be rather puzzled by Bourne's choice of tongue, 'his diction all Latin and his thoughts all English. Bless him! Latin wasn't good enough for him. Why was he not content with the language which Gay and Prior wrote in?'[6]

The attraction that Bourne held for these two poets (whilst clearly indicating something of his valuable qualities) was in many respects a personal matter for them both; in Cowper's case it could be said that Bourne's influence helped to direct the course of his own poetry. Landor, in 1820, was not persuaded of Bourne's virtues, and his denigration (the *Eclectic Review* in 1808 had also thought too much fuss was being made)[7] needs to be carefully weighed, as much as the other poet's warm praise.[8]

The purpose of this essay will have been served if Bourne's merits can be clearly seen to refute the bulk of Landor's charge of frigidity and affectation without necessarily endorsing some of the extravagances of Cowper and Lamb. It is a question of defining some of the contexts in which Bourne must be viewed; a question, also, of suggesting some of the ways in which Bourne's poetry can be approached directly.

As a glance at the compendious *Musae Anglicanae*, by Leicester Bradner (1940), will show, Vincent Bourne was by no means alone in the eighteenth century in writing Latin poems. It was a natural pastime of the educated: boys trained at Westminster and Eton went on to Oxford and Cambridge where they continued with their neatly turned exercises, producing the kind of verse which nobody, apart from Mr Bradner, has bothered to remember. If we look at most of their productions we can see why. Even a popular collection such as the *Carmina Comitialia Cantabrigiensia*, edited by Bourne in 1721, hardly sparkles (except where Bourne himself takes over), and it was no compliment to Bourne when a 'new edition' of his poems, published by subscription in 1772, included indiscriminately and without question, many of the Cambridge poems as the work of Bourne himself. (It was not until 1840 that the Rev. J. Mitford's relatively scholarly edition consigned such pieces to oblivion, and took the trouble to point out just what Bourne had published and when; it is a relief to realize that all those quasi-Lucretian poems – 'Existentia Entium incorporeorum colligi potest Lumine Naturae'; 'Rationes Boni et Mali sunt aeternae et immutabiles'; 'Fluxus et Refluxus Maris pendent ab Actionibus Solis et Lunae' etc. – are not Bourne's work. Even so, this did not prevent Arthur Benson, in 1895, from writing about 'Iter per Tamesin' as though it were by Bourne, when there is no authority textually, and no reason stylistically, for such an assumption.)[9] There were other collections, all indicative of a dearth of real poetic talent. Much more interesting are the Latin poems written by poets who normally wrote in English, such as Swift and Prior, Gray and Johnson, where some connection can be seen between the two modes. The rigours of the exercise were in themselves salutary: not many poets would have gone as far as Gray, whose first ambition, according to Dr Johnson, 'was to have excelled in Latin poetry', but several of them recognized the advantages of adapting their thoughts to an alien idiom.[10]

Dr Johnson was aware that not enough people took any notice of the 'modern writers of Latin poetry': they were 'a class of authors who are too generally neglected'.[11] Certainly not everyone was persuaded of the benefits of such poetry. When Addison's *Poems on Several Occasions* appeared in 1719, it contained a Preface by Christopher Hayes (the translator of Addison's Latin *Dissertation* on Roman poetry), in which the 'general Disuse and Corruption of the *Latin Tongue*' was lamented; the University collections seemed to be the best, and the best of these were published in *Musae Anglicanae*, of which work Addison's poems were 'the most shining ornaments'. Hayes was rather on the defensive, bearing in mind no doubt the hostility in some quarters to this form of exercise:

> I will not say that it is absolutely necessary to be a good *Latin Poet* in order to become a good *English one*, but I am sure that he who imitates the Antients in their own Language will slide more easily into their way of Thinking, adopt their Graces by Degrees, and beautifully transplant them into his Mother-Tongue, and these are no vulgar Beauties in an *English* Poem.

But when the poet Thomas Tickell contributed a preface to another edition of Addison's poems in 1721, he championed the classics more impressively by pointing out how the qualities of 'Augustanism' – such as 'correctness' and 'propriety' – came into English poetry through the influence of the ancients; a grounding in the classics was consequently the 'good-breeding of Poetry'. Of Addison he remarked that 'he was admired as one of the best authors since the Augustan age'.[12] Hayes and Tickell were aware of the implications of their comments, at a time when the whole basis of neoclassical theory was being questioned. It is in this larger context of debate that Vincent Bourne's poetry needs to be seen.[13]

It is no surprise to find that James Beattie, who, echoing Richard Hurd in his emphasis on the rules of poetry, displayed a sublime confidence in the logical construction of a poetic theory, was delivering in 1769 'Remarks on the Utility of Classical Learning'. Whilst acknowledging that 'genius displays itself to the best advantage in its native tongue', he wishes that more people cultivated the talent of Latin verse writing:

> for it has often proved the means of extending the reputation of our authors, and consequently of adding something to the literary glories of Great Britain. Boileau is said not to have known that there were any good poets in England, till Addison made him a present of the *Musae Anglicanae*. Many of the finest performances of Pope, Dryden, and

Milton, have appeared not ungracefully in a Roman dress. And those foreigners must entertain a high opinion of our Pastoral poetry, who have seen the Latin translations of Vincent Bourne, particularly those of the ballads of *Tweed-side, William and Margaret* and Rowe's *Despairing beside a clear stream*; of which it is no compliment to say, that in sweetness of numbers, and elegant expression, they are at least equal to the originals, and scarce inferior to anything in Ovid or Tibullus.

Vincent Bourne is in distinguished company, and all on the strength of his translations of decidedly second-rate verse. The emphasis placed by Beattie on elegance and sweetness of expression encouraged the frequent divorce of form and content. (In this connection, it was easy for the eighteenth century to prefer someone to Ovid and Tibullus: Ovid was offensive to the general taste, and the lyric poets tended to be ignored. Vergil and Horace were often the only authors mentioned in discussions of classical poets, and moralistic considerations prevented Catullus and Propertius from being read and accepted. The divorce of form and content is perfectly apparent in Henry Felton's praise (1713) of the 'Softness and Delicacy' of Catullus' verse, whilst he draws back in horror at the 'Coarseness of his Thoughts too immodest for chaste Ears to bear'.[14]) This is in many respects the most damaging aspect of the reliance on classical imitations, and its debilitating influence may be seen in the numerous theoretical works which plod painfully through all the various permissible turns of expression. Dryden had pointed out how wrong this elevation of 'colouring' was, when expression was essentially secondary;[15] and in 1718 Charles Gildon took issue with Edward Bysshe on this very point.[16] Bysshe had gone so far as to say that the chief art of the poet consisted in the 'Beauty of *Colouring*' and not in the 'matter'; Gildon saw the folly of this, but its dangers were rampant as late as 1772, when the Advertisement for the collection of prize poems, *Musae Seatonianae* (which included five poems by Christopher Smart), began: 'If the present Age is not celebrated for Poetical Genius, it is remarkable for Poetical Taste, even the most refined.' This sense of refinement was a debased version of the decorum that was so essential a part of neoclassical theory. It is helpful to bear this in mind when looking at Bourne's clean-lined, decorous poems.

In the *praefatio* to the second volume of *Musarum Anglicanarum analecta* (1699), Addison, its editor, declared revealingly that he had made his selection of poems on the basis of elegance rather than substance of argument. The work bears this out, with most of the poems sporting forbidding titles: 'Heroes Britannici'; 'Mensa Lubrica, *Anglicè* Shovel Board'; 'In Diatribas Medico Philosophicas de Fermentatione & Febribus'; 'In Artem volandi'; 'De Paeto, sive Tabaco'. Dr Johnson had warned against this fundamental danger of neo-Latin verse: any such poem was to some degree an attempt at a *tour de force*, and it was not long before the incongruity was played on, even by Addison in poems such as 'Battle of the Pygmies and Cranes', 'The Barometer', and 'A Bowling Green'. Johnson declared with some truth:[17]

> When the matter is low or scanty, a dead language, in which nothing is mean because nothing is familiar, affords great convenience: and, by the sonorous magnificence of Roman syllables, the writer conceals penury of thought, and want of novelty, often from the reader, and often from himself.

(This had its repercussions on English poetry.) It is worth pointing out that Bourne seldom succumbs to this temptation, if only because Latin is, for him, a natural way of expressing himself. The desire to be clever does not arise. Addison's work itself, for all the praise lavished on it, ultimately disappoints. He adopts the high style and, within its limits, maintains a certain elegance and poise, but as we should expect of such poetry, it offers little else. Very much public poetry, treading the well-worn paths of eulogy, it has its own peculiar attractions, but these tend to pall amidst the mass of similar verse churned out. The chief merit of such poetry was summed up by Dr Johnson when he commended Edward Smith's 'Ode on Pocock': 'It expresses with great felicity images not classical in classical diction.'[18]

This was clearly thought to be the interest of Bourne's translations; Cowper was especially impressed by these versions of poems by Rowe, Crawford, Mallet and Prior, and a separate publication in 1728 consisted of the versions 'Thyrsis et Chloe'

(a translation of Mallet's celebrated 'William and Margaret'),
'Votum' (a translation of Walter Pope's tiresome poem 'The
Wish'), and 'Corydon Querens' (a translation of Rowe's
'Colin's Complaint'). These versions (which include several
from Prior and one based on Gay's 'Sweet William and Black-
eyed Susan') are extremely competent and fluent, but they
tell us little that is interesting about Bourne, beyond his
evident ability to translate another man's thoughts into an
alien idiom, and make them ring true. We cannot seriously
regard them as more than successful exercises; apart from
anything else Bourne does not choose many poems that are
really worth translating.

Cowper's own translation of Bourne's poems show how
misleading it is to talk in terms of style *per se*: just as Bourne
creates a rather different poem when he translates Prior's
'Chloe Hunting', for example, so Cowper has to take liberties
in order to capture some of the essence of Bourne's poetry.
But, in translating, he inevitably imposes the linguistic tension,
typical of a diction conscious of the classics, which Bourne
evades by writing in Latin. At the same time, his wanting to
translate Bourne at all suggests an awareness of other than
stylistic qualities. Cowper was certainly aware of the difficulties:
a part-time Latin versifier himself, he knew the difference
between an English turn and a Latin one. English readers
expected more than they would get from a straightforward
translation of the Latin; Cowper expressed his doubts when a
translation of Bourne was mooted:[19]

> I find it disagreeable to work by another man's pattern.
> . . . Again *that* is epigrammatic and witty in Latin which
> would be perfectly insipid in English and a translator of
> Bourne would frequently find himself obliged to supply
> what is called the *turn* which is in fact the most difficult
> and the most expensive part of the whole composition,
> and could not perhaps, in many instances, be done with
> any tolerable success. If a Latin poem is neat, elegant
> and musical, it is enough; but English readers are not so
> easily satisfied.

Nonetheless, Cowper tackled a handful of Bourne's poems,
and the choice of poems is a reflection of the common bond
between them – poems to birds, mockingly humorous poems

on a slight moral theme, poems to creatures not usually celebrated in poetry. An interesting example is 'Familiarity Dangerous', a version of Bourne's 'Nulli te facias nimis Soda-lem'. Cowper's poem is poised and witty:

> As in her ancient mistress' lap
>   The youthful tabby lay,
> They gave each other many a tap,
>   Alike dispos'd to play.
>
> But strife ensues. Puss waxes warm,
>   And with protruded claws
> Ploughs all the length of Lydia's arm,
>   Mere wantonness the cause.
>
> At once, resentful of the deed,
>   She shakes her to the ground
> With many a threat, that she shall bleed
>   With still a deeper wound.
>
> But, Lydia, bid thy fury rest!
>   It was a venial stroke;
> For she, that will with kittens jest,
>   Should bear a kitten's joke.

The affinity between this and Gray's 'On a Favourite Cat' is clear; it is a nicely turned, inconsequential, unpretentious poem, obviously shallower than Gray's but with its own feline charm. The poet plays up to our expectations, using the form to contain and emphasize the humour; the final stanza achieves a quality of self-evident logic which derives as much as anything from the tone adopted, as the rhyme plays its subtle part in the overall effect. The poem is successful on its own terms of verbal aplomb: the youthful tabby set off against its ancient mistress in the first stanza, the vivid account of the arm scratching, the quick female response, and the author's ironical attitude to the episode as a whole.

The Latin gives us something rather different:

> Palpat heram felis, gremio recubans in anili;
>   Quam semel atque iterum Lydia palpat hera.
> Ludum lis sequitur; nam totos exerit unges,
>   Et longo lacerat vulnere felis anum.

Continuo exardens gremio muliercula felem
Nec gravibus multis excutit absque minis,
Quod tamen haud aequum est. – Si vult cum fele jocari,
Felinum debet Lydia ferre jocum.

For a start, it is briefer: Cowper has had to extend himself
in his third and fourth stanzas, filling out what is stated with
much greater clarity and economy in the Latin. Bourne
displays his customary flair for balanced antithesis in the
opening lines – a common ploy which usually, as here, serves
to point up a relationship. *Palpat*, reiterated, should not go
unnoticed, for behind the meaning of 'stroke, paw' lurks
the implication of 'flatter, wheedle': by his choice of word,
Bourne suggests the uncertain relationship of the two protagonists, as the eagerness with which the old lady repeats her
fondling strokes hints at the insecurity and underlines the
irony of the sudden attack. This is glossed over by Cowper.
The reversal is also neatly caught in the juxtaposition of *ludum*
and *lis*.

A comparison such as this underlines what Cowper had
said about translation. What is especially striking about
Bourne's poem (having admitted its obvious slightness) is
the economy, the lack of poeticizing, the lack of imagery, the
lack of anything other than what immediately concerns him:
all the frills are gone. This is a quality of all Bourne's work;
it is a quality lost, or at least altered radically, in Cowper's
version. (Equally, we can see what Cowper gains.) Bourne's
Latin is not classical or even imitative: he writes individua-
listically, gaily, without restraint, drawing on a wide range of
vocabulary, much of it beyond the usual poetic pale. We do
not get the Horatian weightiness of Johnson's Latin poetry.[20]
The tone is light-hearted without being scintillating; although
it seems to be work of the surface, it has its own underlying
sense of what is fitting and expected. If there is an ethos in
poetry like this, it is ultimately rather different from what we
find in Cowper, or any other eighteenth-century poet. The
idea, fostered by Lamb, that Bourne is a Latin Prior, does
not bear close scrutiny.

Earlier, in the seventeenth century, Edmund Waller had
put well the problem of poets who were then trying to write
in English; his definition reveals one particular quality of

neo-Latin verse which is especially relevant for the eighteenth century, and the distinguishing feature of Bourne's poetry:

> Poets that lasting marble seek
> Must carve in Latin, or in Greek;
> We write in sand, our language grows,
> And, like the tide, our work oerflows.
>
> ('Of English Verse')

The timeless quality of the classical languages, their inscriptional, marmoreal nature, was something that Dr Johnson, again, was quick to appreciate, as the episode over the inscription for Goldsmith's tomb shows. It was essential that such an inscription should be in Latin (not many agreed):[21]

> the language of the country of which a learned man was a native, is not the language fit for his epitaph, which should be in ancient and permanent language. Consider, Sir; how you should feel, were you to find at Rotterdam an epitaph upon Erasmus *in Dutch*!

The relevance to Bourne of this peculiar quality of Latin inscription may be seen when we look at his poetry: it is a source of some of his strength, as well as some of his weakness. The tendency is to reduce and simplify. This can have its advantages, but it can also lead to inconsequence. The problem with which Bourne has to cope is how far the basically lapidary quality can lend his verse a characteristic and deliberate weight and poise, and how far it can obscure latent life. Some of Bourne's epitaphs conveniently illustrate the problem.

Two of these (amongst Lamb's favourites) are addressed to dogs, and seem to hint at some of the traits we demand from the form – brevity, truthfulness, sincerity. Here is one of them:

> Qui observantiam et fidem,
> Ubicunque spectentur,
> Amare non dedignaris,
> PHYLLIDI, cani obsequentissimae,
> Per undecim annorum spatium
> Hero in venatibus et terra et aqua
> Comiti et adjutrici sagacissimae,
> Vix hanc invidebis urnam;
> Herilis utpote gratitudinis
> Inusitatius fortasse, sed condonabile, testimonium.

(If you are prepared to admire respect and faithfulness wherever they may be seen, you will hardly despise this burial urn for Phyllis, a most obedient dog, for eleven years the friend and most keen helper for her master in the chase in water and on land, seeing that it is witness to her master's gratitude, perhaps a rather strange witness, but pardonable.)

There is a particular blend of praise and reticence, pride and modesty which reaches its fulfilment in the concluding two lines. Such an epitaph, with its three well defined sections each signifying a slight shift of thought and mood, is held together by the emotional logic of the initial 'Qui', from which the rest follows naturally. Where essentials are all that matter, emotion and sentimentality are not indulged. There is an unstated stoic acceptance of death.

The other poem on the same theme is more complex, in that the owner is a blind man and the dog his leader. The problem here is one of the poet's realizing the master's love and gratitude, and the reciprocal affection, without imbuing him with self-pity; it has essentially to be a dramatic piece, in order that the reader can accept the relationship. Bourne cleverly indicates the inseparability of the two, whilst hinting that all the safety and protection has now disappeared:

> Pauperis hic Iri requiesco Lyciscus, herilis,
> Dum vixi, tutela vigil columenque senectae,
> Dux caeco fidus: nec, me ducente, solebat,
> Praetenso hinc atque hinc baculo, per iniqua locorum
> Incertam explorare viam; sed fila secutus,
> Quae dubios regerent passus, vestigia tuta
> Fixit inoffenso gressu; gelidumque sedile
> In nudo nactus saxo, qua praetereuntium
> Unda frequens confluxit, ibi miserisque tenebras
> Lamentis, noctemque oculis ploravit obortam. . . .

Lamb translates this serviceably:[22]

> Poor Irus' faithful wolf-dog here I lie,
> That wont to tend my old blind master's steps,
> His guide and guard; nor, while my service lasted,
> Had he occasion for that staff, with which
> He now goes picking out his path in fear
> Over the highways and crossings, but would plant,

Safe in the conduct of my friendly string,
A firm foot forward still, till he had reach'd
His poor seat on some stone, nigh where the tide
Of passers-by in thickest confluence flow'd:
To whom with loud and passionate laments
From morn to eve his dark estate he wail'd.

Requiesco is all right for the dog, but hard on the old man, still
pauper and *caecus*. The dog realizes the man's loss, and this comes
out in the juxtaposition of past and present. But even whilst he
was alive, he was only helping his master to find a good place to
beg. It is a moving picture, of benignity begetting benignity, the
dog at his master's feet, picking up the scraps of food offered:

Ploravit nec frustra; obolum dedit alter et alter,
Queis corda et mentem indiderat natura benignam.
Ad latus interea jacui sopitus herile,
Vel mediis vigil in somnis; ad herilia jussa
Auresque atque animum arrectus, seu frustula amice
Porrexit sociasque dapes, seu longa diei
Taedia perpessus, reditum sub nocte parabat.

Nor wail'd to all in vain; some here and there,
The well-dispos'd and good, their pennies gave;
I meantime at his feet obsequious slept;
Not all-asleep in sleep, but heart and ear
Prick'd up at his least motion; to receive
At his kind hand my customary crumbs,
And common portion in his feast of scraps;
Or when night warned us homeward, tired and spent
With our long day and tedious beggary.

The final lines of the poem capture this interdependence:

Hi mores, haec vita fuit, dum fata sinebant,
Dum neque languebam morbis, nec inerte senecta,
Quae tandem obrepsit, veterique satellite caecum
Orbavit dominum: prisci sed gratia facti
Ne tota intereat, longos deleta per annos,
Exiguum hunc Irus tumulum de cespite fecit,
Etsi inopis, non ingratae, munuscula dextrae;
Carmine signavitque brevi, dominumque canemque
Quod memoret, fidumque canem dominumque benignum.

These were my manners, this my way of life,
Till age and slow disease me overtook,
And sever'd from my sightless master's side.
But, lest the grace of so good deeds should die,
Through tract of years in mute oblivion lost,
This slender tomb of turf hath Irus rear'd,
Cheap monument of no ungrudging hand,
And with short verse inscribed it, to attest,
In long and lasting union to attest,
The virtues of the Beggar and the Dog.

The idea of the poem as inscription permeates the structure, for the poem the master had inscribed is the poem that we are reading. Bourne appreciates the schizophrenic logic of the medium, and quietly exploits some of its possibilities. The technique of the epitaph and the inscription is transformed here into a poetry of compassion and quiet resignation, whilst the poet himself remains at a distance, gently shifting the focus. Although the monumental aspect is here tempered by a readiness to expand, Bourne realizes that expansion serves to emphasize the suspended quality of the emotion.

In his shorter poems (and most of Bourne's poems aren't very long), Bourne explores some of the implications of this stylistic quality, although often only tentatively. Many of his poems consist of no more than a few elegiac lines, often based on a fairly common, stock theme. Several of the topics that occur are also to be found in the collections of Westminster School poems, *Lusus Westmonasterienses* (1730, 1734, 1740 and 1750), and a comparison between some of the versions of similar themes is quite instructive. A diet of such pieces soon palls; what is especially unpalatable is the anonymity of the majority of them, consciously worked exercises at their best, but no more. It would be hard to imagine any real poetry flowering in such barren ground. Paradoxically some of the poems that Bourne produces in this vein are amongst his best, most characteristic, work; it is as though he accepts the challenge of this very restricted form (with its obvious relation to the epigram, but without any of its verve), and transforms it into something personally felt. Although his frequent use of the form inevitably suggests something of his imaginative limitations, this polishing of it seems to be an acknowledgment by Bourne of the form's inherent virtues. He knows what he can do well. His unpretentious humanity can save an apparently slight poem.

Some of these common motifs allow a very human, and humorous, response from Bourne. Comparisons are more apt than analyses in pointing out Bourne's particular qualities: in the following poem (from *Lusus Westmonasterienses*) on the theme 'Inest sua gratia parvis', note especially the lack of any sense of urgency, of any grappling with a real issue:

> Corporis humani varios circumspice nexus,
>> Pars facit officium parvula quaeque suum.
> Crura licet solidum sustentent fortia corpus,
>> Deme pedis digitum, fortia crura labant.

(Consider the various connecting links of the human body: each little piece does its job. Strong legs might hold up the whole body; but take away a toe, and the strong legs totter.)

Beside this, Bourne's effort, with its reference to the battle of the pygmies and cranes, does at least have some awareness of tradition, of a perspective in which the general maxim can be fitted.

> Bellator fuit exiguis Pygmaeus in armis,
>> Et tenui infestas cuspide figit aves.
> Securum tamen hunc praestat contracta figura,
>> Seu sors adversa est, sive secunda favet.
> It fama ad caelum, si victor ab hoste recedat;
>> Si non, ad caelum fertur in ore gruis.

(There was a Pygmy warrior, fighting in minute arms; he transfixes the hostile birds on his slender spear. His tiny form guarantees his safety, whether fate is against him or not. If he returns victorious from the enemy, his fame wings to heaven: if not, he's carried there in the beak of a crane.)

The lightness of the touch is important to the effect of the whole, as the rather grandiose opening changes to laughter at the end. This lightness runs throughout these little pieces, and is frequently their chief justification. Bourne never resorts to flippancy in his gentle probing of human folly; the corollary to his rejection of satire (explicit in his poem on Hogarth) is his warmth of sympathy, and this is often effectively stated only by implication. For example, he seizes on the episode of Poly-phemus and Odysseus, under the title 'Dant animos socii' – another common topic – and draws a damaging contrast between Odysseus alone and Odysseus with his friend Dio-medes; he does so, however, by relying on the ingredients of the story itself, the pun on the name *Outis* (no man), so that judgment is reserved:

> Vidit ut instantem Polyphemum solus Ulysses,
> Quae modo tam validae contremuere manus.
> Qui totidem, qui tanta heros Diomede peregit
> Cum socio, solus cum fuit, *Outis* erat.

(When Ulysses, by himself, saw Polyphemus bearing down on him, how his hands shook! He had, with his friend Diomedes, frequently performed heroic deeds; but when he was alone, he was nobody.)

Man's pretensions all come to nothing; Bourne was sure of this, and was content to base much of his poetry on the tragi-comedy inherent in such a view of life. Great men fall; cities crumble; reputations fade. These themes run through his work; addresses to glow-worms, silkworms and snails tend to be at the expense of poor mortals; the swallow, nest-building, shows more architectural skill than a Vanbrugh; those who lay on lavish spectacles for the dead are ridiculed; six feet of earth are as good as a pyramid; those busily collecting butterflies, noting the different markings and colourings, are wasting their time; the most beautiful woman is the plainest; the Thames has been polluted by the foul effluent of an affluent society; Stephen Duck, the thresher poet, is, by his unpretentious modesty, a reproach to greater poets. It is no surprise to find one poem entitled '*Panta Gelos*' ('everything's a laugh'). Bourne does not automatically turn to conventional comforts, any more than he rushes into the arms of the Church that wanted him. Each poem that he writes in this vein is a careful, quiet attempt to capture the futility of it all, the difficulty of living: yet he seldom shows complete despair. For he tames his fears and anxieties, just as his poems tame and temper the potential conflicts beneath their surface. He makes life manageable by reducing its difficulties to the level of homely sayings, with their own truth and logic. His is not an art that explores or expands; it defines and restricts, in an ironic acceptance of limitations. Bourne's voice is confident, but never strident or assertive, and the confidence is reflected in the neatness of the operation.

Bourne quite clearly thought about the role of poetry, and art in general, and what its relationship to life should be; of course this was a common preoccupation of writers better than Vincent Bourne. The long-established doctrine of *ut pictura poesis* lay behind much of the descriptive verse of the time, and naturally it affected the more basic question of art's vision of reality. We cannot expect Bourne to say anything really profound on this commonplace topic, but what he does say is an indication of the seriousness with which he views poetry.

There are some poems in which Bourne tackles head-on the problems of the artist; for instance there is 'Denneri Anus' (translated by Cowper) in which he describes one of Denner's paintings in some detail. It is a portrait of an old woman, which smoothes out the wrinkles: old age is transcended in the process of being captured on canvas.

> Nec stupor est oculis, fronti nec ruga severa;
> Flaccida nec sulcis pendent utrinque gena.
> Nil habet illepidum, morosum, aut triste tabella;
> Argentum capitis praeter, anile nihil.

(There is no dullness in her eyes, and no fierce wrinkle on her brow, nor do her cheeks hang down flabbily on either side, deeply furrowed. The picture has nothing disagreeable, morose or sad about it; apart from the silver hair, nothing aged.)

Bourne is genuinely amused by the public reaction: he may be touching on conventional topics, but he achieves a rare freshness of detail and spirit:

> Spectatum veniunt, novitas quos allicit usquam,
> Quosque vel ingenii fama, vel artis amor.
> Adveniunt juvenes; et, anus si possit amari,
> Dennere, agnoscunt hoc meruisse tuam.
> Adveniunt hilares nymphae; similemque senectam,
> Tam pulchram et placidam dent sibi fata, rogant.
> Matronae adveniunt, vetulaeque fatentur in ore
> Quod nihil horrendum ridiculumve vident.

(People come to look: those whom novelty attracts, or report of skill, or love of art. The young people come along, and if an old woman could inspire love, Denner, they think your woman would deserve it. Laughing girls come too, and hope that the fates will give them a similar old age, so beautiful and placid. Ladies come, and say that they see nothing in the old woman's face that is dreadful or absurd.)

This carefully placed sequence of detail leads up to the concluding statement, important for its sureness and finality:

> Quantus honos arti, per quam placet ipsa senectus;
> Quae facit, ut nymphis invideatur anus!
> Pictori cedit quae gloria, cum nec Apelli
> Majorem famam det Cytherea suo!

(How great is the charm of an art through which even old age can give pleasure, which makes an old woman envied by girls! What glory goes to the artist, since Venus gives no greater fame to her own Apelles!)

Apelles is the subject of another poem, 'Lacrymae Pictoris', in which sorrow is contained by art. The painter's son, *sua gaudia*, has died, and the father's reaction is a comment on Bourne's own epitaphic poems:

> 'Hos accipe luctus,
> Moerorem hunc,' dixit, 'nate parentis habe.'

('My son,' he said, 'accept this token of grief and sorrow.')

The image that he creates takes on a life of its own, defying the fact of death. Bourne is consciously refuting the belief of someone like Pomfret, who in his 'To a Painter Drawing Dorinda's Picture' declared, 'No art can equal what's by Nature done.' Bourne was too steeped in the neoclassical tradition to accept that sort of thing; his poem, significantly entitled 'Reconciliatrix' and addressed to a work by the celebrated Sir Godfrey Kneller, emphasizes this point:

> Crescentes laudes natura inviderat arti;
> Et sibi rivalem nescia ferre parem;
> Divinam effinxit nympham, et formam addidit ori,
> Cui Cypriae posset cedere forma deae.

(Nature envied the growing eulogies for art, and did not know how to accept a rival. She fashioned a heavenly girl, and gave her a beautiful face, to which the beauty of Venus could yield.)

The strife between art and nature is overcome by Kneller's statue, which reconciles the two forces. Here again, the tradition plays its part: Pope was ashamed of his epitaph on Kneller, but it was saying much the same thing:

> Kneller, by Heav'n and not a Master taught,
> Whose art was nature, and whose Pictures thought;

so it began. It ended:

> Living, great Nature fear'd he might outvie
> Her works, and dying, fears herself may die.

The much maligned Prior, in his poem on a 'Flower painted by Varelst', captured the paradox rather more successfully.

Another poem of Bourne's, again with a long tradition behind it, which hints at the futility of such strife, is 'Stradae Philomela' (translated quite successfully by Cowper as 'Strada's Nightingale'). Bourne is clearly nodding at Crashaw's superbly structured 'Music's Duell', itself a free translation of a Latin poem by the seventeenth-century Jesuit Famianus Strada. The sort of contest embodied in the poem became a common seventeenth-century allusion, and the popularity continued into the eighteenth century (see for example the 'Fifth Pastoral' of Ambrose Philips (1765) in which Colin Clout vies with the nightingale) and even the nineteenth century (as in Clare's poems on 'The March Nightingale' and 'The Mock Bird', where the approach is quite different, though the origin is the same). Bourne's poem seems rather drab in such company:

> Pastorem audivit calamis Philomela canentem,
>   Et voluit tenues ipsa referre modos;
> Ipsa retentavit numeros, didicitque retentans
>   Argutum fida reddere voce melos.
> Pastor inassuetus rivalem ferre, misellam
>   Grandius ad carmen provocat, urget avem.
> Tuque etiam in modulos surgis, Philomela; sed impar
>   Viribus, heu impar, exanimisque cadis.
> Durum certamen! tristis victoria! cantum
>   Maluerit pastor non superasse tuum.

(Philomela heard the shepherd playing on his pipes and wanted to repeat the slender notes herself. She tried the notes, and tried again, and learnt to echo the clear sound faithfully. The shepherd, unused to having a rival, challenges the poor bird, urging it on to loftier song; and you, Philomela, rise to the tunes he calls. But alas! you haven't the strength, and are unequal to the task: you fall lifeless. A hard contest! A sad victory! The shepherd would have preferred not to have beaten you at singing.)

However lame this might strike us, the significance of its implications was not lost on Bourne; the ambiguities of this relationship seem to have fascinated him, to the extent that he devoted a number of poems to the question, and these poems help us to understand the rest of his work, and his attitude to it. Quite often the themes of reflection and reciprocity take over whole poems, in which the style and syntax become part of the process of enactment, as the identities of the protagonists in the 'drama' are gradually merged. This is especially true of a poem ('Idem agit idem') in which a cat plays with its reflection in a mirror. In 'Canis et Echo' (Swift wrote a Latin poem on the same topic incidentally) a dog sees the moon reflected in the Thames, and barks at it, whereupon his own reflection barks back. He goes on barking until he exhausts himself. Other poems that remain on the level of occasional pieces cover rather the same ground ('Simile agit in simile'; 'Agens et patiens sunt simul'). But others explore the ambiguity. Bourne appears to be genuinely perplexed by the conflicting forces in the world, or at least in his tiny corner of it. In 'Certamen Musicum' he describes the bells that ring on either side of the Thames: no one could say which was the louder. But what appears on first hearing to be futile strife is in fact harmony, as opposites are reconciled, this time by the musical analogy:

> Octo trans Tamisin campanis diva Maria;
> Cis Tamisin bis sex diva Brigetta sonat.
> Haec tenues urget modulos properantius aedes,
> Alternat grandes lentius illa modos.
> Nec quis in alterutro distinguat littore judex,
> An magis haec aurem captet, an illa magis.
> Tantae est harmoniae contentio musica; turris
> Altera cum numeros, altera pondus habet.

A tuneful challenge rings from either side
Of Thames' fair banks. Thy twice six Bells, Saint Bride,
Peal swift and shrill; to which more slow reply
The deep-toned eight of Mary Overy.
Such harmony from the contention flows,
That the divided ear no preference knows;
Betwixt them both disparting Music's State,
While one exceeds in number, one in weight.

(Lamb's version)

If Bourne seems to be asserting the need for harmony in a world
where opposition and contrasts abound, we must set against this
the realistic conclusion of another poem that springs from the
same premise, 'Si propius stes, te capiet minus'. It begins

Londini ad pontem prono cum labimur amne,
Quam tua dat turris dulce, Maria, melos!

(When we glide down the river to London bridge, what a
sweet sound your tower gives out, St Mary!)

But the gaiety of the poem gives way to this:

Talis ab harmonia surgit distante voluptas;
Sin turrim introeas, omnia clangor erit.

(Such delight arises from the distant harmony. But if
you go into the tower, there will be an almighty din.)

It is distance that provides the harmony. It is by no means
fanciful to regard Bourne's verse as an attempt to see and
listen from a distance.

The philosophical tone of most of these shorter poems (and
the longer ones too – Bourne achieves a consistency of outlook
without becoming a bore) can be seen in his poem about the
relative merits of tragedy and comedy, in which he describes
the two masks that so often go together:

Hic sese in risum, patulo sine dentibus ore,
  Solvit, et humanas res facit esse jocum:
In lacrymas fusus, vultuque heu! tetricus ille
  Rebus in humanis nil nisi triste videt.
Ridenti aut flenti credis? si credis utrique,
  Sunt res humanae flebile ludibrium.

(This one dissolves into a grin, his toothless mouth wide
open, and makes a jest of human affairs. The other, tears
galore, and oh, dear! what a sour expression, sees nothing
that isn't mournful. Which do you believe, the smiler or
the weeper? If you believe them both, humanity is a
pathetic farce.)

Bourne appears to be a healthy sceptic, refusing to rule
out the possibility of a compromise; or rather, life makes this
particular refusal. It says much for Bourne that he recognizes
this to be a personal truth so far as he is concerned. It gives
rise frequently to an elegiac quality (nothing soft-centred)
that is to be found in many of his best poems. Even when he is
writing with a medieval spring and lightness, as in 'Corolla' –
a poem with its own characteristic individuality – there is an
unforced tightness of control which allows him to slip in very
quietly and discreetly the undertones of mortal decay which
traditionally lend poignancy to such themes. It would be
misleading to suggest that this is mere imitation, mere reliance
on a genre; rather, Bourne, modestly enough, revives the genre,
by reaching back to a previous age, and in so doing, he dismisses the claptrap of an outmoded pastoral form. D. Lewis's
version of the poem shows this up for what it is, demonstrating
how far removed Bourne is from the petrifying artificiality
of conventional eighteenth-century diction. 'Corolla' ('The
Wreath') begins with an exuberant catalogue of flowers which
will go to make up a wreath for Phyllis. This forms the bulk of
the poem, bursting across the line-endings, until the remem-
brance of mortality draws him up:

> Sed florescere
> Cernit eadem
> Phyllida forma,
> Quique recedit,
> Quique supervenit,
> Alter et alter.
>
> Non datur aetas
> Omnibus una,
> Nec decet omnes
> Una superbia;
> Cedite Phyllidi,
> Cedite, flosculi.

Cedite, sed ce-
dendo dierum
Quo fuga ritu
Pergit, eodem
Dicite et annos
Ire, perire.

(But each succeeding year, one after another, sees Phyllis
flourishing with the same beauty. One age is not given to
everyone, nor does the same glory suit everyone. Yield,
flowers, to Phyllis, yield; but in yielding tell her how,
just as days fly from us, so the years fade and are gone.)

If we can see in this poem (and also in the effective 'Soli-
tudo Regia Richmondiensis') the determination to avoid
pastoral affectations, we can also see the resignation and the
sadness, however gently hinted. When Bourne addresses his
mind to the specific question of death, the melancholy runs
much deeper. To some extent he was obsessed with the problem
of how to face death; many of his poems, as we have seen,
take the form of epitaphs, several others look ahead to death,
and the two letters that were first printed with the 1772 edition
(whatever their origin) are both concerned with this problem.
The rather cocky tone of one letter ('I am just come from
indulging a very pleasing melancholy in a country church-
yard. . . . Every monument has its instruction, and every
hillock has its lesson of mortality') needs to be set against
the anxiety of the other, written to his wife shortly before his
death ('Here I am lost in amazement and dread! . . . The
prospect into futurity is all darkness and uncertainty'). All his
talk about death as the great leveller does not help him in his
'weakness, folly, and sin'. It is not surprising that he achieves a
quality of personal involvement in those poems that arise from
a death or a reminiscence of someone dead. In 'Anus Saecu-
laris' (translated by Cowper) he takes the specific occasion
of the death of an old lady on her hundredth birthday, and
creates out of it something extremely personal and moving.
Handling a common theme, in that someone's death sparks
off reflections on one's own mortality, he manages to steer
clear of anything that we get from the 'grave-yard school',
turning it into a rather soured comment on life. The poem

expresses a generalized vision of life and death, suggesting (*Nil inest rebus novitatis*) a tempered world-weariness in what amounts to a fine balance between profundity and near-colloquialism:

> Singularis prodigium o senectae,
> Et novum exemplum diuturnitatis!
> Cujus annorum series in amplum
> > Desinit orbem!
>
> Vulgus infelix hominum, dies, en!
> Computo quam dispare computamus!
> Quam tua a summa procul est remota
> > Summula nostra!
>
> Pabulum nos luxuriesque lethi,
> Nos, simul nati, incipimus perire;
> Nos statim a cunis cita destinamur
> > Praeda sepulchro.

Cowper gets the spirit:

> Ancient dame, how wide and vast,
> > To a race like ours appears
> Rounded to an orb at last,
> > All thy multitude of years!
>
> We, the herd of woman kind,
> > Frailer and of feebler pow'rs,
> We, to narrow bounds confin'd,
> > Soon exhaust the sum of ours.
>
> Death's delicious banquet – we
> > Perish even from the womb,
> Swifter than a shadow flee,
> > Nourish'd, but to feed the tomb.

It emerges towards the end of the poem that he does not envy this old woman, but hopes he has only to live half as long; life is really pretty unpleasant:

> Integram aetatem tibi gratulamur;
> Et dari nobis satis aestimamus,
> Si tuam, saltem vacuam querelis,
> > Dimidiemus.

Thee we gratulate; content,
Should propitious Heav'n design
Life for us, as calmly spent,
Though but half the length of thine.

Bourne succeeds in conveying at the same time his feeling and respect for this old woman, who is not at all tainted by life: he combines admiration with a strong sense of his own inadequacies, and human frailty in general.

A more varied effect is achieved in 'In Obitum Roussaei', written in his Cambridge days, in 1721, in memory of a college servant. Here Bourne confronts death with mild humour; in the opening lines, whilst there is an acknowledgment that death comes to us all, through the Stygian gloom we can make out the busy Roussaeus, directing the river traffic as efficiently as he had done in Cambridge. The acknowledgment is in effect put in its proper place:

Alme Charon, (nam tandem omnes, qui nascimur et qui
    Nascemur, tua nos cymba aliquando manet,)
Per ripas fer circum oculos, omnesque recense
    Manes, ad Stygias qui glomerantur aquas;
Prospice, si crassam fors exploraveris umbram,
    Non est in toto crassior umbra loco.
Luctantem cernes, animasque hinc inde minores
    Turbantem, ut cubito pandat utroque viam.
Squalidus et pinguis totus, tibi navita dextram
    Tendet, ad Elysii trajiciendus agros.

(Kind Charon (for your boat awaits us all sooner or later, those now living and those yet unborn), cast your eyes around the banks of the river, and review all the spirits who are congregating by the Styx. Have a look – if you can by any chance peer through the thick shade; in the whole place there is not a thicker shade. You will see him struggling, driving the lesser spirits in all directions, to open up a way with each elbow. Quite filthy and fat, your sailor will offer you his hand, to get you across to the Elysian fields.)

The mourning youth of Cambridge make what they know is a vain plea for the return of Roussaeus to their clime (*nostro caelo*); but if this cannot (as it will not) be granted, then, at least Charon shouldn't ask for a fee for the crossing, not that Roussaeus would have any money anyway. The solution is to let Charon and Roussaeus share the duties of rowing the boat: the two will be indistinguishable. There the poem ends, refusing to take death too seriously:

> Adde quod (ut similes estis) dubitabitur, utrum
> Roussaeus geminus sit, geminusve Charon.

(Moreover, as you are so alike, it will be hard to tell which of you is which: you'll be twins.)

Comparable to this is the poem 'Ad Davidem Cook', the nightwatchman at Westminster School (1716). Amongst other things, this poem indicates Bourne's early precocity, as it was apparently written before he went up to Cambridge. What emerges here, apart from the affection of the portrait, is the clever use of detail, the feeling of a classical background but a contemporary setting, the lack of condescension, the humanity of the whole. Bourne's style is balanced, phrase and clause answering each other, so that the whole address becomes a rather formalized ritual. This is especially true of the opening lines, which stress the nature of what is to follow:

> Indicium qui saepe mihi das carmen amoris,
> Reddo tibi indicium carmen amoris ego.
> Qui faustum et felix multum mihi mane precaris;
> Dico atque ingemino nunc tibi rursus, ave.

> For much good-natured verse received from thee,
> A loving verse take in return from me.
> 'Good morrow to my masters' is your cry;
> And to our David 'twice as good,' say I.

(Lamb's version)

The poem demonstrates Bourne's constant refusal to strive for effect, his determination to avoid the extravagant gesture: details are sufficient to give us an idea of the man, and it is characteristic of Bourne that he should conclude his catalogue (but it is no *mere* catalogue) with mention of the 'friendly hand of death'. The man commemorated is shown to be wise and stoic.

Multa docens juvenes, et pulchras multa puellas,
  Utile tu pueris virginibusque canis:
Conjugium felix monitis utentibus optas,
  Cunctaque quae castus gaudia lectus habet.
Tu monitor famulis sexus utriusque benignus,
  Munditias illis praecipis, hisce fidem.
Omnibus at votis hoc oras atque peroras,
  Ut dominis cedant prospera quaeque tuis.
Unum hoc prae cunctis meminisse hortaris, ut imis
  Summa etiam exaequet mortis amica manus.
Quid tibi pro totidem meritis speremus? amori
  Quisve tuo aequalis retribuatur amor?
Tuque tuusque canis si nos visetis, uterque
  Grati eritis nobis, tuque tuusque canis.
Mille domos adeas, et non ignobile munus
  (Nulla minus solido) dent tibi mille domus,
Quemque bonum exoptas nobis, laetumque Decembrem,
  Esto tibi pariter laetus, et esto bonus.

Lamb condenses this, but gets the drift of it:

To youths and virgins they [your verses] chaste lessons read;
Teach wives and husbands how their lives to lead;
Maids to be cleanly, footmen free from vice;
How death at last all ranks doth equalise;
And, in conclusion, pray good years befal,
With store of wealth, your 'worthy masters all'.
For this and other tokens of good will,
On boxing day may store of shillings fill
Your Christmas purse, no householder give less,
When at each door your blameless suit you press:
And what you wish to us (it is but reason)
Receive in turn – the compliments o' th' season!

At a time when the neoclassical tradition was being challenged
in favour of originality and 'genius', Vincent Bourne was
demonstrating that a steeping in the classics need not result
in dull artificiality: rules meant little to him. It would be
foolish to make great claims for his poetry: its very nature
eschews such claims. But it is the prerogative of minor poets
to know their particular skills and to apply them patiently and
diligently. Bourne's poetry is modest, entertaining and human.

So long as neo-Latin poetry is read then Bourne must have a place, and not too lowly a one, at the table.

Notes

1 British Museum Add. MS. 32689, fol. 296; Add. MS. 32713, fol. 428. Bourne's poems were dedicated to the Duke of Newcastle.
2 His epitaph, significantly emphasizing the 'silence which he loved', runs: *Pietatis sincerae/Summaeque humilitatis/nec dei usquam immemor/nec sui,/in silentium quod amavit/descendit/V.B.*
3 Bourne is not a bestseller today. In this essay I have tried to give a fair sample of his verse, without letting the essay become an anthology; most libraries, however, house unread copies of his work.
4 Cowper to Rev. William Unwin, 23 May 1781: *Correspondence of William Cowper*, ed. Thomas Wright, 1904, I, p. 310.
5 'The Latin poems of Vincent Bourne', *Englishman's Magazine*, September 1831, p. 63.
6 Lamb to Wordsworth, 7 April 1815: *The Letters of Charles and Mary Lamb*, ed. E. V. Lucas, 1935, II, p. 154.
7 *Eclectic Review*, IV, September 1808, pp. 832–4.
8 Landor, *Idyllica Heroica decem*, 1820, p. 212.
9 Arthur Benson, 'Vincent Bourne', *MacMillan's Magazine*, 71, 1895, pp. 423–30. For the Lucretian influence on English poetry see Wolfgang Fleischmann, *Lucretius and English Literature 1680–1740*, Paris, 1964. Two of the poems poached from the Cambridge anthology and attributed to Bourne were by John Jortin (1698–1770): the Ode *Qualis per nemorum nigra silentia*, and *Ad Tempus*, both poems of some accomplishment, but sombre and Gray-like.
10 Johnson, *Lives of the Poets*, ed. G. B. Hill, 1905, III, p. 421.
11 *Ibid.*, III, p. 182.
12 For an interesting account of this development, see James W. Johnson, *The Formation of English Neo-Classical Thought*, Princeton, 1967.
13 The context cannot be fully explored here: a useful survey is by R. S. Crane, 'English Neoclassical criticism: an outline sketch', *Critics and Criticism*, ed. Crane, University of Chicago Press, 1952, pp. 372–88.
14 Henry Felton, *Dissertation on Reading the Classics and Finding a Just Style*, 1713, p. 35.
15 'Preface to the Fables' in *Essays* of John Dryden, ed. W. P. Ker, Oxford, 1926, II, p. 252. See generally, J. W. H. Atkins, *English Literary Criticism: 17th and 18th Centuries*, 1951.
16 Charles Gildon, *The Complete Art of Poetry*, 2 vols, 1718; Edward Bysshe, *The Art of English Poetry*, 1702.
17 Johnson, *Lives*, II, pp. 82–3.
18 *Ibid.*, II, p. 12.
19 *Correspondence*, I, pp. 309–10.
20 See Susie Tucker and Henry Gifford, 'Johnson's Latin poetry', *Neophilologus*, XLI, July 1957, pp. 215–21; also Caroline Goad, *Horace in the English Literature of the Eighteenth Century* (Yale Studies in English

LVIII), New Haven, 1918. Johnson and Bourne both translated a poem by William Oldys, 'The Fly, an Anacreontick'. The differences are instructive: Bourne avoids the rather ponderous tone adopted by Johnson. It is also significant that whilst Walter Pope, in his poem 'The Wish', makes frequent allusions (in his notes) to classical writers, mainly Horace, Bourne, in his translation of the poem, does his utmost to avoid them.

21 See R. W. Ketton-Cremer, 'Lapidary Verse', *Proceedings of the British Academy*, XLV, 1959, pp. 237–53.

22 Lamb's translation of the first line of this poem blurs the fact that *Lyciscus* is the dog's name: Vergil has *Lycisca* in his third eclogue; *non-ingratae . . . dextrae* in the third line from the end means, rather, 'of a hand not ungrateful'.

VI
The Latin Poetry of Walter Savage Landor

Andrea Kelly

I The background

Walter Savage Landor symbolized for Yeats the complete man of action who 'topped us all in calm nobility when the pen was in his hand, as in the daily violence of his passion when he laid it down'.[1] He stood alongside Donne in his turbulent energy and eloquence. He needed both, and an exceptionally robust constitution as well, to maintain the prodigious literary activity that was spread out over nearly three-quarters of a century. He was born in 1775, nine years before the death of Dr Johnson, and a few months before his own death in 1864 he received as a visitor, almost as a pilgrim, the young Algernon Swinburne. In the course of his long life Landor met a great many of the most noteworthy figures of the age, and his encounters were not confined to men of letters, but extended to all connected with society and the arts, and to politicians, revolutionaries and fellow men of action. His vision, like his range of acquaintances, was wide. Dr Landor, his father, was a well-established member of the Warwickshire squirearchy, and Walter stood to inherit a considerable portion of the family estates. Nevertheless the turbulent events of his life ensured that he spent many years abroad. Though he might declare in verse at regular intervals that the French were rogues and the Italians cowards, he lived in both countries and fought in the Spanish uprising in 1808 (for two months). He was an Englishman, but one with a lively appreciation for all things European.

Yeats's image is drawn from Landor's unquiet personal history,[2] but it also reflects the peculiarly Roman qualities in his writings, their eloquence and strength. These find their greatest scope in the English prose works of his later years, notably the *Imaginary Conversations*. But earlier on in his career many ambitious experiments were made in Latin. His epic, *Gebir*, published in 1798, was followed in 1803 by a Latin version, *Gebirus*, which was composed concurrently with the English.[3] *Gebir* had some distinguished admirers. Shelley, for instance, 'would read it aloud to others, or to himself, with a tiresome pertinacity'.[4] It is an oriental romance with revolutionary overtones and its political radicalism attracted the unfriendly attention of the *Anti-Jacobin Review*. Landor's next attempt in a comparable genre was on a much smaller scale. In 1806 he published a small volume of poems entitled *Simonidea*. The Latin section contained a short narrative poem, 'Pudoris Ara', 'The Altar of Modesty', which was the first of a number of 'idyllia' whose subjects were taken from ancient fable and mythology, generally the lesser known episodes. These, translated into English several decades later, became the core of his *Hellenics*,[5] which are considered by some to be the high point of his poetic career. Already in this first poem the element of 'imaginary conversation' is present in a lively, subtle dialogue between Leda and her daughter, Helen. Landor's insight into personality and his remarkable imagination for antiquity are shown to much better advantage within a single episode than in the more slow-moving, expansive progression of epic, with its necessarily philosophical and political overtones.

I have concentrated on Landor's short lyric poems because, in their wealth of personal and topical allusions, they need a more detailed introduction than *Gebirus* or the 'idyllia'. Unlike the longer poems, the lyrics are not usually accessible through English versions. A detailed comparison, however, between the Latin idylls and their later English counterparts would throw valuable light both on Landor's Latin style, and its influence on his feeling for the English language. 'Pudoris Ara' is a case in point.[6] The Latin poem is in one respect a show piece, 'doctus' in the Catullan sense. There are verbal echoes of most of the classical Latin authors, and Landor makes liberal use of patronymics, archaic place names and an assortment of traditional epithets for his chief characters. Several of the more indirect allusions he does not attempt to translate in the English versions. Landor's style remains his own in spite of these borrowings. But beyond this Landor's debt, in spirit at least, is to Ovid, for the witty handling of a story after Ovid's own heart: Helen of Troy's first elopement from home, and Leda's chagrin as she recognizes in her own daughter a potential rival. The Ovidian quality of the wit is rooted in Landor's verbal dexterity. Puns, for instance, are an important source of humour and psychological insight in the poem, and they are unfortunately confined to the Latin version. These delicately define the relationship between mother and daughter. In the opening paragraph the implications of Leda's command 'Ede tuum . . . ordine casum' are lost in the English 'tell me all',[7] 'casum' implying as it does, the idea of Helen's 'fall' or 'overthrow'. The Latin too preserves a robust quality in its brevity: 'Helenam Aegida raptam'. The participle cannot be so rendered in the English 'whom Theseus lately bore away', but its conciseness defines Helen graphically, and ironically anticipates her future elopement with Paris. It will be found that this precision and wit is impeded in the English versions by their Latinate diction and syntax, such a weighty style allowing Landor none of the licence he freely takes in the Latin. The Ovidian sentiment is, therefore, partially lost. As the natural movement of the verse is thwarted, spontaneity disappears, and with it the linguistic flexibility necessary to enhance moments of deliberate reticence. In other idylls with more serious 'heroic' themes (e.g. 'Corythus' and the lengthy 'Ulysses in Argiripa') this conflict in the English versions between style and content is not so marked, but the impression made is still very different from that of the Latin original.

The most concerted period of composition in Latin, effectively from 1813 to 1820, was devoted almost entirely to the idylls, and was followed by the richest period in Landor's English career. 1824 to 1847 saw the appearance of *Imaginary*

Conversations, Pericles and Aspasia, The Pentameron and the English *Hellenics*. And yet when Landor published his first collection of Latin idylls in 1815[8] he was already forty years old. The period of transition was marked by the troubles at his Llanthony estate and his consequent removal to Italy where, for the next five years, he seems to have embarked on a policy of withdrawal. He published only in Latin, and this exclusiveness markedly influenced the thought and style of the English works that followed. In 1820 Landor published the *Idyllia Heroica Decem*. This was his most ambitious and also his final attempt to present Latin verse to the English public as a viable literary concern. The volume contained, besides the ten idylls, a large number of short Latin lyrics on a great variety of subjects: addresses to friends, fellow artists and public men, descriptions of places he was fond of, fables, love lyrics, political poems (with particular reference to Italy), satirical verses often of a very personal nature, eulogies, epigrams, *sententiae* and epitaphs.

After 1820 Landor submitted to pressure from his friends and publishers and abandoned any new major excursions in Latin. Henceforward his Latin composition was confined to lyrics. In one sense it was a restriction, in another it was a step towards the refinements of technique and sentiment that distinguished many of his later small poems. In 1847 he published his last exclusively Latin work, *Poemata et Inscriptiones*. This was a largely retrospective collection intended as a companion to the English *Works* of 1846. It contained, with some revisions, *Gebirus*, the idylls, all the short poems published between 1800 and 1820 and the others written since that time. It is the most accessible and comprehensive volume for the modern reader, and it is also the most confusing, containing as it does the miscellany of a lifetime. As Leicester Bradner[9] suggests, a fairer introduction to Landor's short poems would be through the two later English volumes that contain sizeable sections of Latin verse: *Dry Sticks, Fagoted* (1858) and *Heroic Idyls* (1863). Here Landor's epigrammatic technique is at its best, the tone is more mellow, and the Latin sections, being small and confined to the compositions of a relatively short period, form recognizable units, complementing the larger sections of English verse. For his earliest period *The Poems of Walter Savage Landor* (1795)[10] and *Simonidea* (1806) are of similar value, though unfortunately they are less accessible.

Landor was acquainted with Anglo-Latin poetry from quite an early age. Removed from Rugby School after a violent disagreement with Dr James, the headmaster, he was still too young for Oxford, which he entered in 1793. In the interim he studied for a time with William Langley, rector of Fenny Bentley in Derbyshire. Here he first became acquainted with the Anglo-Latin poets. He translated Buchanan's *Jephthah* into English verse and Cowley's English poems into Latin Sapphics and Alcaics, a task which must have impressed upon Landor the potentialities and also the limitations of each language. With William Benwell at Oxford Landor's reading of the modern Latinists, including European authors, increased, and in 1795 he declared with pride:[11]

Mihi equidem, haec opera pendenti, videtur Britannicis volumen colligi posse quod nequaquam cedet iis aliarum omnium gentium.

(It occurs to me, studying these works, that it would be possible to compile a British anthology in no way inferior to those of other nations.)

He never did compile an anthology, but in 1808 he wrote to Robert Southey: 'We really do need some Elegant Extracts of the modern latinists. Many fine specimens are recoverable. I wonder some German has not done it.'[12]

All the major Anglo-Latin poets are discussed, if somewhat cursorily, in the course of his Latin essays:[13]

Principes sunt Buchananus, Oënus, epigrammatum scriptor suis temporibus non injucundus, et Miltonus, et Maius, qui *Pharsaliae* supplementum addidit, et Jortinus, et Graius, nostraque aetate Tuedelius, adolescens longe doctissimus, Graeco carmine Sapphico memorabilis, et morum suavitate et corporis pulchritudine et immatura morte.[14]

(The best are Buchanan, Owen – a gifted writer of epigrams in his day – Milton, May – who added an extra book to the *Pharsalia* – Jortin, Gray, and in our own time,

Tweddell – the most learned young man of all, remarkable for his Greek verses in the Sapphic metre, his gentle disposition, his physical beauty, and his untimely death.)

The unfortunate and long-lamented John Tweddell,[15] whose *Prolusiones Juveniles* appeared in 1793, shared with Landor a mutual friend in Samuel Parr. In the same essay Landor's unfavourable remarks on Vincent Bourne are surprising:[16]

Novimus quem Tibullo ac Propertio praetulit bonus Cuperus . . . Vinnius autem . . . nihil admodum habet suum, et, aliena quum Latina faceret, frigida est plerumque concinnitatis affectatio.

(We know whom the good Cowper holds in greater esteem than either Tibullus or Propertius . . . Vincent, however, totally lacks originality, and when he imitates other Latin authors he is without warmth, and aspires to mere elegance.)

He also dismisses without much ceremony Sir William Jones, philologist, and Judge of the High Court at Calcutta:[17]

Jonesius . . . thus pingue Arabum Persarumque ita odoratus est, ut rosam verbenamque non senserit; nec viderit ab ipso Apolline hoc suis omnibus edictum: Simplice myrto nihil adlabores. Poeta vix mediocris fuit, vir prudens, judex integerrimus, civis optimus.

(Jones was so overcome by the heady perfumes of Arabia and Persia that he could not smell the rose and tamarisk; nor did he realize that Apollo himself had instructed his poets: Do not attempt to improve on the simple myrtle. He was an indifferent poet, a wise man, a judge of great integrity and the best of citizens.)

Landor refers here to the odes Sir William had translated from the Chinese, Arabic and Persian into Latin.[18] He had translated even more into English, and Landor held these in no higher esteem. He could do as well himself he claimed, and in 1800 he had produced a small book called *Poems from the Arabic and Persian*, supposedly translated into English from a French intermediary text. Every poem was, in fact, Landor's own work.

The one contemporary Latinist for whom Landor always had the greatest respect and admiration was Robert Percy Smith. As an undergraduate in the early 1790s Landor had read Smith's Cambridge Tripos poems on the systems of Plato, Descartes and Newton, and his prize ode 'Mare liberum'.[19] An ardent admirer of Lucretius, Landor recognized in these poems the masterful spirit which transmutes scientific concepts into poetry, the same spirit in which Shelley was to write. Smith, like Landor, found that his ability was well suited to the short narrative poem, and within this form he was to Lucretius what Landor in his 'idyllia' was to Ovid. Landor's poem 'Ad Fratrem', first published in *Simonidea* in 1806, contains an early tribute, and in the *Heroic Idyls* of 1863 he wrote:[20]

Saecula vix alium bis nona tulere poetam
Qui Musas Italas audita voce vocaret,
Omnes exilium Nasonis triste dolentes,
Denique vir surgit carmen sublime Lucreti
Exsuperans, et humi prosterans omne priorum
Quot genuit cretas ignavo semine tellus.

(Hardly one poet appeared, in eighteen hundred years, who might command attention from the Muses of Ancient Italy, still sadly grieving for the exiled Ovid. Then there came a man surpassing the sublime poem of Lucretius. He levelled to the ground all that had been sterile of the earth's offspring in the works of earlier poets.)

One of the most significant differences between the Latin careers of Landor and Smith is that Smith belonged to an anthology tradition. He belonged, that is to say, to a small literary élite confined to certain public schools (in Smith's case, Eton) and the universities. Landor avoided the cult of the prize poem, so that even at Oxford his writings were never anthologized. He was ambitious, rather, for a European reputation as a Latinist. Writing to Southey in 1819 he declared: 'Hearing that all the poets in France and Germany are contending for the prize declared by the Academy of Stockholm to be given for the best ode on the accession of Bernadotte, I am resolved to set myself against the continent.'[21] The ode 'Ad Gustavum Regem Suedorum', finally published in *Poemata et Inscriptiones* in 1847, was unsuccessful. As R. H. Super remarks, 'It can hardly have aided his cause that Bernadotte ascended the throne not as Gustavus but as Karl Johann.'[22] Landor did not compete again. He was free now to write as he wished, that is, in unconventional forms, energetically, and on every conceivable subject. But in turning from the universities he lost a great part of his audience, for Anglo-Latin verse, as Leicester Bradner points out, was rapidly becoming either 'the pastime of scholars or the eccentricity of unusual undergraduates'.[23] He published, therefore, at his own expense, and always at a loss.

Landor stood apart from the mainstream of the eighteenth century too, by turning away from exclusive imitation of the Horatian ode and epistle. His ode and bucolic 'coefficients' are relatively low. His favourite Roman authors were the great favourites of Renaissance writers: Lucretius, Catullus and Ovid. It is significant that Landor's understanding of the Renaissance was on a par with his sympathy for antiquity. Lucretius appealed to his basically humanistic, unmystical temperament. In Catullus he found passion, but also grace. In fact, it was only the grace that remained when he translated some of the 'carmina' into English,[24] and he came nearer Catullus' intensity of tone in his own more personal poems. In both Catullus and Lucretius he admired the pristine strength of the Roman language and compared it to the strength of the English language at the time of Milton: 'Each had attained its full perfection, and yet the vestiges of antiquity were preserved in each.'[25] Catullus, again, was his model for satire, along with Martial, and in this field he allowed himself considerably more licence in his Latin writings than in the English. Ovid, however, was the great favourite of his youth and never lost pride of place. In old age Landor would quote the *Tristia*, and hail Ovid as a fellow exile. In him he found wit, lightness of touch, stylistic simplicity and delicate psychological insight (especially into the female character). He found, too, a wealth of fable and mythology, and that idyllic, pictorial quality of arrested motion which he singles out specially when commenting on the *Metamorphoses*: 'What a gallery of pictures is here! what a floor of mosaic! what a ceiling of arabesques! Is there any poem, excepting the *Odyssea*, that presents so many figures, so many attitudes?'[26]

While, as a child, Landor was reading the Latin and Greek

classics in the original for the first time, he was also assimilating their influence in an indirect, but perhaps more profound, fashion, through the English tradition itself. As a boy, he remembers, he played truant from Latin and Greek for Cowper's 'sweeter Task':[27]

> Spenser shed over me his sunny dreams:
> Chaucer far more enchanted me;

and later on there followed Shakespeare, Milton and Pope. Landor was approaching the Greek and Latin classics within that ethos of urbanity distilled by poets of the preceding century, an urbanity typically accompanied by a waspish satirical strain that Landor fully appreciated. An urbanity, too, that in many poets had been transmuted from classical models into purely native sentiment, even in Anglo-Latin poetry. In his first published Latin essay of 1795 Landor quoted enthusiastically and at length from the poems of an 'unknown author', in fact, the 'Festum Lustrale' of Benjamin Loveling.[28] He singled out too for its humour Addison's mock-epic *epyllion* on the battle of the pygmies and the cranes.

Landor's sensitivity to tradition, great though it was, did not prevent him from developing a highly individual style. For Landor, as Connop Thirlwall pointed out, resembled no other author, ancient or modern. His style 'is the style of Landor and it is marked with the stamp not only of his intellect but of his personal idiosyncrasy.'[29] Thirlwall continues: 'No doubt the author's poetical faculty is more largely developed in the longer compositions; but the shorter are more deeply impressed with the signature of the man; not always indeed in the most winning aspect. . . . Now and then harmlessly playful, but much oftener instinct with the bitterest sarcasm.' These shorter poems have never been edited or annotated, and being of an occasional nature, they can be difficult to follow, especially when Landor chooses to be stylistically obscure. In the case of Landor's political and satiric verse, several poems were sent to newspapers and journals of the day, and their topicality is lost on the modern reader. Leicester Bradner has commented: 'He is a poet who is impressive in anthologies and disappointing in the bulk. . . . A judicious selection of the idylls and epigrams would do much to raise Landor's reputation as a Latin poet.'[30] A judicious selection is certainly needed, but one that represents the man in all his moods and undertakings, not simply the bereaved lover or the stoic philosopher of the English anthologies. Landor imparted an engaging, sometimes an alarming directness of address to even his most commonplace verses and he touched on contemporary issues with a lively and discerning mind. An important aspect of his writings is their sheer bulk; this immense productivity lies behind each small poem and is sustained over a lifetime. Something of the man and the daily violence of his passion is lost, if selection is too rigorous. It would be a pity to cage such characteristic expansiveness within too rarefied an anthology, even in the interests of calm nobility.

II Politics and polemic

Landor drew his political ideals and inspiration directly from the days of Cromwell and the Commonwealth. His politics were generally assertions of principle rather than discussions of policy and therefore his tone was frequently didactic or even prophetic. Accordingly, he had little rapport with his own countrymen. The simplicity of his message divorced him, for the most part, from the intricate and secondary workings of English domestic policy and placed him instead in the company of revolutionary and nationalist movements on the Continent. In English politics his criticism was exercised chiefly on the ethics of particular statesmen. In all these various struggles he was primarily conscious of one, grand, overriding principle of freedom which, he was quite clear, would only be triumphant at the cost of many lives:[31]

> 'Liber eris' Homini Spes perfida dixit in aurem:
> De coelo auditur vox altera, 'Desine falli:
> Praetereunda prius tibi sunt mortalia secla,
> Tunc sperare licet cum libertate quietem.'

('You will be free' whispered deceitful Hope in the ear of Man. But from the heavens another voice is heard: 'Do not believe it. Centuries must pass before the human race may hope to enjoy peace as well as liberty.')

'Libertas' and 'justitia' were frequently personified in his poems, sometimes triumphant, but more often in retreat:[32]

Justitiam picta Pax est amplexa tabella.
Ut bene! dixit et haec, dixit et illa, 'vale'.

(This picture shows Justice and Peace embracing. Just
so! They are both saying 'farewell'.)

This principle of freedom Landor saw enshrined in the latest
attempt by Englishmen to overthrow the monarchy:[33]

O diem! jucundam et illustrem! quae Tyrannidis nubila,
diu collecta semperque hominibus gravia, luce pura laeta
salubrique dissipavit! Quae vidit identidem vigentes
Justiam ac Poesin: quae vidit, ut uno verbo complecter
omnia, Miltonum.

(O glorious and joyful day! That day on which the clouds
of Tyranny, so long gathered together in unceasing malevo-
lence towards mankind, were dispersed by a pure, glad-
some, beneficial light. The day which saw Justice and
Poetry flourish side by side. In one word that embraces
all, the day that saw *Milton*.)

Milton had justified tyrannicide in *The Tenure of Kings and
Magistrates* (1650) by appealing to Seneca's authority:

There can be slain
No sacrifice to God more acceptable
Than an unjust and wicked king.

Experience had led Landor to believe that most kings were
unjust and wicked. In the *Poemata et Inscriptiones* of 1847 a poem
is dedicated to Henri Grégoire, French revolutionist and ex-
bishop of Blois,[34] who had proposed in the National Convention
a motion for the abolition of kingship in the words: 'kings are in
the moral order what monsters are in the natural'. In the same
volume is an epitaph for Edmund Ludlow, one of King Charles
I's judges who signed the warrant for his execution and who
subsequently died in Vevey:[35]

In Ludlonis Sepulchrum Vibisci
Libera gens olim te, Ludlo invicte, recepit,
Et non ingrato condidit ossa solo.
Hoc unum est meritis pro talibus . . . occidis exul.
Debueras patriae charior esse tuae.

(*On the Tomb of Ludlow at Vevey*
A free people once welcomed you, indomitable Ludlow,
and gave burial to your bones in a friendly soil. To die in
exile – this was all your reward for such devoted service.
You should have been more highly valued by your homeland.)

Landor's views were well known to the English public, so that
when in 1858 the Italian patriot Felice Orsini attempted to
assassinate the Emperor Napoleon III and the Empress
Eugénie on their way to the Paris Opera, Landor found himself
the object of many violent accusations which he was finally
driven to repudiate in a letter to *The Times*.[36]

Landor harboured particular animosity towards Ferdinand
II, King of the Two Sicilies from 1830 to 1859. This was
King 'Bomba' whose treatment of political prisoners in Sicily
was exposed to Europe in Gladstone's *Letters to Lord Aberdeen*.
The revolutionary Bandiera brothers, executed by Bomba
are among the many Italian patriots commemorated in
Landor's poetry.[37] The domestic and political intrigues of
Ferdinand VII, King of Spain from 1808 to 1833, were also
recorded:[38]

> En venit iste fugax qui semper ab hoste minaci
> Abdidit os pavidum deseruitque suos!
> At ferro intrepidus matremque patremque petivit,
> Uxoresque jacent vermibus esca duo.

(This is the runaway who could be counted on to hide his
cowardly face at the sight of a dangerous enemy, and to
desert his men. But he was brave enough to threaten
mother and father with the sword. His two consorts are
dead also, and eaten by worms.)

His Latin poems, in fact, contain attacks on most of the sove-
reigns of his day, exceptions being made for Victor Emmanuel
II (King of Sardinia-Piedmont from 1849, King of Italy from
March 1861) and the exiled Czartoryski of Poland (b. 1770,
d. 1861), both of whom he respected as leaders committed to
their people's good. Pride of place among villains is given to
the English Georges:[39]

Georgius IV
Heic. jacet,
Qui. ubique. et. semper. jacebat
Familiae. pessimae. homo. pessimus
Georgius. Britanniae. Rex. ejus. nominis. IV
Arca. ut. decet. ampla. et. opipare. ornata. est
Continet. enim. omnes. Nerones.

(George IV

Here sleeps the man who, while he was alive, consistently slept everywhere. The rotten offspring of a rotten family, George, King of England, the fourth of that name. It is right that the sepulchre should be large and sumptuously decorated, it contains a whole family of Neros.)

Of all the political struggles Landor espoused in his long life, the nearest to his heart was that of Italy. It is noticeable that when he returned there as a very old man in 1858 the political content of his next (and last) volume of poems was much higher than in previous years. In Italy he had a close view of the struggle between a people bent on liberty and unity, and the reactionary forces grouped round various small monarchies and the papacy. The latter was constantly under attack by Italian nationalists as one of the instruments through which Austria maintained its domination over the peninsula, and Landor was consistently and violently anti-clerical. He saw superstition as the handmaid of tyranny, the one perpetrated by priests and the other by kings and tyrants in a gross conspiracy to dupe and subdue the people. Thus when Napoleon III betrayed Italy to Austria in 1859 by the treaty of Villafranca Landor was swift to align him with Pius IX's right-hand man, Cardinal Antonelli:[40]

Si mendacia mane vesperique
Discit Napoleo, atque voce clara
Cuncta edicta refert, stupere noli;
Antonellius huic fuit magister.

(If, day and night, Napoleon learns new lies, and can go back on all his earlier agreements unashamedly, do not be surprised. Antonelli was his teacher.)

Pius IX himself, originally the liberal pope, had greatly dis-
illusioned Landor by the reactionary policies he adopted after
the political upheavals of 1848. In 1847 Landor had dedicated
to him his English volume, *Hellenics,* and *Poemata et Inscriptiones* in the same year contained a poem in his honour.[41] In
1863, however, he appeared in a different light:[42]

> Exul eris, fraudesque tuae caedesque patescent . . .
>   Vive Dei oblitus; non erit ille tui.

(The day will come when you will be an exile. Your murder
and treachery will be brought to light. Continue to forget
God. He will not forget you.)

The political role of the poet is as often directly discussed as
implied in Landor's poetry:[43]

> Reges, impia turba, non timetis
> Vel ferro violare literatos?
> At quum Corsus adesset, in latebras
> Ceu damae pede vos cito tulistis:
> Hi fortem populum suum vocabant
> Ut vos eruerent pavore hiantes,
> Vestrisque oribus hi probe inserebant
> Verba ardentia bellici laconis.

(Listen kings, you ungodly rabble, are you not afraid even
to threaten with the sword your men of letters? Remember, when Napoleon came from Corsica, you took to your
hiding places with the swiftness of the mountain deer.
These men banded together to rout you out, as you shook
with fear, and then they fitly put into your mouths the
fiery words of Spartan battle.)

He frequently decries the ill-treatment of poets and philosophers by tyrannical rulers, but, like Horace, has confidence
in the durability of literary fame:[44]

> Longa regibus est manus, poetis
> Multo longior

(Great is the power of the king, but the poet's is greater)

Landor had his own problems with the state authorities. For

instance, in 1820 the censor at Pisa deleted three passages from the *Idyllia Heroica Decem*. A few copies are extant which contain a supplementary leaf with the censored sections: a poem denouncing Florence's niggardly treatment of Dante, and his memory,[45] a passage of tribute to Alfieri, Italian tragedian and nationalist, and a passage praising Cardinal Consalvi (of the liberal days of the papacy) at the expense of other Italian statesmen. To this Landor added a malediction of Pressiner, the censor. At no time did his relationship with the Tuscan government and its officials even approach cordiality.

In his letter to *The Times* concerning Orsini and tyrannicide (17 March 1858) Landor had stated, 'I detest and abominate democracy, the destroyer of republics.' Inseparable from his concept of the people was his conviction of their need for a leader, without whom, on occasion, they might either be inert and gullible, or senselessly violent. The greater part of the population of Italy, for instance, in the first part of the nineteenth century seemed almost complacent under Austrian rule. Landor spent many years exhorting and decrying the people by turns:[46]

> Vobis nil reliquum est boni malive,
> Rursum Insubribus in jugum redactis,
> Praeter flere patique! Restat unum,
> Quod non annumerare vis: mereri.

(Now that you Milanese have been subjugated once more, you say there is nothing left, either good or bad, except to weep and endure. There is one thing left, though you do not wish to admit it: to deserve it.)

Landor finally greeted the appearance of Garibaldi with the enthusiasm he had also shown to Bonaparte, Riego of Spain, Kossuth of Hungary, and the other charismatic leaders of his day:[47]

> Unus homo Romae cunctando restituit Rem;
> Restituet non cunctando (deus adjuvet!) alter.

(One man [Fabius], by delaying, saved the Roman state. Now, with God's help, may another save it once more without any delay.)

And behind each of his heroes he saw the shadow of Cromwell:[48]

> Te victimis assuetus humanis Iber,
> Te Gallus, omne cui sacrum est ludibrio,
> Expavit: ipso ex funere erepta face
> Per Galliam tua umbra perque Iberiam
> Se sustulit, per ultima Alpium juga,
> Pietatis ultrix.

(It was you [Cromwell] who struck terror into the heart of the Spaniard, hardened as he is to human sacrifice, and into the heart of the Frenchman, though he holds all things sacred in derision. Your spirit moved through France and Spain bearing the torch snatched from your funeral pyre. The champion of righteousness and liberty, it crossed the very furthest Alps.)

Napoleon Bonaparte, like Cromwell, had started his ascent to power as a military leader. Having gained control of the state, his objectives proved quite different. Landor had originally seen him, in the light of the American War of Independence, as another George Washington, his earliest republican hero. As it became obvious that the liberator of the French people was aspiring to become emperor, Landor was outraged. In 1800 he published anonymously a booklet entitled *Iambi, Primi ad Moraeum de Cambacerio et Bonaparta. Posteriores ad Cambacerium Cos, Subjiciuntur Quaedam Alia.* Invoking in his preface Catullus' treatment of Caesar and Mamurra as a precedent Landor attacked Napoleon and Cambacérès violently, transferring his allegiance to the new republican hope, General Moreau:[49]

> Valeat furentis vetula moecha Barrasi:
> Valeatque qui buxeta cuncta Corsicae
> Adusto in ore, in aestuante fert sinu
> Venena cuncta (scit Canopus) Colchidos.
> At tu, Moraee, si sapis, redi domum.
> Sortem haud iniquam praestitere dii tibi:
> Haud contigerunt omnibus, Germanice,
> Pudica conjux et verecundi lares.

(Let the aged whore of debauched Barras enjoy her glory. [Barras was Captain Bonaparte's colleague when he organized the defence of Toulon. He arranged Napoleon's marriage to his own cast-off mistress, Josephine de Beauharnais.] And let him flourish too, who carries the box plantations of Corsica in his scorched face, and all the poisons of Colchis in his seething grip – as Canopus knows. [Canopus: a town near Napoleon's base in Egypt, Alexandria. It was named after the pilot of the vessel of Menelaus, who died on the coast of Egypt from a snake bite. After the Egyptian Campaign Napoleon was accused of ordering lethal doses of opium for sick troops who could not be transported.] But you, Moreau, would be wise to return home. It is not a hard lot that the gods have prepared for you, O Conqueror of Germany. Not everyone can claim a faithful wife and a modest hearth.)

At the end of his life, Landor regarded Napoleon III as a similar combination of might, shrewdness and corruption, and finally came to the conclusion that the French had the government they deserved.

If some of the attacks in Landor's English poems are dangerously near the mark, he allows himself even greater freedoms in his Latin verse. It was a trait that Byron noticed and pointed out in a note to Canto 2 of 'The Island', June 1823: 'It is to Mr Landor, the author of "Gebir", so qualified, and of some Latin poems, which vie with Catullus or Martial in obscenity, that the immaculate Mr Southey addresses his declamation against impurity.' The virulence of Landor's attacks on Bonaparte is echoed in many other poems whose subjects range from the English statesmen of his day, and the behaviour of Caroline, Princess of Wales, in Italy ('Rufa in Novo Como') to his own private enemies. Prominent among these are various literary critics and rivals, and the lawyers of Llanthony. The stormy course of events at his estate in Wales had left Landor very bitter towards the Welsh nation as a whole and the legal profession in particular. 'The laws of England are made entirely for the protection of guilt,'[50] he wrote to Southey, and he set his opinion out in verse too:[51]

> Est noxa nulla praeter innocentiam,
> Tutisque vivitur omnibus praeter probos.

(Nothing is criminal except innocence, and, provided you are not honest, you can get by very well.)

Most of these more private poems are an uneasy mixture of personal attack and a more public declamatory style. When, however, he abandons impassioned factual accusations, Landor produces good caricatures, some of the best satire being at the expense of various Italian nationals. But he is most devastating when he holds both his fury and his distance and assumes his public voice:[52]

Eldon

Officiosus. erga. omnes. potentes. praeter. deum
Quem. satis. ei. erat. adjurare
Criminibus. capitalibus. quorum. numerus
Opprobrio. fuit. legibus. gentique. plura. subtexuit
Aureorum. decies. centena. millia
Litibus. audiendis. acquisivit.

(Eldon

Obsequious to all who wielded power, except God, by whom he was content to swear, the number of offences he made punishable by death was shameful. Some measures were taken against crime, but more against the people. He made a million pounds by hearing lawsuits.)

The Earl of Eldon, Lord Chancellor almost continuously from 1801 till 1827, was an enemy of the new radicalism and the initiator of many repressive policies. Another of Landor's political enemies, George Canning, is dealt with in a similar fashion.[53] Landor not only despised his politics, but his literary abilities as well. Canning, in fact, rivalled Landor in the ease and frequency with which he could produce topical verse, both Latin and English.

Death was not necessarily a prerequisite for an epitaph from Landor, who considered the desirability of certain people's decease to be in itself sufficient. In the *Poemata et Inscriptiones* of 1847 the 'Inscriptiones' themselves follow on three sections of occasional poems entitled 'Hendecasyllabi', 'Iambi' and 'Minora varia'. While these latter divisions may seem on occasion somewhat arbitrarily chosen, the 'Inscriptiones' do form a quite distinctive group. They are formal epitaphs, each one set out as if for engraving on a memorial plaque or tombstone. Those for George IV and Eldon have already been quoted. The 'Inscriptiones' reveal themselves as well suited to political attack, the finality of the epitaph lending authority to the terse, epigrammatic statement of facts. Moreover, they could be used in quite a different vein. There is, for instance, in this collection, a warm memorial to General Pasquale di Paoli, the Corsican patriot whom Boswell had visited in 1765,[54] and there are several more intimate epitaphs for Landor's own friends. In yet other poems the element of attack, while it may be present, is of secondary importance. In the *Imaginary Conversations* of 1824 (vol. 2), appended to the conversation of General Lacy and Cura Merino, are several 'Inscriptiones' in Latin on the restoration of Ferdinand VII of Spain to absolute power, at the bidding of the Holy Alliance. The revolutionaries who had effected three years of comparative freedom in Spain were hunted down in their hundreds, among them, General Riego. The poems of 1824 were reprinted among the 'Inscriptiones' of 1847. Among them, at least one is reminiscent of Simonides and the heroes of Thermopylae:[55]

Super Milites Hispanos regio jussu Interemtos
Viator
Ossa. quae. calcas
Regis. Fernandi. jussu
Fracta. tormentis. erant
Pro. parentibus. et. liberis
Pro. aris. et. focis
Pro. legibus. et. rege. pugnavimus
Lubenter. quiesceremus, libertate. parta
Amissa. precator. quiescamus.

(*For the Spanish soldiers executed by the order of the king*
Traveller, the bones on which you tread were broken by torture at the command of King Ferdinand. We were fighting for our parents and our children, for our homes and our household gods, for our constitution and our king. We would gladly have rested with the birth of liberty. Having lost her, pray let us rest anyway.)

The 'Inscriptiones' of 1847 are set out as formal epitaphs, but informal verse memorials, both intimate and public, will be found right through Landor's work. Some of these are satirical. There is, for instance, a short poem in mock-heroic style on the

death of the 'warrior of Walcheren', the second Earl of Chat-
ham, whose expedition in 1809 to destroy Napoleon's arsenal
and fleet ended in disaster.[56] Others are poems of tribute.
Whatever the tone adopted, Landor is most successful when he
maintains it in simplicity. This is why the epitaphs in particular
are good. In the following poem, not an epitaph this time, it is
his personal enthusiasm for Arndt, the German poet and
patriot whom he met in Bonn in 1832,[57] that inspires both his
politics and his poetry, and gives unity to the poem:[58]

Ad Arnetium, Poetam Praeclarum

Qui liberasti Gallicis latronibus,
 O Arneti, Germaniam,
Regesque turpi contremiscentes metu
 Tuo excitasti spiritu,
Ferrumque conflasti ingeni magni ignibus,
 Iners fodinis Noricis,
Resurge! reges vulneratorum latus
 Calcant suorum militum,
Et liberam vetant domum ingredi quibus
 Ipsi fuere liberi.
Olim stetisti, armatus unica lyra,
 Potentibus potentior:
Smintheus Apollo diriget rursus manum
 Contra minores bestias.
Quid expulisse rure pantheram juvat
 Mox devorandos muribus?

(To Arndt, a Great Poet

(Arndt, thou who liberated Germany from French thieves,
and who roused kings, erstwhile trembling with shameful
cowardice, by thy powerful spirit. Thou who drew the lifeless metal from the mines of Bavaria and forged in the fires
a weapon of great strength. Rise up once more! These
kings trample on their own wounded troops and refuse
their rightful home to the sons of free-born men. Once
you stood, armed only with a lyre, mightier than the
mighty. May Smintheus Apollo raise his hand once more
against these lesser animals. What good is it, to have rid
the countryside of the panther, if the inhabitants are soon
to be devoured by mice?)

The image with which Landor closes the last poem is interest-ing on two counts. Firstly, it is an obscure allusion of the kind in which his poetry abounds: Smintheus was one of the surnames of Apollo in Phrygia, where he had destroyed a number of mice that infested the countryside. Secondly, and more important, the use of an image, usually drawn from the animal and natural worlds, to clinch the point of a poem, is a characteristic of Landor's poetry even in poems which are not ostensibly epi-grams. It is particularly characteristic of his polemic, whether aimed at public or private enemies. In the following poem he incorporates with the animal images a pun on 'leo' and 'Napoleon':[59]

De Napoleone et Strasoldo

Icit Napoleo; esurit Strasoldus;
Quis prudens apibusque fructibusque
Ursum non timeat supra leonem?
O vafri domini! O dolus facetus!
Misistis scelerum huc scelus supremum
Ut vobis, ubi veneritis, esset
Saltem unus popularis haustus aurae.

(Concerning Napoleon and Strasoldo

[Landor compares the rule of Napoleon in North Italy with the later Austrian regime, and in particular mentions Strasoldo the Austrian appointed governor in Como in 1818.] When Napoleon strikes, Strasoldo goes hungry. What wise owner of beehives and fruit trees does not fear the bear more than the lion? Crafty lords! Cunning trick! You have sent on this most rascally of scoundrels ahead of you, so that when you arrive you would receive at least one round of applause.)

These images are sometimes confined to one line, and are sometimes presented as full-length fables. Sometimes they are salacious or scurrilous and sometimes they are simple, as this image of peace returned to Italy;[60]

Tandem inter haec arbusta solae
Lusciniae merulaeque certent!

(Finally the only contest in these groves will be between the nightingales and the blackbirds.)

Here the image, though traditional, is far removed from any hidden mythological or allegorical significance. Among the political poems there are several such lyrical descriptions of the Golden Age returning to the liberated countryside. These poems often contain personifications of justice, plenty and liberty. Where the personifications are extended there is generally some tension. 'Liberty' and 'justice', even in the guise of the goddess Astraea, are less convincing figures in an evocation of modern Italy than the more factual account of the Princess Belgiojoso leaving her beautiful home near Como to man barricades and direct military hospitals at the siege of Rome in 1849 (Landor wrote an English version of this poem):[61]

> Trivultiorum filia nobilis!
> Nuper benigno lumine Larium
> Lustrans, reliquisti paternae
> De proavis ditionis Alpes, . . .
> En! vulneratis illam adhibes manum
> Quam gloria esset tangere regibus,
> Nec dentium stridorem acutum
> Nec saniem refugis nigrantem.[62]

(Noble daughter of the Trivulzi! A short time ago you bathed Como in a blessed light. Now you have left the Alpine heights, the lands governed by your fathers. . . . See! you rest your hand on the wounded, that hand it were an honour for kings to touch. You do not shun the gnashing of teeth and the dark blood.)

Fables, epigrams, personifications and *sententiae* all suggest the predominantly didactic manner of Landor's political writings. Similarly, his sense of history was of a succession of personages exemplifying by their actions certain unchanging principles. To this view nothing alters except the characters, which is why Gustavus Adolphus (Landor's anti-Austrian hero of the Thirty Years' War), Cromwell, and the kings of modern Europe can all stand side by side in one poem,[63] and why Joan of Arc ('Virginem Aurelianensem') and Charlotte Corday ('Cordata') can provide inspiration for modern generations. Landor sought a personal exemplar in his own pedigree: through his mother's side he traced his ancestry, somewhat tenuously, back to a certain Sir Arnold Savage who, in the

reign of Henry IV, had asserted the financial independence of
the Commons by insisting that the king should redress griev-
ances before Parliament grant him any money:[64]

> Parietibus pictis, populo quos curia monstrat
> Nescio quot proceres obtinuere locum.
> At tibi nulla datur sedes, Arnolde Savagi,
> Quo sine nulla esset curia: fortis eras;
> Fortis eras sapiensque, et (territus ante) senatus
> Praeside te vires sumpsit, erantque tuae.
> Solus nempe audax audacemque ante tyrannum
> Fatus es, adsurgens, ista silente domo.
> 'Voce loquor populi: dum jura infecta manere
> Tu sinis, haud aeris subsidia ulla dabit.'

(On its walls the chamber records for the nation the images
of former members of the House. But no place is given to
you, Arnold Savage, without whom there would have been
no House. You were brave, brave and wise. With you as
their leader the terrified Commons drew on your strength
and took fresh heart. For you alone were bold enough to
face a bold tyrant. Rising up in the silent chamber you
announced: 'I speak with the voice of the people. While
you allow laws to stand unenforced, they will give you no
money.')

More disinterested are two sketches, one of Hannibal and one
of Brutus, that attest simply to Landor's lively imagination and
appreciation for antiquity. Both are cast as short, dramatic
scenes: Hannibal dreaming of the oath sworn to his father
against Rome, and Brutus facing Caesar's ghost before
Philippi.[65] They provide an interesting gloss on the dramatic
ability displayed in Landor's *Imaginary Conversations*.

Finally it is in Italy that Landor's feeling for a people and
their culture, both ancient and modern, is most fully integrated
with his political idealism:[66]

Ad Mantuam

> Quod cunas dederis O Mantua clara Maroni,
> Semper erit merito gloria prima tibi.
> Quod lethum dederis Hofero, latrone jubente,
> Heu nimium cedit gloria dedecori.

(*To Mantua*

You were the cradle of Vergil, bright Mantua, and that will always rightfully be your chief glory. But you also put Hofer to death at the orders of a brigand and so, alas, your glory must greatly yield to shame.)

Hofer, the Tyrolese patriot shot by the Austrians at the direct order of Napoleon Bonaparte, stands in Mantua alongside Vergil. Charles Borromeo still watches over Milan, though now it is occupied by the Austrian Whitecoats. In Florence, where Milton visited Galileo, Landor's heroes, Dante, Savonarola and Alfieri watch Garibaldi and Manin and the patriots as the new Italy is born.

III The personal poems

If Landor's urbanity expressed itself most often in polemic or satire, it did, nonetheless, have its gentler aspects. His power to fashion a warm and graceful compliment without abandoning simplicity is remarkable. His attentions are marked by an appealing courtesy and lightheartedness that can transform even the most occasional of poems. In 1826, for instance, on a visit to Naples, Landor met Sir William Gell, the classical archaeologist. Later he published a poem addressed to Sir William which, after a lyrical description of the return of spring to the Italian countryside, afforded a glimpse of the famous scholar mixing business with pleasure:[67]

> Tu prope Parthenopen tua, jucundissime Gelli,
> Ebrius agricolae sincero melle Maronis,
> Sub patula fago aut tiliae fragrante susurro
> Aut ulmo aut platano, felicia somnia fingis
> De Laestrygonibus, Cyclopibus, atque Pelasgis.
> His tibi perdomitis, calcatis arcibus exi;
> Respirare licet strataque quiescere lauro:
> Solerti posthac studio expectare licebit
> Quicquid Cecropidis comoedia prisca leporum
> Exhibuit.

(Not far from your own dear Naples, my charming Gell, you rest, intoxicated by the undiluted honey of farmer Vergil's *Georgics*, lying under the spreading beech tree, or the lime with its fragrant whisper, or the elm, or the plane tree. Here you spin happy dreams of the Laestrygonians, the Cyclops, and the Pelasgians. You have conquered them all. Now come out from their ruined citadels. Allow yourself to draw breath, and relax upon the strewn laurels. Later on you can enquire with your shrewd insight into the wit of ancient Greek comedy.)

Such poems knowingly recall the spirit of camaraderie and witty erudition that distinguished Catullus and his circle. Landor admitted himself and his friends into this élite and took it upon himself to continue the tradition. The memory of his sojourn in Como (1816–18) remained throughout his life both a source of pleasure and poetry. It was his villa at Fiesole, however, which evoked his very best attempt at Catullan playfulness, albeit in the form of an Horatian ode:[68]

> O villa laetis undique collibus
> Stipata! turri quis minio latus
>   Sic decoloravit flagrante,
>   Quis viridi tibi peste frontem?
> Alecis (aiunt) venditor improbus
> In immerentes opprobrium intulit,
>   Nec tale passas dum penates
>   Nobilior dominus colebat.
> Atqui per istos perque alios deos
> Te testor! aegrae, villula, dedecus
>   (Si qua est mihi virtus) levabo,
>   Restituens speciem priorem.
> Id mox agendum: tu modo (nam sumus
> Soli, nec uxor nec puer audiet)
>   Dic Africi insanos amores,
>   Mensola quem pudibunda fugit;
> Unde ille, saxo vinctus, iter grave
> Nec qua solebat ducere cogitur,
>   Dum Nympha per canum salictum
>   Populeasque vagatur umbras.
> Te scire certum est; nempe super lacum
> Stetisse, in herbisque ire palustribus
>   Vidisse praedonem, represso
>   Jam pede, jam celeri sequentem.

Referre si vis facta, refer cito;
Tu permanebis plurima saecula
Sylvasque subter Faesulanas
Multa, negata mihi, videbis.
Ut sint fugaces te nihil attinet
Horae; mihi harum Fata fugacium
Paucas reservarunt, sedenti
Qua profugum petit amnis amnem.

(My house, circled closely by the happy hills! Who has so
discoloured the side of your tower with bright red paint,
and your façade with this horrible green? They say he
was a rascally fishmonger who bore a senseless grudge
against the household gods. They had not suffered any
such indignity when in the care of a more noble master.
By these, and by all the other gods, I swear to you, my
little house – if I can claim any strength – to remove this
sorrowful shame and to restore your former appearance.
This will soon be done, in return you need only tell the
story of Africus' wild love – for we are alone, neither wife
nor child may overhear – and how the modest Mensola
fled from him. Weighted down then by a heavy stone
he was constrained to set forth on a solemn and unac-
customed journey, while the Nymph wandered through
the poplar shades and the foam-flecked willows. That you
know is certain, for you stood looking out over the lake,
you saw the thief creep through the marshy grass, now
stopping, now pursuing swiftly. Tell me how it happened,
if you will, and tell me soon, for you will remain many
centuries in the shade of the forests of Fiesole, and you
will see many sights denied to me. The fleeting hours are
of no concern to you, but Fate has left very few of them to
me, sitting here, where one rivulet chases, and the other
seeks to escape.)

John Forster records of the Villa Gherardesca: 'The valley
of the Ladies was in his [Landor's] grounds; the Affrico and
the Mensola [the metamorphosed lovers in Boccaccio's *Ninfale
Fiesolano*] ran through them; above was the ivy-clad con-
vent of the Doccia overhung with cypress; and from his
iron entrance gate might be seen Valdarno and Vallombrosa.'[69]

Landor's delight in these associations is well conveyed by his poem. The house is addressed affectionately as an animate being and the gods are invoked with a mock solemnity reminiscent of 'Phaselus ille'. The legend of the Nymph of Fiesole recalls Ovid as well as Boccaccio and is introduced with a suitable lightness of touch ('nec uxor nec puer audiet'). Finally both address and legend fade imperceptibly into a recollection of the advance of years upon the author, and we are left with Landor in a typically statuesque pose, on this occasion not overstated and well in balance with the rest of the poem.

This well-informed playfulness extended too into literary discussions and erudite puns. Francis Hare, the eloquent friend of his days in Florence, was nicknamed Lagöe, a reference not only to the Greek 'lagos' but to the Latin 'lepus' (hare), very similar to 'lepos' or 'wit'. 'Lepos', a prerequisite of the Catullan school, was something that not all poets were fortunate enough to possess:[70]

> Tentare rursus, O Lagöe, me jubes
> Thebaida; cur haec perpeti coegeris
> Crudeliora quam Thebe patrata erant?

(You order me to try the *Thebaid* again, Lagöe. Why do you force me to suffer cruelties worse than Thebes itself endured?)

Elsewhere we find Landor's old schoolfriend Walter Birch enjoying with Reginald Heber the vigour of Landor's attack on the Llanthony lawyers.[71] Several such incidents involving Landor's friends and their literary pursuits are recorded throughout the poems.

Many different shades of formality and intimacy will be found in Landor's poetry, and all are maintained by a precise, though not a chilling or inflexible, sense of decorum. An almost reverent tone is adopted towards distinguished contemporaries, but this is always quickened by a genuine enthusiasm for achievement. Several such eulogies are inspired by personal anecdote. There was, for instance, the occasion on which Landor passed through Lucca without realizing that Sismondi, the historian, was living there. This caused him much regret:[72]

> Sismonde, laetas Pisciae valles equis
> Raptus quaternis praeteribam, nescius
> Ibi esse solum cui darem dextram virum
> Quot pinguem Etruriam incolunt: sortem dole
> Sismonde, vatis qui dolere sat nequit.

(Sismondi, I sped straight past the happy vales of Pescai, drawn in my four-horse carriage. I did not know there lived there the one man, of all those dwelling on rich Etruscan soil, with whom I would have shaken hands. Grieve, Sismondi, for the bad luck of this poet, who cannot grieve enough.)

Again, when Hans Andersen toured England in June 1847 Landor stopped his *Poemata et Inscriptiones*, as it went to press, to include this compliment at the end of the section entitled 'Iambics':[73]

> Jam lineis in hos iambos inditis
>   Virgata quaeque pagina est,
> Tamen morari prelum agentes obsecro,
>   Ut ingeni clari viro,
> Qui me cubantem tres dies gravedine
>   Refecit optimo libro,
> Servent honoris gratia paulum loci
>   (Quanquam situ sit ultimo)
> *Andersini*, per Italos et Atticos
>   Viam secuto floream.

(Now each page lined with these iambics is ready for the press, I beg the printers, however, to delay a moment. I want them to reserve a small place of honour (although it is at the end of the section) for a noble and illustrious man, who revived me with his wonderful book after I had been in bed with a cold for three days; a place for Andersen, who has followed a flower-strewn path through Italy and Greece.)

Hans Andersen's tour was a great success, and he was seen off from Ramsgate pier by Charles Dickens. Meanwhile Landor must have been, as always, unpopular with the printer for his last-minute alterations.[74]

Of Landor's more intimate poems, the later ones concerning 'Ianthe', Jane Sophia Swift, have with justice always been the most admired. But there are earlier more rhetorical poems addressed to his brother, Robert, and to his friend, Southey, that contain the raw material of youthful ambition and idealism. The reflective tone of these poems distinguishes them immediately from the witty, direct addresses to the Anglo-Italian literati. Nor had Landor yet learned to express the totality of his innermost feelings in a four-line epigram. 'Ad Robertum Fratrem' of 1806[75] runs to over a hundred lines. After exhorting his brother to prepare himself for the struggle against France, he pictures their life of Horatian calm in the days of victory. He goes on to attack Canning and to praise 'Bobus' Smith. Finally, he pictures the fame of the brothers Landor in the years to come:[76]

> Hoc nostrum est; uni volvenda pepercerit aetas.
> Omnia sub numero sunt interitura dierum,
> Ut brevis iste lacus, modo qui pluvialibus austris
> Natus erat, flectique infra non palluit herba,
> Illicet autumni foliis operitur, obitque.
> Sed manet ingenium: quid nobilium atque potentum
> Sollicitemus opem?

(This is what fate offers us. Together we will be spared throughout the circling of one great age. All sublunary things must be buried in the passage of days. So with this short-lived lake, which just now has been born of the rainy east wind; beneath it the grass has not paled, the leaves of autumn cover it, it dies. But genius endures. What work of nobility or strength may we undertake?)

'Curious that great men should so run in pairs,' he once commented. 'Will they ever talk of the two Landors, myself and Robert?'[77] The military and literary achievements of other brothers never passed unnoticed and they provided the themes of several later poems.

The early poem 'Ad Fratrem' is one of Landor's most grandiloquent, and draws heavily upon Vergil and Horace to lend solemnity to the occasion. In a poem written in 1815 to Southey retrospect has already taken over from youthful anticipation and is suitably expressed in elegiac couplets. This was the metre in which Landor was at his most lucid and in which the more intimate poems of his old age were written. In the following extracts he has told his friend not to ask for more verses. Youth and poetry have both escaped him. He contrasts the onset of old age with the gentle progress of autumn:[78]

> Aurea lux, radios properanti condere, Soli est,
>   Suavis odor tiliae cui folia aura rotat;
> Et juvat in sylvas, si quid juvat, ire sonantes,
>   Inque fugam versas rore cadente feras.
> Tempore non alio est quam tali mitior annus,
>   Cur aliter claudat languida vita diem?

(The light of the sun is golden as it hurries to bury its beams. The scent of the lime tree is sweet as it turns its leaves to the breeze. It is a relief, if anything can be a relief, to walk in the whispering woods, the wild animals put to flight in the falling dew. No other time of year is so mellow, why should feeble life close its day so differently?)

This lament re-echoes throughout Landor's poems. The thought was remodelled in the first verse of an English poem to Ianthe:[79]

> Mild is the parting year, and sweet
>   The odour of the falling spray;
> Life passes on more rudely fleet,
>   And balmless is its closing day.

Most of Landor's poems to Southey are in the nature of epistles. Sometimes, as in the poem just quoted, he takes the opportunity to reflect on his own situation, generally with sad relish. There is a poem offering consolation on the death of Southey's son,[80] and another lamenting a prolonged silence on Southey's part.[81] On one occasion in particular he enthusiastically praises Southey's epic, *Joan of Arc*, which, he claims, will expiate the criminal behaviour of the English towards one of his favourite heroines.[82] Everywhere Landor's warm admiration for his friend's ability is eloquently expressed. Perhaps this is the more so because of the scathing criticisms to which Southey was subjected from various quarters and which Landor took personally. His gratitude for his friend's

encouragement at the outset of his literary career lived on
after Southey's death and was concisely expressed by Landor
as an old man:[83]

> Laudare quae calens juventa scripseram
> Primus fuisti, forsitan neque ultimus,
> Utcunque id est, haec pauca parvaque accipe
> Lantonianis involuta nubibus
> Quae dissipaveris benigno lumine.

(You were the first to praise the eager verses of my youth,
and perhaps you were not the last. Be that as it may,
accept these few small efforts, shrouded in the mists of
Llanthony, which once dispersed before your generous
light.)

Landor retained a great affection for all the places in which
he had lived, especially as a child, and he had many home
thoughts from abroad. He wanted his children, born in Italy,
to see England.[84] In the following poem he recalls the river
Arrow that ran near the family estate in Ipsley, Warwickshire:[85]

> Fluviorum trepidantum
> Nova percurrere regna,
> Adeuntumque cubile
> Panopes Cymodocesque
> Neque visus mihi quisquam
> Neque regnantibus undas
> (Fateantur modo verum)
> Alius pulchrior, Arro!
> Ubi qualisque revisam
> Tua jucunda fluenta?

(Of all the shimmering rivers that run through far-off
lands and out into the haunts of the Nereids and sea
nymphs, I have seen none so beautiful as you, my river
Arrow, and neither have the deities of the waves – in
confessing this they speak only the truth. When and how
shall I see once more your laughing waters?)

As it happened, the return to England was sudden, and in
unhappy circumstances. In 1835 Landor, already sixty years
old, with twenty-four years of marriage behind him, separated

from his wife. Retaining for himself only enough money on which to live modestly, he travelled to England, without his children. When he returned to Florence twenty-three years later, once more an exile from England on account of a law-suit, he was treated with a singular lack of kindness by his family. The attitude of his children, in particular, upset him deeply. So, he walked out again, only this time he was eighty-three and penniless. It was the Brownings who came to the rescue and looked after him for the last five years of his life.

Given these circumstances, the bitterness of several of the poems of Landor's old age is understandable. The libel suit brought against him by Mrs Yescombe of Bath was a particu-larly scandalous affair,[86] and the eagerness with which his political opponents sprang to attack him makes unpleasant reading even today. The Latin poems, besides bitter and specific polemic against the people who had caused his mis-fortunes, include several epigrams on the scarcity of honesty and justice amongst men, and on the prevalence of envy, with its desire to harm a man of good repute:[87]

> Persequitur mala Fama bonam, mox calcibus instat,
>   Denique sub pedibus candida palla jacet.

(Evil repute is swift to follow on good, and to overtake it, so that at last its white robe lies trodden under foot.)

These poems, however, are surprisingly few, and the eloquent pride that had typified all his earlier works is still very much in evidence. A good example of the tone is found in the volume of 1858:[88]

> *Gloriae Contemptor*
> Qui gloriam se praedicat contemnere,
> Solusque truxque more rustici domo
> Suapte delitescit, ille fallitur:
> Sorex eadem glorietur gloria.
> Nomen futurum est unico magni viri
> Qui gloriam, sed nactus, aspernatus est.

> (*The Man Contemptuous of Fame*
> That man is deceiving himself who claims that he despises fame, that he is a hermit and an ascetic, best suited to

life in a rustic hideaway. The very field-mouse may glory in fame of that kind. The title is reserved only for the truly great man who, having already achieved fame, chooses to turn his back on it.)

The same sentiment is expressed in the Imaginary Conversation between Cicero and his brother: 'Glory can be safely despised by those only who have fairly won it: a low, ignorant, or vicious man should dispute on other topics.'[89]

Landor's return to England in the early 1830s had been considerably brightened by his friendship with Rose Paynter. Rose and Sophie were daughters of Mrs Paynter, the half-sister of Rose Aylmer, whose death in 1800 had inspired Landor's most famous English poem, 'Ah what avails the sceptred race'.[90] As Super remarks, 'no laureate ever served royalty better than Landor served the younger Rose and her family. Her birthday, the nineteenth of January, became a saint's day on his calendar.'[91] Several birthday verses, and others commemorating Rose's painting, her travels, and finally, her children, will be found among the Latin poems. In the following one, the title contains a pun on 'suave-olens', 'sweet-smelling' and 'suaviolum', a 'little kiss':[92]

Daphne Suave-olens in Vase Fictili
Daphnen odoram quae tuis natalibus
    Florere gaudet, accipe.
Quamvis et imbres et nives Aquarii
    (Vides) reformidat parum,
At sedem in horto da, prope aedium fores,
    Apriciorem caeteris.
Flores favere parvulos haud dedecet,
    Utcunque vix aptos sinu:
Verum haud dolebunt illud infortunium
    Si, naribus quando applices
Calicem rubentum, laeta odore melleo,
    Possint labella tangere.

(Sweet-scented Daphne in an Earthen Pot
Please accept this sweet-smelling daphne which is happy to flower on your birthday. Although, as you see, it scarcely fears the rains and snows of January, give it a place in your garden more sunny than the rest, near the doorway

to the house. It is most becoming to fondle infant flowers, though not yet suited to the bosom. They will not lament their bad fortune, however, if, when you lift the blushing vase to your nose to enjoy the honeyed scent, they may touch your lips.)

Landor's most constant companion during this period, however, was Pomero, a small Italian dog who barked incessantly, went into ecstasies when he heard his native language being spoken, and quite frequently sat on the top of his master's bald head. Landor addressed several poems to him:[93]

> Veni, atque laudes accipe, Pomero,
> Quales mereris; quotquot enim canes
> Usquam fuerunt Transpadana
> Aut alia regione creti,
> Primum obtinebis tu merito locum . . .

(Approach and hear your praise, Pomero, which you have well deserved. For of all the dogs born beyond the Po, or in any other region, you will rightly hold pride of place.)

Landor was very fond of all animals and disapproved deeply of blood sports. He prided himself, especially, on the care he took of the aged horses on his Llanthony estate. He had not sold them off, but had provided generously for their retirement:[94]

> Nec trahere plaustra, nec media urbium via
> Quassare inanem ad os ligatum sacculum.

(They do not have to pull carts, or shake an empty nose-bag in the city streets.)

His love of animals was, in fact, one aspect of his sympathy for the whole of the natural world. His was not a vision of nature 'red in tooth and claw'. The 'Inscriptiones' include a reflection on the harmony of nature:[95]

> *In Domo Vapore Tepido pro Floribus Temperata*
> Hominum. satis. superq. multi. viderunt. Naturae. nemo
> Hospes. ingreditor
> Et. in. parvis. eam. ut. in. maximis. mirabilem
> Pio. animo. heic. et. ubique. contemplator.

(*In a Hot House of Flowers*

Many have seen as much and more than they care for
of man, no one of nature. Let the guest enter and contem-
plate with awe how wonderful she is, in small things as in
great, here, and everywhere.)

Landor's return to England in 1835 had heralded a period
of intense literary activity during which he produced much
of his finest English prose. Of his work in general he had once
remarked, 'Poetry was always my amusement, prose my study
and business.'[96] Landor was certainly an orator, and he carried
over into his poetry the rhetorical manner of his prose. This
is a distinguishing feature of the more topical poems. Read in
quantity they will be found to express an integral part of
Landor's thinking, though the prose has the advantage of
continuity and sustained striving after artistic effect on a
grand scale. T. S. Eliot has remarked on a comparable 'unity
of a very complicated kind' in the work of Rudyard Kipling:
'the significance of the "poems" would be lost [without] the
background of the "verse", just as the significance of the
verse is missed except in the context of the prose'.[97] Later on
in Landor's life the composition of lyrics, both English and
Latin, did assume relatively greater importance. By this time
he had refined his rhetoric to a point where he could produce
intimate personal poetry which was not necessarily, by the
same token, melodramatic. Early and late, his poetry is remarkable for its singular lack of *Angst*, and in this respect it can
again be compared with Kipling's.[98] In his later years Landor
underlined this detachment by his increasing simplicity of
style. The Ovidian couplet, a favourite metre in his earlier
poems, is used extensively once more, combined with the epigrammatic technique of the 'Inscriptiones'. Landor's themes are
progressively fewer, more distinct, and more intimate.

One theme that predominates is that of the approach of
old age. He anticipates the day when he will finally cease to
write, in a scene taken from his domestic routine:[99]

> Tandem laborum desino, neque amplius
>   Mea charta sub stylo crepat.
> Caenae, sodales, parva ut est, accumbite,
>   Ego interim dormitum eo.

(At last I abandon work, no more does my quill scratch
on the paper. Sit down to the meal, my friends, small
as it is. Meanwhile I will go to sleep.)

The image of dining with his friends was a favourite one with
Landor. In a different context, discussing his literary reputation, he had once claimed: 'I shall dine late, but the dining
room will be well lighted, the guests few and select.'[100] His
lost youth and old age are the protagonists in these verses.
The personifications are very well integrated:[101]

> Una, Senecta, viximus multos dies,
>   Una atque amice viximus:
> Quietiorem inveneris siquem locum,
>   Id dic in aure, tunc abi.

(We have lived together, Old Age, for a long time, and we
have lived together as friends. When you find some quieter
place, whisper it in my ear, and then depart.)

The first lines of this poem are translated at the beginning of
a longer English version: 'Welcome, old friend! These many
years/Have we lived door by door.'[102] There is a companion
poem, also translated, entitled 'Ad Juventam':[103]

> Revocare te, Juventa, nequaquam licet,
>   At sponte cum Somno redis;
> Quotiesque virga leniter papaveram
>   Spirante sopito adstitit
> Adstas et ipsa: tum labella, olim meis
>   Aptata, rident cominus:
> Signum silenter interim Somnus dedit
>   Et avolant ambo simul.

> I may not call thee back; but thou
>   Returnest, when the hand
> Of gentle Sleep waves o'er my brow
>   His poppycrested wand;

> Then smiling eyes bend over mine,
>   Then lips once prest invite;
> But sleep hath given a silent sign
>   And both, alas! take flight.[104]

It is hard here to separate the warmly conceived image of lost youth from Landor's memory of Ianthe. She, indeed, presides over a great many of the poems, even when not referred to by name.

Although Landor had early formed a Dickensian habit of writing impromptu epitaphs for himself[105] he in fact outlived most of his dearest friends by many years. While their deaths are often commemorated in his Latin and English lyric verse, there are few formal epitaphs actually intended for inscription on a monument. Landor seemed only to write such epitaphs on request, and even then he preferred to write them in English. However, he was prevailed upon to provide a Latin epitaph for the grave of a very close friend, Lady Blessington:

> Infra sepultum est id omne quod sepeliri potest
> mulieris quondam pulcherrimae.
> Ingenium suum summo studio coluit,
> aliorum pari adjuvit.
> Benefacta sua celare novit; ingenium non ita.
> Erga omneis erat larga bonitate;
> peregrinis eleganter hospitalis.
> Venit Lutetiam Parisiorum Aprili mense:
> quarto Junii die supremum suum obiit.
> [MDCCCXLIX]

A letter written to the *Athenaeum* in January 1850 to expose an unauthorized revision of the epitaph was republished in *Last Fruit Off an Old Tree* in 1853. It contained the revision, the original quoted above, and a translation:[106]

> *To the Memory of Marguerite, Countess of Blessington*
> Underneath is buried all that COULD be buried of a woman once most beautiful. She cultivated her genius with the greatest zeal, and fostered it in others with equal assiduity. The benefits she conferred she could conceal, her talents not. Elegant in her hospitality to strangers, charitable to all, she retired to Paris in April, and there she breathed her last on the 4th of June 1849.

He also discussed the genre as a whole:[107]

It may be thought superfluous to remark that epitaphs

have certain qualities in common; for instance, all are encomiastic. The main difference and the main difficulty lie in the expression, since nearly all people are placed on the same level in the epitaph as in the grave. Hence, out of eleven or twelve thousand Latin ones, ancient and modern, I find scarcely threescore in which there is originality or elegance. . . . Nothing is now left to be done but to bring forward, in due order and just proportions, the better peculiarities of character composing the features of the dead, and modulating the tones of grief.

By comparison with Lady Blessington's epitaph, Landor's published 'inscriptiones' of 1847 are more of a literary and political exercise, though a few references will be found to personal friends. There is, for instance, a memorial for Francis Hare.[108] More typical, however, is the epitaph written for Southey in English[109] while Landor records his grief and his memories of their friendship less formally in Latin verses.

It is in Landor's love poetry that one finds his most appealing elegies. As the satiric Martial could write the tenderest of epitaphs for a child, so the turbulent Landor was at his most gentle in the imagined presence of Ianthe, who had died in 1851:[110]

> Saepe meam dextram, neque erat rejecta, tetendi,
>   Ultro tu mihi da, sit mora nulla, tuam.

(Often have I offered you my hand, nor was it rejected. Now in your turn stretch out yours to me, and may there be no delay.)

Not all the poetry written for Ianthe, however, was in so serious a strain. Some verses recall the more playful moments of their brief romance in Bath:[111]

> Dura! cur iterum abruis sedile
> Quod junctis genubus tibi apparavi?
> Satisne esse putas prope adsedere
> Vel collo dare dexteram reclini?
> Me spes, ut levioribus, fefellit.
> At saltem liceat (grave invidenti)
> Saxum sternere molliore musco.

(Hard-hearted girl! Why do you rush away again from the seat I have prepared for you here on my knees? You think it enough to sit near me or rest your arm on my leaning shoulder? Hope has deceived me, as she has done less worthy fellows. But at least allow me – with very bad grace – to strew this stone seat with softer moss.)

Earlier poems contain more intense expostulation. There is a long poem of this kind, first published in 1815, which contains a plea later translated by Landor into English verse:[112]

Vita brevi est fugitura, prior fugitura venustas,
  Hoc saltem exiguo tempore duret amor!

Soon, O Ianthe! life is o'er,
  And sooner beauty's heavenly smile:
Grant only (and I ask no more),
  Let love remain that little while.[113]

The same volume contains a poem describing his journey to Spain in 1808. He explains that his sorrow is not caused by the leaving of friends or homeland:[114]

Dura puella meas exercuit unica curas,
  Illa mei spatium pectoris omne tenet;
Et quoniam mentem non verteret, ire coegit
  Quo vocat abreptus turbine Martis Iber.

(A hard-hearted girl is the sole cause of my misery. She occupies my heart entirely. Because she would not change her mind I am forced to go where Spain, torn in half [by civil war] is sounding the trumpets of battle.)

Landor comforted himself with the thought of her sorrow and remorse over his battle-scarred, lifeless body.

Other poems, less intense in tone, are addressed to a variety of young ladies with suitably classical names. These verses are generally playful and satirical by turn, for Landor derived considerable (literary) pleasure from petitioning obdurate maidens and from detailing the devious workings of the female mind. Catullus, Horace, and Ovid are all recalled, and Petrarch too, but to these Landor adds a humour of his own:[115]

Expectans ego te diem per omnem
Heic sedi, miser, aut steti, Coroni!
Aut, vertens celerem gradum, ambulavi,
Et spinae folia ultimasque frondes
Discerpsi unguibus improbe inquietis,
Interque otia dentibus momordi
Siccis, atque siti aspero palato.
'Sit vobis male, pessimae volucres,'
Dixi, nam trepidus pedes venire
Frustra credideram tuos . . .

(I have been standing and sitting here waiting for you and feeling wretched all day, Coronis. I have paced swiftly up and down, picking off with my ruthless, restless fingernails the leaves and topmost sprigs of thorn bushes. Meanwhile I have consumed my leisure with a dried-out mouth and my palate harsh with thirst. 'May evil befall you, you wretched birds,' I cried out, because I had trembled for nothing, believing I heard your footsteps approach.)

He goes on to explain how he mistook the sound of the birds' flight for the approach of his mistress's footsteps. Through all such interludes, however, Ianthe remained his constant muse. In later life his tone was never anything but reverently loving:[116]

Praeteritos annos revoco mihi pectore tristi,
   Quos prius haud sineres triste manere diu.
Mortua sis aliis, mihi non morieris, Ianthe!
   Hoc jurare jubet, dum sepeliris, Amor.

(I recall with a sad heart those bygone years which formerly you would not have allowed to remain sad for long. You may be dead for others, Ianthe, but for me you will never die. This, Love is glad to claim, as you go to your burial.)

He had intended the volume of 1858, *Dry Sticks*, to be his last, and right at the end he placed this dedication:[117]

Id satis est, placuisse tibi, te semper amasse;
   Si possim, haud alio nomine clarus ero.

(It is enough to have pleased you, to have loved you always.
If I might, I would have no other claim to fame.)

This modest statement is, however, most certainly belied
by the achievements of the last major English poet to write
in Latin, Walter Savage Landor.

Notes

1 W. B. Yeats, *Mythologies* (London, 1959), p. 328.
2 The standard modern biography of Landor is by R. H. Super,
   Walter Savage Landor. A Biography (New York, 1954). There is also
   Malcolm Elwin, *Landor. A Replevin* (London, 1958). The Victorian
   biography, in two volumes, was written by John Forster, *Walter
   Savage Landor, A Biography* (London, 1869). Much shorter is a very
   readable biographical and critical essay by Sidney Colvin, *Landor*
   (London, 1881).
3 For a detailed account of Landor's publishing history see R. H. Super,
   The Publication of Landor's Works (London, 1954), Supplement to the
   Bibliographical Society's *Transactions*, No. 18.
4 Forster, I, p. 114.
5 Landor made two translations of the Latin idylls. See *Hellenics*
   (London, 1847) and *Hellenics* (Edinburgh, 1859).
6 *Simonidea* (Bath, 1806), pp. 81–91. More accessible is a later edition
   (revised) in *Poemata et Inscriptiones* (London, 1847), pp. 4–10.
7 Landor, *Poetical Works*, ed. S. Wheeler, 3 vols (Oxford, 1937), II,
   pp. 203–10 (translation of 1847); pp. 528–35 (translation of 1859).
8 *Idyllia Nova Quinque Heroum atque Heroidum* (Oxford and London, 1815).
9 Leicester Bradner, *Musae Anglicanae* (New York and London, 1940),
   pp. 315–25. An assessment of Landor's Latin verse and his place in the
   Anglo-Latin tradition.
10 Only one of the Latin poems in this volume was ever reprinted, the
   rest were omitted from the big collection of 1847.
11 *The Poems of Walter Savage Landor* (London, 1795), p. 208.
12 Forster, I, p. 220.
13 Besides the essay of 1795 just quoted, *Idyllia Nova Quinque* (1815),
   Idyllia Heroica Decem (1820), and *Poemata et Inscriptiones* (1847) all contain assessments of the Anglo-Latin poets.
14 *Poemata et Inscriptiones*, p. 290.
15 T. J. B. Spencer, *Fair Greece Sad Relic* (London, 1954), pp. 205–7. An
   account of Tweddell's 'untimely death'.
16 *Poemata et Inscriptiones*, p. 300.
17 *Idyllia Nova Quinque*, p. xxiv.
18 In 1800 there was published in Calcutta *Poems in Three Parts*. Part the
   first was the Latin poetry of Sir William Jones, with an English
   version.
19 Smith's Tripos poems were printed on sheets and distributed to the

audience, as was the normal custom. Apart from their appearance in the scholarly journal, *Museum Criticum*, 2 vols (Cambridge, 1826), they had no other form of publication till the 1839 Eton collection of Latin philosophical poems: *Fasciculus carminum stylo Lucretiano scriptorum*. The most comprehensive collection of the Latin poems appeared posthumously in 1850: *The early writings of Robert Percy Smith, with a few verses in later years*, ed. R. V. Smith.

20   *Heroic Idyls* (London, 1863), p. 289.
21   Forster, I, p. 446.
22   Super, *Biography*, p. 146.
23   Bradner, p. 340.
24   Landor, *Poetical Works*, ed. S. Wheeler, various translations of Catullus in vols II and III.
25   From an essay by Landor, 'The poems of Catullus', first published in the *Foreign Quarterly Review*, July 1842; reprinted in *The Complete Works of Walter Savage Landor*, ed. T. Earle Welby, vols 13–16, ed. Stephen Wheeler, 16 vols (London, 1927–36), XI, p. 193.
26   Forster, II, p. 380.
27   Landor, *Poetical Works*, ed. S. Wheeler, II, p. 414.
28   *Poems of Walter Savage Landor* (1795), pp. 209–15.
29   Thirlwall is quoted by Richard Monckton Milnes, Lord Houghton, in his *Monographs, Personal and Social*, 2nd ed. (London, 1873), pp. 147–9.
30   Bradner, pp. 322–3.
31   *Dry Sticks* (1858), p. 209.
32   *Poemata et Inscriptiones* (1847), p. 235.
33   *The Poems of Walter Savage Landor* (1795), p. 208.
34   *Poemata et Inscriptiones* (1847), p. 196.
35   *Ibid.*, p. 232, first published in 1815 in *Idyllia Nova Quinque*.
36   Super, *Biography*, pp. 447–9.
37   *Heroic Idyls* (1863), p. 323. See also note on Bandiera brothers in Landor, *Poetical Works*, ed. S. Wheeler, II, p. 542.
38   *Poemata et Inscriptiones* (1847), p. 235.
39   *Ibid.*, p. 259.
40   *Heroic Idyls* (1863), p. 280.
41   *Poemata et Inscriptiones* (1847), p. 178.
42   *Heroic Idyls* (1863), p. 315.
43   *Poemata et Inscriptiones* (1847), p. 177.
44   *Ibid.*
45   Reprinted without alteration in *ibid.*, p. 143.
46   *Ibid.*, p. 141.
47   *Heroic Idyls* (1863), p. 301. Landor here adapts Ennius.
48   *Poemata et Inscriptiones* (1847), p. 203.
49   *Iambi* (1800), p. 6.
50   Forster, I, pp. 407–9.
51   *Poemata et Inscriptiones* (1847), p. 181.
52   *Ibid.*, p. 261.
53   *Ibid.*, p. 260.
54   *Ibid.*, p. 263.

55 *Ibid.*, p. 257.
56 *Ibid.*, p. 240.
57 See *Poetical Works*, ed. S. Wheeler, II, p. 431, for a record of the meeting.
58 *Poemata et Inscriptiones*, p. 201.
59 *Ibid.*, p. 142.
60 *Heroic Idyls* (1863), p. 304.
61 *Poetical Works*, ed. S. Wheeler, II, p. 320.
62 *Heroic Idyls* (1863), pp. 316–17.
63 *Poemata et Inscriptiones* (1847), p. 203.
64 *Heroic Idyls* (1863), p. 292.
65 *Poemata et Inscriptiones* (1847), pp. 135–6 and 141–2.
66 *Ibid.*, p. 236.
67 *Ibid.*, p. 229.
68 *Ibid.*, pp. 247–8.
69 Forster, II, p. 224.
70 *Heroic Idyls* (1863), p. 308.
71 *Poemata et Inscriptiones* (1847), p. 169.
72 *Ibid.*, p. 189.
73 *Ibid.*, p. 205.
74 See Super, *Biography*, pp. 369–70.
75 Reprinted with alterations in *Poemata et Inscriptiones* (1847), pp. 223–5.
76 *Simonides* (1806), pp. 97–8.
77 Forster, II, p. 527.
78 *Poemata et Inscriptiones* (1847), p. 227.
79 See *Poetical Works*, ed. S. Wheeler, III, p. 117.
80 *Poemata et Inscriptiones* (1847), p. 126.
81 *Ibid.*, p. 154.
82 *Ibid.*, p. 237.
83 *Heroic Idyls* (1863), p. 313.
84 *Poemata et Inscriptiones* (1847), pp. 250–1.
85 *Ibid.*, p. 246.
86 Super, *Biography*, pp. 433–62.
87 *Heroic Idyls* (1863), p. 285.
88 *Dry Sticks* (1858), p. 215.
89 Landor, *Complete Works*, ed. T. E. Welby and S. Wheeler, II, p. 143.
90 See *Poetical Works*, ed. S. Wheeler, III, p. 77.
91 Super, *Biography*, p. 289.
92 *Poemata et Inscriptiones* (1847), p. 199.
93 *Dry Sticks* (1858), p. 211. For Pomero's death and epitaph, see Super, *Biography*, p. 429.
94 *Heroic Idyls* (1863), p. 339.
95 *Poemata et Inscriptiones* (1847), p. 263.
96 Super, *Biography*, p. 355.
97 *A Choice of Kipling's Verse*, ed. T. S. Eliot (London, 1941), p. 13.
98 A study of the similarities between Kipling and Landor would be well worth while.
99 *Heroic Idyls* (1863), p. 309.
100 Forster, II, p. 345.

101 *Dry Sticks* (1858), p. 204.
102 See *Poetical Works*, ed. S. Wheeler, III, p. 247.
103 *Dry Sticks* (1858), p. 204.
104 See *Poetical Works*, ed. S. Wheeler, III, p. 247.
105 Super, *Biography*, p. 213.
106 *Last Fruit Off an Old Tree* (1853), pp. 330–1. See also Super, *Biography*, p. 390.
107 *Last Fruit Off an Old Tree* (1853), pp. 331–2.
108 *Poemata et Inscriptiones* (1847), p. 262.
109 Super, *Biography*, pp. 346–7.
110 *Dry Sticks* (1858), p. 222.
111 *Heroic Idyls* (1863), p. 332.
112 *Poemata et Inscriptiones* (1847), p. 209.
113 See *Poetical Works*, ed. S. Wheeler, III, p. 122.
114 *Poemata et Inscriptiones* (1847), pp. 213–14.
115 *Ibid.*, pp. 173–4.
116 *Heroic Idyls* (1863), p. 286.
117 *Dry Sticks* (1858), p. 230.

Index